I Am Net Worthy

The Financial Master Plan for Millennials

Chris Smith

Copyright © 2018 by Awesome Financial Future, LLC

ISBN 978-1-7320237-0-3

This work is intended to provide accurate and authoritative information in regard to the subject matter covered. However, the ideas and strategies outlined herein are intended to be generally illustrative and may not be suitable for every individual, every circumstance, or every situation. It is sold and/or distributed with the understanding that the author is not engaged in rendering legal, accounting, tax, insurance, financial, real estate, securities investment, or other professional services of any kind. Laws and practices often vary from state to state, and if such assistance is required by the reader, the services of a competent professional person or firm should be sought.

No warranty is made with respect to the accuracy or completeness of any of the information contained herein. The author specifically disclaims any liability, loss, or risk, personal or otherwise, that is incurred as a consequence, directly or indirectly, of the use or application of any of the contents contained herein.

Contents

2   **Chapter 1**
    The Million Dollar Plan

22 **Chapter 2**
    The Three-Phase Path to Financial Independence *with Amber Berry*

50 **Chapter 3**
    Money Basics *with Monica Viera*

80 **Chapter 4**
    Budgeting and Your Magic Number *with Nick Matiash*

104 **Chapter 5**
    Cars *with Samantha Poelstra*

134 **Chapter 6**
    Houses *with Dion Beary*

162 **Chapter 7**
    Long-Term Investing *with Colby Howard*

196 **Chapter 8**
    Your Financial Dashboard *with Claire Boyte-White*

258 **Chapter 9**
    The Right Things in the Right Order *with Claire Boyte-White*

Preface

The entire I Am Net Worthy book, website, app, and series is about taking care of the money you earn, wisely, safely and successfully, to get you onto a solid, proven path to a bright financial future. How you earn your money is up to you—this book is not about employment, job tips, or career-path management. But building a strong financial future is about more than just earning an income; you have to know what to do with the money you earn.

The financial world in the United States in the 21st century is more challenging, more complex, and more confusing than ever before—partly because it's become much more of a do-it-yourself financial world. Financial independence is every bit as possible now as it ever was, but it's more important than ever to have a solid plan and enough practical financial knowledge to work it. This book is designed to deliver the most important things you'll need to know to put yourself in firm control of your financial future.

We'll emphasize the most important decisions, actions, and habits you'll need to get off to a strong start early in your financial life. And if your financial life is already well underway, but you have the feeling it might need a serious reboot, you'll find what you need here.

Gimmicks, secrets, little-known tricks, and get-rich-quick schemes are everywhere. It can be tough to separate legitimate personal-finance information from the worst kinds of scams that aren't just ineffective but financially dangerous. Everything explained in this series is solid, proven, and well established.

Everyone's financial life is different, but no matter your individual circumstances, you'll greatly improve your chances of achieving your financial dreams by establishing a solid understanding of the most important personal finance core principles first. That's what you'll get here, delivered in a concise, fast moving, no-nonsense style.

If you're looking for a more traditionally presented textbook-style approach to personal finance for young adults, see *Securing Your Financial Future: Complete Personal Finance for Beginners* (Rowman & Littlefield, 2012), also by Chris Smith. You'll also find lots more information, tools, and resources to help you on your way at IAmNetWorthy.com, and in the Net Worthy Navigator app.

The financial future belongs to the Net Worthy! And the Net Worthy path is built on a series of essential points of knowledge called the Net Worthy Nuggets. There are 83 Nuggets in all, grouped by subject into the 9 chapters of this book. Ready? Let's get Net Worthy!

Chapter 1

The Million Dollar Plan

by Chris Smith

Net Worthy Nugget #1.1

If you save and invest $500 a month for 40 years, you'll end up with a one-million-dollar fortune.

Net Worthy Nugget #1.2

Compound interest is the single most powerful financial force, and it's the most important to understand.

Net Worthy Nugget #1.3

What you do—or don't do—in your 20s and 30s has a tremendously disproportionate effect in determining how financially well-off you'll be in the long run.

Net Worthy Nugget #1.4

Compound interest works for you when you save and invest—and it works against you when you borrow. Borrowing money is the financial, mathematical, and moral opposite of saving and investing it.

Net Worthy Nugget #1.5

The single most important measure of your overall financial condition is called "net worth."

Net Worthy Nugget #1.6

You should calculate your net worth regularly in order to track your progress and compare it to your goals.

Net Worthy Nugget #1.7

The single most important goal in your financial life—the "object of the game"—is to accumulate enough net worth to achieve financial independence.

Net Worthy Nugget #1.8

You can look rich, or you can become rich—but not both.

Net Worthy Nugget #1.9

Once you've established an income, the best way to grow your net worth is to adopt a two-step approach: saving and long-term investing.

Net Worthy Nugget #1.1

If you save and invest $500 a month for 40 years,
you'll end up with a one-million-dollar fortune.

The idea of turning $500 a month into a million dollars may surprise you, but it's doable—and anyone can do it.

Even better: the fortune that you'll build will be worth one million dollars *after* taxes and *after* inflation. "After taxes" means that you'll have paid any taxes you owe along the way, as you were saving and investing, so at the end of the 40 years, your fortune is all yours to spend however and whenever you want. That's because you'll be saving and investing in a Roth IRA—more on that later.

The "after inflation" part is even more incredible. Over the past few decades, inflation in the United States has averaged 3-4% per year. That doesn't seem like much, but over 40 years, it really adds up. If prices go up by 4% per year for 40 years, something that costs $100 today will cost $290 then. That means that in this million dollar plan, the balance in your investment account won't be $1 million, but it will actually be $2.9 million. Because 40 years from now, it will take $2.9 million to buy what $1 million buys today.

To keep things simple, let's use round numbers for your age. Say you start saving on your 20th birthday. You save $500 a month, each and every month, which comes to $6,000 per year. Over 40 years, the grand total you're saving into this plan will total $240,000. But on your 60th birthday, the balance in your investment account will be $2.9 million, or about equal to $1 million of today's dollars. It's like inheriting a fortune from a rich relative, except that relative is you.

The key to growing $500 per month, or just $240,000, to $2.9 million is compound interest. The math behind compound interest is simple, but the results of that math are shocking. Call it mathemagical or "the empirical miracle"—either way, it's the indispensable factor to growing your investments.

The million-dollar result doesn't depend on some unrealistically high rate of return or some unrealistically low estimate for inflation. This calculation assumes a 10% per year rate of investment return and a 4% per year estimate for inflation, resulting in a 6% "real" return, which are conservative assumptions by all historical standards. In other words, it's considerably more likely that your $500 per month save-and-invest plan will result in *more* than a million dollars, not less.

Net Worthy Nugget #1.2

> Compound interest is the single most powerful financial force, and it's the most important to understand.

It's important to realize that the impressive results of the million dollar plan are not the result of some highly sophisticated investment strategy, but one that is pretty simple. There's no need to subject yourself to a lot of risk, rely on sketchy gimmicks, or hope for good luck or good timing. This investment strategy is simple, safe, and well established. In fact, it's so dependable that the million-dollar result could have been achieved over *any* 40-year period in the past century.

The math behind compound interest is basic, but powerful, and you'll want to understand a few very predictable characteristics that factor in.

The first is this: compound interest may be astounding in the end, but it's a notoriously *slow starter* that will require some patience before you see its effects. The graph below shows the investment balance at end of each decade of investment:

The Million Dollar Plan
All in $K

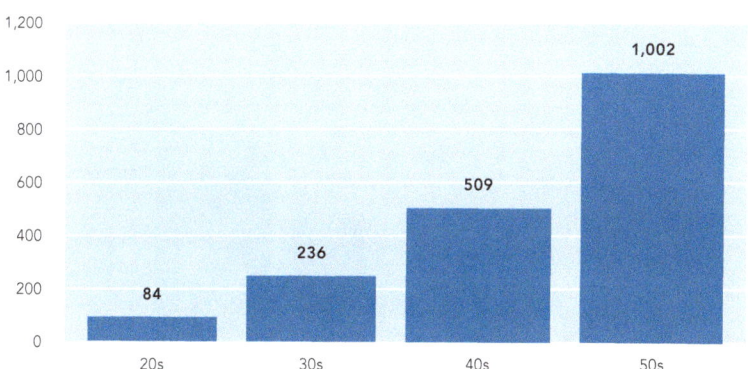

It would be easy to get discouraged after only the first 10 years. Those early results really don't look that impressive: $60,000 invested, and an $84,000 balance. But that's how compound interest always works—maddeningly slowly at first until it picks up a little steam, and eventually the numbers start getting enormous.

So to declare the plan a failure at age 30 after just 10 years of investing would be a huge mistake, because even if it may not look like it, things are progressing exactly as they should. You won't need a fancy investment strategy, but you will need patience.

Net Worthy Nugget #1.3

What you do—or don't do—in your 20s and 30s has a tremendously disproportionate effect in determining how financially well-off you'll be in the long run.

Let's break the million-dollar-plan chart down a little bit more. Below, the bars are segmented to show which decade's investments account for what portion of each bar. The darkest shade represents the money saved and invested during your 20s, the slightly lighter shade represents your 30s, and so on. The far-right bar shows the million-dollar balance waiting for you on your 60th birthday.

The Million Dollar Plan
All in $K

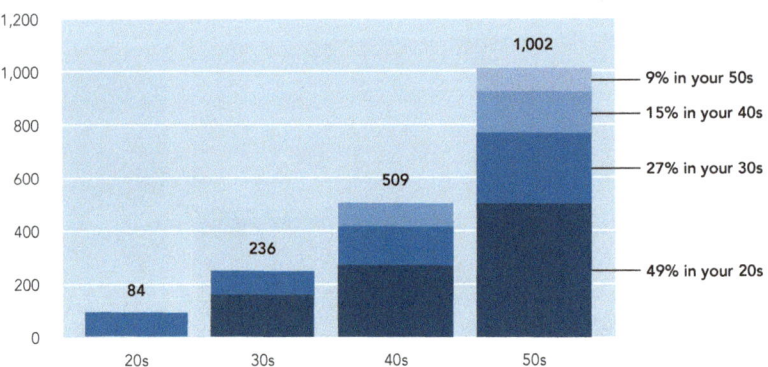

Consider it: Even though the amount you saved and invested was exactly the same throughout—each month, each year, and each decade—the results are not evenly balanced. Roughly half of the million-dollar balance on your 60th birthday comes from the money you saved and invested in your 20s, while only 9% comes from what you saved and invested most recently, in your 50s. Compound interest hasn't had nearly as long to work its magic on your 50s investments as it has on your 20s investments, and the results really show it.

Assuming that having this $1 million at age 60 was a very important goal to achieve financial independence, keep these two main points in mind:

1. Waiting until your 40s or even 50s to even begin thinking seriously about saving and investing—like most Americans tend to do—is NOT likely to be an effective strategy.

2. And if you had to pick one decade to skip saving and investing altogether, the very last decade you'd want to skip is your 20s—and it's not even close!

While it's true that good financial habits are easier to form before you've had a chance to develop any bad ones, that's not the main reason the early part of your financial life is so disproportionately important to your long-term financial picture. Instead, it's mostly because that's just how the math behind compound interest works. Compound interest takes time to work its magic, so the sooner you get the clock ticking on savings and investments, the more growth you'll see.

The idea that the early years matter the most inspires mixed reactions. Some people are motivated to start saving and investing right away. Others point out that the 20s can be the hardest decade of all to save and invest—your working life is just beginning and incomes are lowest. That's without considering the fact that many begin their financial lives with daunting levels of student loan or other debt. But almost everybody says I'm glad I know this now, *but I wish I'd known it earlier!*

If you're discouraged to learn about the magnified effect of the earliest parts of your financial life, take heart. Now that you understand this, even the smallest steps in the right direction will make a big difference later.

Spotlight: The Power of the First Decade

A Mini-Case Study

Amy and Beth are identical twins. Amy studied the million dollar plan carefully and started investing right away, at age 20, with $500 per month—but then she abruptly stopped, after just ten years, at age 30. Beth took much longer to get motivated and didn't begin until age 40. To make up for the lost time, Beth doubled down, saving and investing $1,000 per month, and kept that going until age 60.

Amy invested $500 per month for 10 years, while Beth invested $1,000 per month for 20 years—that's twice as much, for twice as long. The only thing going for Amy is that she started earlier in life and gave compound interest more time to work. If Beth and Amy decide to compare their account balances over slices of 60th birthday cake, you wouldn't be surprised to learn that even though it's close, Amy still comes out on top. *There's just no substitute for a strong, early start.*

Wait, I'm Over 20! Am I Too Late?

A Note from Chris

No, no, a thousand times no—you're not too late! Our million-dollar example uses nice round ages because that makes the plan simple to explain and follow. The 40-year investment timetable is easy to divide up neatly into decades, and it's easy to compare the progress in each. But it's just one example of a long-term savings and investment strategy; there are countless other ways you can set up your own plan. Compound interest doesn't care how old you are when you start. The math works just the same whether you start at age 20, or age 80, or anywhere in between.

There are three main variables at play:

1. When you start

2. How long you continue

3. How much you save and invest each month

Each of the three variables plays a role; the more aggressive you are with any one of them, the more flexibility you'll have with the others. The idea is to play around with all three variables until you find the combination you're most comfortable with.

Fortunately, that's pretty simple to do. The simplest way of all is to use the "Million Dollar Plan Calculator," in the Net Worthy Navigator App. It's specifically designed to let you try out different starting points, ending points, and investment levels, and see how much each combination leaves you in your investment account balance. It won't take long for you to develop a solid understanding of how the tradeoffs work.

Let's say that hypothetical reader Connor is starting at age 35 instead of age 20. The Million Dollar Plan Calculator helps him understand the tradeoffs he faces and choices he can make.

- He could save $500 per month for 40 years, and that will yield a one million dollar fortune—but he'll be age 75 by then, quite a bit later than his dream retirement date. (He knew that without even using the calculator.)

- If he wants to stop working at age 60 instead, like the original Million Dollar Plan, the required monthly savings jumps from $500 per month to $1450, to make up for the late start.

- If that seems a little steep, he can set his monthly savings to an even $1000, and that will get him to a million dollars in 30 years, when he's 65.

- He might also want to take into account that the younger he is when he stops saving and investing, the more he'll likely need—because those savings will need to last for a longer time.

If Connor doesn't think any of those choices seem appealing, he might be tempted to put the decision off for a few more years, but that just makes his challenge even tougher. He'd be much better off if he just chooses *something*—and gets started *now*.

And so will you.

Net Worthy Nugget #1.4

Compound interest works for you when you save and invest, and it works against you when you borrow. Borrowing money is the financial, mathematical, and moral opposite of saving and investing it.

Compound interest may be enormously powerful, but it's also two-faced. It can work for you or against you, and either way, the math works the same—predictably and relentlessly. In the same way that an early saver/investor can become discouraged because the early returns seem deceptively low, the same thing can happen in reverse to an early borrower. The classic example is credit card debt. At first, interest charges on unpaid balances seem so low it's easy to underestimate just how dangerous this kind of debt is. Millions of people have gotten into serious credit card quicksand, which can take years, or even decades, to resolve.

This point is simple to state and simple to understand, but it's not always so easy to apply. One of the fundamental principles of personal finance is to save and invest as much as you can and borrow as little as you can. Just as saving and investing early in your financial life is particularly helpful, borrowing early in your financial life is particularly unhelpful.

Net Worthy Nugget #1.5

The single most important measure of your overall financial condition is called "net worth."

Understanding how something works is one thing, but measuring it is another. It's easy to measure your height in feet and inches, your weight in pounds, or your speed in miles per hour. The ability to accurately measure something is fundamental to managing and improving it.

Luckily, there is a simple, well-established way to measure your financial condition. Despite the complexity, the ebbs and flows, and the mixture of different types of accounts and arrangements, your whole financial condition can be boiled down into a single number called "net worth." It can be expressed as a single number at any point in time, which means you can see, unambiguously, if your financial condition is getting stronger or weaker compared to previous measurements. And, it means you can set goals—long and short term—and measure your progress toward them.

Most people have heard the term "net worth" but don't really know what it means. Imagine an ordinary, everyday bathtub. The water coming in from the faucet represents your income. The water flowing out through the drain is your spending and the lifestyle your spending supports. Finally, the water level in the bathtub is your net worth—and that's what really matters. Your goal is to steadily increase your net worth, year after year. If you do, eventually you'll have "enough." In other words, there will be so much water in the bathtub you can choose to turn the faucet all the way off if you want to.

The Net Worth Bathtub

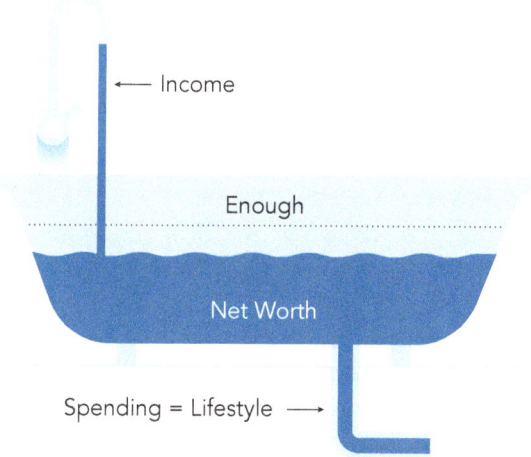

The bathtub model makes it obvious: the only way to keep the water level rising is to consistently spend less than you earn, year after year. The water level also represents your financial power—not power over other people, but power in the sense of having more freedom, independence, and choices in your life. The more water you have in your bathtub, the more financial power you have, so you don't want to casually give away that power to the cable company, or the car dealer, or anybody else. Only give away your power—that is, only spend—if you're sure what you get in return is not only worth it but also the best way of meeting the need in question. When you think of it that way, hanging on to your power becomes more and more appealing. You'll fill up your bathtub faster that way.

Net Worthy Nugget #1.6

You should calculate your net worth regularly in order to track your progress and compare it to your goals.

The bathtub analogy offers a good conceptual idea, but how do you actually *calculate* your own net worth? The accounting definition is "assets minus liabilities," but an easier way to think about it is:
NET WORTH equals *what you OWN minus what you OWE.*

Some of the things you own are easy to quantify into specific dollar amounts. Your checking and savings account balances, for example. Another example is money that is owed to you, that you're highly confident of collecting but haven't received yet—like an income tax refund when you've filed the return but haven't gotten the check yet. Other things you own can be trickier to place a value on, though. Say you own a car, free and clear. You paid $10,000 for it several years ago. Today, according to Kelly Blue Book, you could count on getting $6,000 for it—but only if you spent $500 to renew the registration, get it spiffed up into sellable condition, and run an ad. But you have no intention of doing that, because to you, that car is priceless. So, what value do you put on the car when calculating your net worth? Is it the original $10,000, the market value of $6,000, or your own sky-high opinion? The answer is $5,500—the price you could reasonably expect to get for the car today, minus an estimate of whatever expenses you'd reasonably have to incur in order to convert that car to cash.

That's the thought process to use for everything in the what-you-own category: if you had to "shut down" your financial life and convert everything you own into cash at reasonable market prices, what would the total be? Of course, this involves a fair bit of estimation, especially for things like real estate, but as long as you use the same estimation methodology each time you look at your net worth and stick with middle-of-the-road values, you'll be fine.

As a practical matter, it's just not worth the effort to catalog every last paperback book and jar of peanut butter in your possession. The typical solution for this is a single catchall line item, where you include an estimate for all of your lower-valued items collectively. If you sold everything you own in an imaginary garage sale, there would be dozens of individual items that would sell for less than $100. Just lump all of those items together, take a rough guess at what all of those "less than $100 items" would add up to, and don't spend more than a couple of minutes on it. (Try not to be too sad to realize that you originally paid more than $100—maybe *way* more— for lots of these items. Consider it money well spent to learn something valuable about how quickly newly purchased items can lose their appeal, along with their resale value.)

What about "intangible" assets, like your education? Your skills? Your support system of friends, family, and loved ones? Your network of professional contacts? The short answer is: all of those assets are important to your financial future, but none of them are included in your net worth calculation. These types of assets might, and hopefully will, eventually lead to better job opportunities, higher income, more stability, and so on, and when those things happen, your net worth will be improved. Until then, they don't count (at least where money is concerned).

Next, consider what you owe to others. Again, some line items will be simple to quantify. For student loans, credit card debt, car loans, and the like, just list the current balance. The amounts are usually much bigger when it comes to real estate, but the methodology is the same: just list the current mortgage balance. What about an apartment you're renting? Let's say you're two months into a one-year lease. To estimate that, you need to take a look at the actual language in your lease, and ask: if I moved out now, how much would I owe the landlord? Usually, there is some kind of penalty for breaking the lease, such as a month's rent, the forfeiture of deposits, or both. Finally, there could be any number of bills to think about—bills you've received but haven't paid, expenses you've incurred but haven't been billed for yet, and ongoing monthly bills like cell phone plans, cable or satellite TV plans, and more.

Ultimately, you'll apply the same general thought process you did when calculating what you own: if I knew that this were to be my last month on Earth, and I wanted to settle all my debts before departing: what would it take to square up all of my accounts with the various people and businesses I owe?

It may sound like a giant, complicated exercise just to come up with a single number, but relax. There's a learning curve to these calculations, and the first time or two might be pretty time-consuming. But once you've blazed the trail and know where to go to look everything up, the process is fairly simple, especially with many of today's financial and budgeting tools geared to automate big parts of the calculation. The Net Worthy Navigator App features a calculation tool that includes clear, simple instructions for each input; it's called (of course!) the Net Worthy Calculator. Using the app, you'll be able to generate a rough net worth calculation surprisingly quickly. By the way, the Net Worthy Navigator is designed with the security of your personal information as a top priority; everything you enter is stored on your local device only, never online.

In any case, knowing your net worth is fundamental—otherwise, you'll have no idea if you're improving it or not. Calculating it each month is probably overkill, since it isn't likely to change much in just 30 days' time. Calculate it at least once a year, though, plus a "before and after" calculation if you're making any major financial transitions, such as moving or making a major purchase like a car or house.

The first time you see your net worth boiled down to a single number may be daunting. You might be looking at a negative number. This can seem scary, depressing, or both, but it's not at all uncommon for young adults in the United States today. The one-two punch of student loans and credit card debt has created a sea of negative net worth. But just because you have a lot of company in other negative net-worthers doesn't mean you shouldn't be concerned. Instead, remember the old advice: when you're in a hole, stop digging. If your net worth is negative, it's crucial to embark on a plan to improve it. It won't turn positive overnight, but the goal is to turn the trend around and make steady, positive progress until you're in the black.

Net Worthy Nugget #1.7

> The single most important goal in your financial life—the "object of the game"—is to accumulate enough net worth to achieve financial independence.

Nobody's going to fill your bathtub for you. It's up to you whether, and when, you'll do it. When your bathtub is empty, and you have no or negative net worth, you are completely *financially dependent*. You might be dependent on your job, on your parents or other friends and family, on public or private assistance, or on some combination. If you have at least a little water in your bathtub, that's a distinct improvement. Even a little water means you could turn the faucet off, or at least down, temporarily, which isn't an option when the bathtub's empty. The more water in your bathtub, the more choices and freedom you have.

And when the water level reaches the "enough" line—enough net worth to cover your living expenses for the rest of your life—that's complete financial independence, that's your goal, and it's great! You can turn the water all the way off and completely walk away from the working world altogether—but only if you want to. You can pursue other types of jobs, even if they pay much less than your previous jobs, if you'd like. You'll be in a position to take more risks and head in a pure entrepreneurial direction. And if you truly love the work you do and would like nothing more than to keep doing it, you can do that, too. Financial independence gives you complete freedom to choose whatever you'd like to do from that point onward.

That's why I don't call this "saving for retirement." Traditional retirement—immediate conversion from 100% work to 100% leisure—is only one of the many choices you'll have when you reach financial independence, and it's one that fewer and fewer people are finding attractive.

On the flip side, if you don't reach financial independence, there are no bailouts. You'll continue to be financially dependent, regardless of your age. Many older people facing this situation respond with a grim determination to "work forever," but in reality, the older you get, the harder and harder it is to remain employed. The combination of health-related limitations and obsolete job skills can be tough to overcome. And, without any job-related income at all, financial dependence truly limits your choices and freedom.

That's not the future you want. You want financial independence and the freedom to choose how you'll spend your time and your money.

Net Worthy Nugget #1.8

You can look rich, or you can become rich—but not both.

The big difference between income and wealth is that income is how much money you bring in, and wealth, or net worth, is how much of your income you've managed to hang on to and put to work for you. The less you spend, the faster your wealth accumulates.

Pop culture, on the other hand, insists that the more you spend, the richer you must be. The rich always seem to have super spendy lifestyles, luxury cars, and either a suburban mansion or a penthouse (or both!). But that kind of lifestyle would drain an average bathtub pretty quickly.

It's true that a tiny percentage of people are *so* wealthy they can spend like crazy and not have to worry about running out. This extremely rare setup still remains popular culture's favorite version of "being rich"—probably because not only is it pretty entertaining, but the idea that "the more you spend, the richer you must be" sounds like the kind of dreamworld that advertisers everywhere would love to convince you is real.

Two much more common types of households are far more important to understand:

1. **The Big Spender.** The big spender makes a pretty high income but spends it all (and maybe even a little more) as soon as it comes out of the faucet. The big spender may

look rich from the outside, but in reality, their bathtub is just as empty as somebody just starting out. As soon as the income stream stops or even slows, the party's over—and probably quite abruptly. Think of all the entertainers, pro athletes, and lottery winners whose financial bubbles have publicly popped. Plenty of people from other walks of life fall into this trap, too—you just don't read about them. Even if the neighbors can't tell from their side of the fence, the big spender is a long, long way from financial independence.

2. **The Big Saver.** The famous book *The Millionaire Next Door* documented the surprising truth about the most typical type of American millionaire. Spendy lifestyle? Not so much. The typical American millionaire has a moderate income, owns a modest home, drives a used car, and has giant investment account balances. And probably also a big smile, because the big saver can withstand any financial crisis—loss of income, a big recession, whatever—and still be just fine. Their neighbors might not have any idea of their financial status, but the big savers are either already financially independent or on a solid path to getting there.

Sadly, there are way more big spenders in the United States today than big savers. It's a shame, because most people have enough income that they could be filling their bathtubs. They simply don't understand that's the object of the game, and they don't know how or where to begin.

After your bathtub is full, being a big spender can work, at least within limits. But being a big spender before your bathtub is full will probably prevent you from filling it in the first place. It comes down to a simple choice: you can look rich today or you can take steps to become rich tomorrow, but not both!

Net Worthy Nugget #1.9

Once you've established an income, the best way
to grow your net worth is to adopt a two-step
approach: saving and long-term investing.

You can fill your bathtub just by spending less than you earn and depositing the difference into a savings account, but if that's all you do, it will take a very long time to reach financial independence. The interest rates on savings accounts are simply too low; your balance would grow, but it wouldn't grow fast enough to keep up with inflation.

The Two Step Plan to Filling Your Bathtub

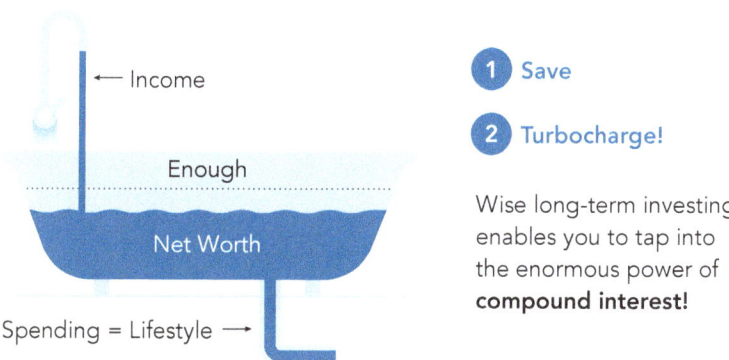

Instead, you need a two-step strategy. Step 1 is to consistently spend less than you earn, which requires solid management of your drain. Step 2 is to speed up the rate at which your fill your bathtub by turbocharging your savings—that is, channeling them into a wisely chosen long-term investment program.

That's why we started this discussion with the million dollar plan. Financial independence is much easier to reach when you've got the enormous power of compound interest working for you.

It bears emphasizing that you definitely need both steps! If you save—even if you save a lot—it's just going to take way too long to fill your bathtub unless you wisely invest those savings. And even if your long-term investment program is executed perfectly, if you're not saving enough, there just won't be enough there to turbocharge.

So, how much is "enough?" How long will it take to fill your bathtub? The next chapters address those questions thoroughly, but for now, just remember that the more you save—month after month and year after year—and the earlier in your financial life you start your saving and long-term investment program, the sooner you can reach financial independence.

A Million Dollar Story

A Note from Chris

I began helping Lisa with her personal finances about five years ago. Lisa is a member of a Native American tribe near the Seattle area. I'd been asked by tribal officials to put together a personal finance workshop for members of the community, and we thought that some one-on-one sessions with a few key community members would be a good way to get started.

Lisa was selected because she was highly respected in the community, and as soon as I met her, I could see why. She looked me square in the eye from the moment we met and spoke in a direct, no-nonsense way. I could tell that if I could win her over, her opinion would carry a lot of weight. But I could also tell that the only way to win her over would be with solid results, not theories or charts.

She was 44 at the time, and she had been a Tribal employee for 15 years. She's a single mom and was working hard to stretch her dollars to provide for her family. So, we started right in with household budgeting. Lisa turned out to be an excellent student, and we got some quick wins right away. I congratulated her on her success and proclaimed that she was ready to move on to the next aspect of her financial picture: her 401(k) account. As soon as I said that, I could see the enthusiasm drain from her face. She found the whole topic of investing confusing and frustrating. She knew people whose retirement savings had been lost in the 2008-09 recession, and she didn't want that to happen to her. But she was also deeply aware of her parents' story of reaching retirement age with little in the way of savings, and she didn't want that to be her future, too. Like so many people, she knew she needed to be doing *something* to start building for her future, but didn't know how to even get started.

Since I knew Lisa was a "show me, don't tell me" type, we went right into her 401(k) account, using the computer in her office. She showed me the low balance in the account and told me frankly she didn't even understand how that balance was calculated, let alone how it got there in the first place. Then we got to the screen showing "Investment Elections," which featured a pulldown menu of 29 different choices for her to put money into—mutual funds, money market funds, on and on. She looked at the menu, then she looked at me and said, "Chris, this might as well be in Chinese. I have no idea what any of these choices even mean. I always get this far and then stop and say I'll come back and choose something later. Well, it's been 15 years, and 'later' hasn't happened yet."

I explained to Lisa that the balance in her 401(k) account will ultimately come down to just three things. First, what percentage of her paycheck she would be willing and able to set aside for her financial future. Second, how long she was willing to keep that commitment in place. And third, that pulldown menu and its 29 choices. I reassured her those menu choices were a lot easier than they looked. But the real question, the one that only Lisa could answer, was the first: the percentage she could save. She'd done a great job freeing up some money in her monthly budget. So I asked how much of that she was willing to put toward her financial future. In typical Lisa fashion, she wanted to take some time thinking it over before deciding.

The next time we met, she had no hesitation. "I can do 15%. Sometimes maybe more, but I wanted to pick something I know I can stick with in good times and bad." I said "Wow!"

I did some quick calculations, keeping everything on the conservative side. I wrote a number down on a piece of paper, folded it in half, and handed it to her.

"Lisa, you're 44 now, and if you keep working until you're 65, that's 21 more years. If you change your contribution percentage to 15% right now, and leave it there until you're 65, the balance that will be in your account is what's written on that sheet of paper." I'll never forget the look on her face as she opened it up and read: $1.1 million.

That was almost five years ago, and Lisa is now well ahead of the pace we established for her that day. Of course, it's not quite the same timing and amounts described in this chapter. She started too late in her financial life for that. On the other hand, she is fortunate to work for an employer who offers a generous 401(k) match (more on that later). She'd also avoided getting into debt, which meant she could start investing right away.

Today, when I do the workshops, Lisa comes in and tells her story, which is always a highlight of the day. It's one thing to learn about a million dollar plan; it's another to hear it firsthand, from someone you know who's actually doing it. She usually closes with, "If I can do it, you can too." Then, she gives me the evil eye, and says, "Hey, Chris, thanks for explaining all that to me. But where were you twenty years ago, so I could be living the good life *now*?"

She's got a point—the earlier you start, the further you can get. But people of all ages are inspired by Lisa's story, because it shows the amazing power of just a little bit of knowledge, the confidence to act on it, and the commitment to stick with it.

Go Lisa, millionaire in progress!

This page intentionally left blank

Chapter 2

The Three-Phase Path to Financial Independence

by Chris Smith with Amber Berry

Net Worthy Nugget #2.1
The financial world that today's young adults face is dramatically different than it was a generation or two ago. Strategies for financial success that worked in the 20th century are ill-suited for the 21st. Yet many of these outmoded principles stubbornly persist as "conventional wisdom."

Net Worthy Nugget #2.2
The financial world of the 21st century requires a long-range approach that begins early in your financial life.

Net Worthy Nugget #2.3
The Net Worthy Path to financial independence includes three distinct phases: red (getting your financial basics in order and preparing to invest), yellow (earn/save/invest/repeat), and green (financial independence).

Net Worthy Nugget #2.4
Your goal is to get out of the red phase and into the yellow phase as soon as you can. To accomplish that, permanently eliminate all your (non-mortgage) debt and build up an adequate emergency fund.

Net Worthy Nugget #2.5

A bare minimum emergency fund of one month's expenses is your initial, and high-priority, goal. Eventually, you'll increase this to 4, 6, or 9 months' expenses, depending on your household risk level.

Net Worthy Nugget #2.6

Pay off debts ASAP! If you have more than one, start with the highest interest debt first, and work your way down.

Net Worthy Nugget #2.7

The yellow phase is where you methodically build net worth. The sooner you start, and the more you save and invest, the easier it will be for you to achieve financial independence.

Net Worthy Nugget #2.8

The green phase represents true financial independence! You reach it when you have sufficient net worth to walk away from your primary job—or not. This 21st century definition of financial independence is entirely different from the old idea of "retirement" and should not be confused with it.

Net Worthy Nugget #2.1

> The financial world that today's young adults face is dramatically different than it was a generation or two ago. Strategies for financial success that worked in the 20th century are ill-suited for the 21st. Yet many of these outmoded principles stubbornly persist as "conventional wisdom."

If we could take a trip back in time to a strange and wonderful destination called the late 20th century, you'd notice right away that this financial world works very differently than the one we're used to today. If we were to poll the people who live in this world to find out the most widely accepted points of financial wisdom, we'd get a list like this:

1. Debt is a normal and necessary part of financial life. As long as you can afford the monthly payments, you're fine.

2. The most important measure of your financial strength and stability, by far, is your income level. It's all about how much you make. "Rich" means high income, "poor" means low income.

3. A college degree is the golden ticket to a high income.

4. A sure-fire sign of a financially well-managed household is a balanced budget. If the outs equal the ins in an average month, all is well.

5. When your income goes up, so should your spending; you've earned it, and you're entitled to spend it.

6. The least important part of your financial life is your 20s and early 30s, because you aren't making much. The most important time is your 50s and early 60s, because they're your "peak earning years."

7. Find a great employer or union, and stick with them for your entire career. You'll be richly rewarded for your loyalty.

8. Renting is for suckers. Since you'll be working for just one employer or union, you'll never need to move, so the decision to buy is a no-brainer. Your home will turn out to be your very best long-term investment.

9. Retirement happens on a specific day, when you don't have to go to work anymore. It's based on your age and time with your employer. The three pillars that make up your retirement funding are your pension, your home equity, and Social Security.

10. Long-term investing is icing on the cake: nice to have for those who can afford it, but not essential.

You might notice something vaguely familiar about this list. It likely sounds a lot like the financial advice that your parents, and others from that generation, are giving you today. No wonder. This list represents the conventional wisdom they learned when they were young adults. Today, they want what's best for you and your future, so they're thoughtfully sharing their accumulated wisdom with you. Their hearts are certainly in the right place, so let's be thankful for that.

There's just one problem. That list doesn't work anymore.

We're *not* saying that buying a house is a bad move nowadays, or that a long stint with a single employer is something to be avoided. What we are saying is that this list is no longer a slam-dunk recipe for success. Buying a house may or may not be a good move. It's a big decision, and you'll need to carefully weigh the pros and cons—and it turns out those pros and cons shake out quite differently now than they typically did a generation ago. Same thing when it comes to sticking with one employer or union for most of your working life. It might be a good move, and it might not—but don't expect anywhere near the same kinds of rewards for long-term loyalty.

And it's not just your parents. Educators, employers, advertisers, financial services companies, the news media, politicians regardless of party—everybody seems to keep on singing from that outdated financial songbook. But today's young adults are catching on. Increasingly, you're realizing that the old rules, and the assumptions behind them, are seriously flawed.

Here's the truth. If you follow this 20th century playlist in the 21st century, the odds are that you're headed for trouble, even if not immediately. You might be able to navigate through your 20s and 30s well enough. But the kicker is that you're likely to end up in your 40s or 50s with very little in your financial bathtub and not enough time left in your working life to do much about it. Today, you can only stop working when your bathtub is full, but not until it is. Your age has nothing to do with it.

Funding Your Golden Years
It's a completely different financial world

Latter 20th Century	Today
Pensions	401(k)s, IRAs
Home equity	Lower ownership % Buying Later, smaller equity
Social Security	Adequately funded?

The left-side strategies in the table above were available to very broad segments of the population, and the strategies were so dependable they were called the three "pillars" of retirement funding. In contrast, the right side, which considers today's most common strategies, is a lot more iffy. While 401(k)s and IRAs are great tax-advantaged ways to build investment balances, they only work if you're willing and able to contribute to them. Home equity can add a lot more savings, but only *if* you're among the shrinking percentage of people for whom it makes sense to buy. Social Security might play a role for you as well, but only *if* Congress ensures there's adequate funding left for it to do so.

It's tempting to think of the 20th century as "the good old days" and wish things still worked that way. In today's financial world, the harsh reality is that if you haven't filled your bathtub, your only choices are to keep on working as long as you can, to depend on others, to downshift your lifestyle, or some combination of the three—no matter what your age is.

You don't want that to be you. But it doesn't have to be.

Believe it or not, the 21st century financial world is really much better than the old one—with one very important qualification. Today, it's a do-it-yourself financial world. And that's a wonderful thing, *if* you know how to do it yourself. If you do, you don't have to live with somebody else's idea of how long you should work, or what your lifestyle should be afterward. You call the shots, not some pension fund manager, not a Social Security payout table, and definitely not a calendar.

It's never been more true that, financially speaking, knowledge is power. With the right knowledge, you can most definitely set yourself up for a financial future that can bring you joy, because you're the one who designs it. You not only decide the destination, but you also are in complete control of how fast you get there. One of the keys to making this easy is to think ahead—way ahead.

The Seeds of Change

A Note from Amber

There was a time when I tried following this old advice. And let me tell you, it most certainly does not work anymore. At least for me it didn't. I pretty much did everything according to plan. In high school, I worked really hard academically and did several extracurriculars so I could get into a good college because my parents and I really thought that was the key to success. Once I got there, I realized I had to pay for it.

-_____-

That's how I ended up with two jobs so I could pay for books and also food (food is nice to have). Thankfully, I was able to skid by with only one loan. But that was the result of having to leave a semi-traumatic housing situation that involved an elderly man and his porn addiction in rapid fashion. Don't be like me, kids: screen your housemates better. #sayNOtocraigslist

Anyway, I couldn't afford to live on my own with the hours I was working. I took out a loan so I could finally put an end to the housemate trauma. This allowed me to offset some costs, and I could finish my last two quarters of school and graduate.

But after that, I couldn't find a job. At least not a full-time one. You may see where this is going, but I ended up with four jobs at once. Believe me, working from 5:00 a.m. to 9:00 p.m. Monday through Thursday, and 7:00 a.m. to 6:00 p.m. Friday through Sunday was one of the worst ideas I have ever had in my entire life. I worked holidays, I had no days off, and I cried. Often. The money wasn't worth it, because I had no time for anything but work, not even just hanging out with friends. I became best friends with my car since I was commuting more than an hour each day. Though I was glad that I could pad my savings and pay off my car, I was very sad.

When I finally did find a full-time job, I remember being elated! I had benefits, so I could finally afford a check-up. I could go to the dentist again without worrying I would have to sell a body part to make it happen. Life seemed good. Until I found out that my so-called job was actually the place where dreams and souls go to die. Though I studied science in college and spent years during undergrad doing DNA-repair research, that's not what my new job called for me to do. Instead, I counted seeds, all day long, in a basement with no windows. And when I say seeds, I mean rice grains, soybeans, arabidopsis siliques . . . You name it, I counted it.

I kept telling myself that I had done everything right. I couldn't make sense of all of this.

How could this, THIS, be the pinnacle of adulting?

I was exchanging the potential for early-onset arthritis for what? An hourly rate that had me frantically scrambling to make ends meet.

I realized that I was never going to be able to do the things I wanted to do if I didn't change something. Eventually I was offered a very small raise in my hourly rate. And you guessed it, they wanted me to do even more seed-counting work with no hope of ever really moving past it. I knew it was time to go. By this time, I was reduced to living in a mobile home community across from the railroad tracks in a rented 350 sq. ft. tiny house. As much "fun" as it was, I had dreams of something normal-sized. When older people would tell me I should just buy a house-because renting is for the birds, I would have loved to tell them to go try buying a house with the wages I was getting. Live more frugally? I would have loved to, but I'd already squeezed out everything I knew how to—I honestly don't know how I could have saved another dollar.

-_- #bittermillennial

Net Worthy Nugget #2.2

The financial world of the 21st century requires a long-range approach that begins early in your financial life.

How's this for a dream-come-true scenario? You're just arriving at the point in life when you're seriously beginning to consider what it would be like to step out of the working world, for good. You've had a nice long run, and you've done a lot to be proud of. But now there are plenty of bucket-list items you'd rather turn your attention to. Now imagine that just as you're about to dismiss all that as an idle daydream, you're informed that you've just received a huge sum of money, no strings attached, from an anonymous secret admirer. And it just happens to be the *exact amount* you need to completely fill your bathtub, grab a piece of cake at your going-away party, and walk out the employer's door for good.

Wouldn't that be awesome? Of course it would. The only thing that might top that would be a little role-reversal, in a daydream where you get to play the secret admirer—the one doing the giving. Imagine how having the financial power to completely change someone's entire future would feel, allowing them the freedom to go off and pursue the life of their dreams without having to stress about money. What you'd really be giving them is the precious gift of time—time to spend with their loved ones and to pursue their deepest passions. You'd feel like Santa Claus.

But that dream isn't so far-fetched, and you don't have to choose. Both dreams come true can be yours—you can be the giver *and* the receiver.

It's just another way of looking at the Million Dollar Plan. Who's the receiver in that scenario? You are, of course, because you're the one who gets to spend that fortune, any way you want to. But, you're also the giver, since it's the younger version of you who's doing all that saving and investing.

Both versions of you are going to be smiling, because you're both living the dream. It isn't just a fantasy. The power of compound interest is very real, and it's perfectly capable of delivering that awesome gift to your future self. Provided, of course, that you give it plenty of time to work its magic. It only takes a few decades.

There are dreamers, and there are doers. If you want to be a doer, you need to get the compound-interest clock started ticking *early* in your financial life. Today would be good. Just imagine how grateful your future self will be.

Net Worthy Nugget #2.3

> The Net Worthy Path to financial independence includes three distinct phases: red (getting your financial basics in order and preparing to invest), yellow (earn/save/invest/repeat), and green (financial independence).

The one thing that can make your financial life more stressful than anything else is competition among your top priorities, all screaming for your attention, all at the same time. Rent needs to be paid, credit card interest is piling up, student loan payments are due, your emergency fund cookie jar was raided long ago, your taxes are almost due and you haven't even started, and it seems like everybody's guilt-tripping you for not having a retirement plan already figured out. And that's just Tuesday. The list of things you need to do financially is already way too long. But what you really need to know is what to do *first*.

There's an old saying that "Time was invented to prevent everything from happening all at once." In other words, sometimes the best way to break a priorities logjam is to build a plan in clear phases, with distinct goals for each phase. That's where the Three-Phase Path to Financial Independence comes in. It's a simple traffic-light model, with a red phase, a yellow phase, and a green phase. And it's your high-level, big-picture map to an awesome financial future.

Your financial life begins when you are completely responsible for your own financial condition, and as soon as you are, you start out in the red phase. Your goal is to get out of it as soon as you possibly can. There are two requirements to getting out. First, you need to build up an emergency fund of cash reserves, your E-Fund, and we recommend a big one. Second, you have to completely pay off all debts: student loans, credit cards, everything, with the possible exception of a mortgage on a house that you live in. We've emphasized how important it is to begin investing early, but the red phase is there because your chances for financial independence are much better if you tackle E-fund establishment and debt elimination first.

The Net Worthy Path
Three phases to financial independence

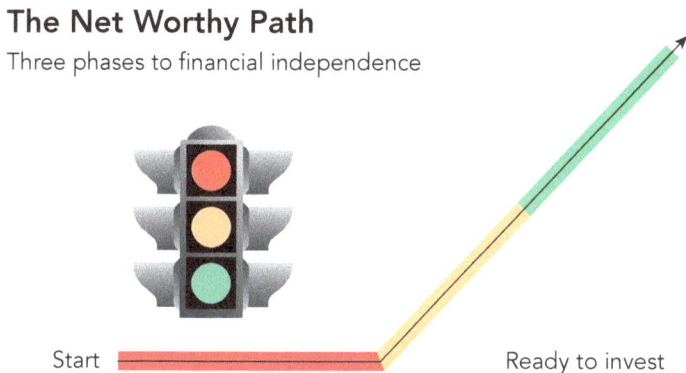

Once you've met those two requirements, then you graduate to the yellow phase. The yellow phase is simple to describe: earn, save, invest, repeat. You keep on doing that until you have enough in your financial bathtub that work becomes truly optional for you. In the yellow phase, you're free to go as fast or as slow as you want. If you want to achieve financial independence really fast, keep living like a starving student. If you want to slow down and enjoy the ride, that's fine too, as long as you keep the water level rising

If you don't have clear phases like these in mind right from the start, you're likely to go through your financial life with one foot in the red and one foot in the yellow, investing a little bit on one hand, paying off debt on the other, and not making any real progress. It's like stepping on the gas and the brakes at the same time, but that's exactly what you'll end up doing if you follow a 20th century financial strategy in the 21st century. Unfortunately, that's become a very common financial fate in the US today.

But if you block your plan out one distinct phase at a time, you *can* get to the green phase, and it's almost automatic if you just follow the steps.

To summarize:

- **Red:** Debt elimination and emergency fund: Your goal is to get out of the red phase and into the yellow phase as soon as you can. To accomplish that, permanently eliminate all of your (non-mortgage) debt and build up an adequate E-Fund.

- **Yellow:** Earn, save, invest, repeat: The yellow phase is where you methodically build net worth. The sooner you start, and the more you save and invest, the easier it will be for you to achieve financial independence.

- **Green:** Financial independence: You reach financial independence when you have sufficient net worth to walk away from your primary job if you choose to (or not). This 21st-century definition of financial independence is entirely different from the old idea of "retirement" and should not be confused with it.

Net Worthy Nugget #2.4

Your goal is to get out of the red phase and into the yellow phase as soon as you can. To accomplish that, permanently eliminate all your (non-mortgage) debt and build up an adequate emergency fund.

It's no surprise that some parts of the path to financial independence are less fun than others. So why not take the most demanding, challenging requirements and tackle them first? That's exactly what the red phase is. Once you've gotten rid of your debt and built up your E-Fund, it's amazing how much better those two tasks will look in your rearview mirror. You'll feel a sense of accomplishment from getting them out of the way, and you'll be able to approach the rest of the path with peace of mind, focus, and confidence. It's the financial equivalent of eating your broccoli first.

Even after you've graduated into the yellow phase, you'll probably face an emergency somewhere along the line, which means you'll need to go back and replenish part of your E-Fund. And, you might not be completely finished with all debt forever. But make no mistake: it's never going be anywhere near as hard as it will be the first time, when you're starting from zero. So, focus on these two tasks, grind 'em out, give yourself a high five, and never look back.

For some of you, though, those two tasks might actually be three. If you work for an employer who matches your 401(k)/TSP-type plan contributions, then thank your lucky stars because that's the best deal in the history of personal finance. It's an offer of free money, pure and simple, deposited directly into your financial bathtub, where it can begin to compound immediately. So, if you qualify, take full advantage. Consider taking advantage of an employer-matched 401(k)/TSP-type plan contribution to be a third red-phase requirement, just as important as building an E-Fund and paying down debt.

What's An Employer Match?

A Note from Chris

Some of you read the phrase "matched 401(k)/TSP-type plan contribution" and your eyes glazed over, your head hurt, and you immediately skipped to the next paragraph. But this nerdy, bureaucratic little phrase turns out to have borderline magical powers.

Let's start with what a "401(k)/TSP-type plan" is. If you're a full-time employee (not a freelancer or part-timer), you may be eligible to divert some of your pay into a special kind of account that allows you to save and invest for your long-term financial independence with the added benefit of some very significant income tax advantages. The most recognizable type of investment account is a 401(k), but there are also 403(b)s, 457s, and TSP (Thrift Savings Plan) accounts, depending on what type of employer you work for. So instead of rattling off that long string of possible account types, we'll just lump them all together and call them "401(k)/TSP-type plans."

Most employers are required to offer these kinds of programs, but some take it a step further and offer an additional feature, called a "match," voluntarily. If you put money into your 401(k)/TSP-type plan account, these special employers will match it. For example, if your employer offers a 50% match, for every dollar you put in, your employer will throw in another 50 cents. Even if it seems like a small number, that's free, extra money on top of your earned income. Your employer may be happily offering to start pouring water directly into your financial bathtub, on top of your pay, and they're just waiting for you to say, "yes, please!" So, if any of this sounds like it might apply to you, contact your employer's payroll, HR, or employee benefits departments. It never hurts to ask, and it might just get you some free money.

Bottom line: Anytime you're eligible for an employer match, *take it!*

The caveat to this discussion is that we're talking "non-mortgage" debt. If you're currently renting and don't have a home mortgage, you can skip ahead. But if you own your home, you'll notice that you're getting a free red-phase pass on your mortgage—it's exempted from the debts you've got to pay off before you can move to your yellow phase. That's because a mortgage is a very special kind of debt. It's relatively low interest, it carries special tax advantages, and it allows you to own a large asset in your name that is very likely to appreciate in value. In other words, it is the exact opposite of credit card debt. You might choose to pay off your mortgage early later, but it's not a requirement for entry into the yellow phase of your financial life.

Bottom line, the red phase isn't necessarily much fun, but you'll never reach financial independence until you knock out these requirements. Depending on how much debt you have, it may take a while to get through it. It might be tempting to put it off, but if you do, it will only get harder when interest is working against you, and interest never rests. Every spare dollar you can scrape together and any extra money that might come your way should go straight toward these critically important red-phase priorities. There's a big pile of broccoli standing between you and an awesome financial future: dig in!

Net Worthy Nugget #2.5

> A bare minimum emergency fund of one month's expenses is your initial, and high-priority, goal. Eventually, you'll increase this to 4, 6, or 9 months' expenses, depending on your household risk level.

Life is full of surprises. Sometimes they're good, but sometimes they're not. When a nasty surprise pops up in your financial life, it can be extremely stressful if you're unprepared for it. One way you can prepare is through insurance. You can directly insure against damage to your car, a fire in your house, or a broken leg. It's a smart move, and we'll get to that later. But you can't directly insure yourself against everything, which is why you have an E-Fund: it's like "all-purpose" insurance, to protect yourself against life's inevitable nasty financial surprises.

Examples might be the loss of your job, unforeseen but mandatory travel expense, uncovered medical or dental crises, or even dealing with a natural disaster. Sometimes the crisis might be a very personal one, like divorce, a surprise pregnancy, or needing to relocate to serve as a caregiver for a loved one; these types of events carry all kinds of emotional challenges in addition to financial ones. Regardless of the cause, financial surprises are so stressful because they hurt you twice. First, there's the emergency itself, which undoubtedly is going to require your full attention to resolve. But then, there's the hole in the middle of your financial month that the emergency caused. How will you beg or borrow the money to pay your bills if all your available cash has been redirected to resolve the emergency? Without an E-Fund, every financial crisis that pops up immediately becomes two.

The need for an E-Fund is so basic you might think everybody except you has one. Sadly, that's not the case. Most people understand the need, and almost everyone has the best of intentions to build up an E-Fund, but so many people just never get around to it. A recent survey done by the Federal Reserve showed nearly 50% of Americans would be unable to cover a $400 emergency. That's the equivalent of a new set of inexpensive tires or a month's groceries for a small family. So, when emergencies happen, people are forced to borrow. That means credit cards. Friends and family. Even the dreaded payday loan. An emergency can kick off a vicious interest-fueled circle that might take years to recover from.

But you'll have a stash of cash at the ready, just in case. You'll keep it somewhere where you can get your hands on it quickly if you need to, but separate from your regular bank account so you're not tempted to spend it. Ideally, you'd like to earn a little bit of interest on it, but you never risk the principal—it's too important. And most of all, you don't touch that money except in the case of a true emergency. The timing chain breaks on your car and it gets towed to the shop for a full engine rebuild? True emergency. A sale that ends just before payday on some really great-looking shoes? Not so much.

So how big does your E-Fund need to be? A simple answer involves figuring an average month's household expenses. So, go back over your household spending for the past several months and come up with a solid estimate for an average month. Be honest about it—if an emergency occurs, you'll be glad you didn't lowball your estimate. Do it now, just some simple addition.

Once you have that figure, understand that first off, *you urgently need a bare minimum of one month's expenses in your E-Fund*. This is a full-on, hair-on-fire, four-alarm financial emergency, and until you can count that money saved up, saving it is your top financial priority.

Once you've successfully built your E-Fund up to the one-month threshold, congratulations. You'll need even more in order to graduate to the yellow phase, but the urgency doesn't need to be as high. How much more will you need? Here's where it gets very individualized, because it depends on your own household risk profile.

Here's how it works:

- Start out by assuming you'll need 6 months' expenses in your emergency fund before you can leave the red phase.

- If your risk profile is lower than average, you can lower the requirement to 4 months.

- If your risk profile is higher than average, raise the requirement to 9 months.

The risk factors to consider include: how many people are in the household, how many of them are earning an income and how many are financially dependent, how susceptible the income earner(s) is/are to job loss, and whether there's substantial supplemental income (on top of your primary job) in the picture. Here are a couple of examples to give you the idea:

- A couple with no dependents or plans to add any, who each earns roughly half the household's income while working in unrelated fields, both of which are relatively "layoff proof" jobs (in a union with seniority, licensed nurse, tenured professor, or similar), who both earn lots of supplemental income on the side—they're good candidates for 4 months' worth of emergency savings.

- A single parent with 5 dependent kids and no supplemental income, in a vulnerable/seasonal/offshorable job in a mature or shrinking industry (say, housing construction worker, bank teller, retail clerk, or a brand-new hire in almost any type of job) should keep 9 months in emergency funds.

As you can tell, there's no one-size-fits-all recommendation for the size of your E-Fund. Your susceptibleness to emergencies, and your ability to recover from them, might be quite different than other people's, and it might be quite different for yourself at different times in your financial life. This is a judgment call, and it's up to you carefully consider all the factors before deciding.

There's a tool in the Net Worthy Navigator App that can help you get a handle on your risk profile quickly, called the E-Fund Risk Assessment Questionnaire. This tool asks you a series of questions, most of them on a 1-to-10 scale, then calculates a personalized E-Fund size recommendation for you. Some of the questions might surprise you and open your eyes to types of financial risks—or your ability to weather a financial storm—that you might not have fully appreciated. It's also a great way to help you recognize when your risk profile changes over time.

No E-Fund? That's No Way to Roll

A Note from Amber

If you want to suffer, don't have an emergency fund. You may not suffer now, if your E-Fund consists of credit cards, like many people I know. But you will suffer when you have to pay it back. And no, increasing your card's credit limit does not count as an expanded E-Fund. Unless you're on a promotional zero-interest period (which is always just temporary anyway), you will pay significantly more for any emergency than if you'd had a well-stocked E-Fund in the first place. And if you're a newer credit card holder, your interest rate will likely be on the higher end. It can get out of hand quickly.

A friend of mine once blew two tires at the same time on the freeway. He'd opted against having roadside assistance on his car insurance, in order to save a little money on his premium. Even worse, he had no E-Fund. At all. All the money to his name was just enough to get a tow to the tire shop and to buy how many tires? Just one. He couldn't afford to get the two that he needed. So he rolled around on three tires, and a "space saving" donut spare. When payday came, he quickly bought the final tire, which meant he couldn't pay that month's rent. This is what life without an E-Fund is like. One bad luck moment on the freeway took him months to finally recover from.

Which Comes First—Pay Off Debt or Build an E-Fund?

A Note from Chris

You've got two dragons to slay to exit the red phase, and the question is which one do you slay first? The biggest one? The one breathing the hottest flames? Or does it even matter?

It matters. To achieve financial independence, you not only have to do the right things, but you have to do them in the right order. (*Chapter 9: The Right Things in the Right Order*, spells out the right sequence of priorities.) There's a lot to consider, but here's a crash course zeroing in on the red phase:

1. **Minimum debt payments.** All your credit cards and other revolving credit accounts have minimum monthly payments, and your installment loans (student loans, car loans, and so forth) have required monthly payments. These come first. Falling short on these carries immediate consequences, so guarding against that is your top priority. We call these "Priority Zero," because they're required, in every sense of the word.

2. **Emergency fund of one month's household expenses.** You'll need much more later, but for now, just sock away the bare minimum to keep you afloat if bad news strikes.

3. **Employer matched 401(k)/ TSP-type plan contributions.** Does your employer match? If yes, it's the deal of the century, and you'd be crazy not to take full advantage.

4. **High interest debt.** High interest means double digit (>10%) APR, and for most people, this means credit card debt. You're already making the minimum payments; now start chipping away at the principle. If your credit card debt is huge, you may want to consider a balance transfer strategy (more on that in Chapter 9.)

5. **Tie between building the rest of your emergency fund and paying off low interest (<10% APR) non-mortgage debt.** It may sound like a cop-out to call this a prioritization tie, but just picture those last two dragons simultaneously keeling over while you stroll serenely into the yellow phase—glorious!

Net Worthy Nugget #2.6

Pay off debts ASAP! If you have more than one, start with the highest interest debt first and work your way down.

Back in Late 20th CenturyLand, student loans were rare and small. It was not unusual to show up bright-eyed and bushy-tailed to begin your financial life with an even-steven scorecard—don't have any money, don't owe any money. Those days are long gone now. Ballooning tuitions mean that student loans are common and large. Most college students start out their financial lives already in the hole, whether they complete their degrees or not.

So far, we've talked at length about student loans, but you may have many different kinds of debt—credit card (or maybe *multiple* cards), car loans, furniture and appliance loans, the ever-popular Bank of Mom and Dad, and more. Obviously, your first priority is to make the minimum payment on each loan, each month. But if the goal is to pay them completely off as quickly as possible to exit the red phase, which do you attack first?

Mathematically speaking, you'll make the fastest progress by tackling the debts with the highest interest rates first. That's why we placed the high interest rate (>10% APR) debt higher on the priority list than single-digit interest. List all your debts, one by one, with the highest APR (annual percentage rate) first. Start at the top, and work your way down. Remember, compound interest works against you when you borrow; by paying off the highest APRs first, you're putting big dents into your fastest growing debts first. This is known as the avalanche method, and that's our recommendation.

There's another approach called the snowball method. It's especially recommended for people who have gotten into very deep debt much faster than they expected, who are facing a disheartening, multi-year task to become debt free. List all your debts in ascending order of the total balance owed. Pay off the smallest balance first, then the next smallest, and so on. This results in some quick, early wins, which can produce a very motivational effect! The avalanche method has the mathematical advantage, and that's the one that will get your debts to zero the fastest. But the snowball method's advantage is that it's motivational, so if motivation is what you're most in need of, give it a try.

After all your debt is paid off, congratulations. Paying off debt is no small feat. The hardest part of your financial journey is over, you're well nourished on broccoli, and it's time for some serious bathtub-filling in the yellow phase.

The Explosion of Student Loans: Very Serious Business

A Note from Chris

The alarming growth of student loan debt over the last decade has meant that it's now "normal" for many to have very substantial debt at a very young age. Normal or not, this can create a huge emotional burden.

The stress can begin long before the first payments are due; sometimes the sheer anticipation of working off a mountain of debt that high can feel overwhelming. Once the first payment notice actually arrives, the anticipation becomes a grim, and sometimes frightening, reality. When this is combined with difficulty finding a decent paying job after leaving school, the situation can seem hopeless. Your mind can swing into survival mode and send you into a panic. Without help, you can begin to spiral out of control emotionally.

In extreme cases, suicide might be considered as the only way out of an impossible financial dilemma. If this is you—or if you think this may describe someone you know and care about—please remember that suicide is a very permanent and painful solution to a temporary situation. There are resources available for your help and support. Below is a toll-free 24hour hotline available for you as well as a link to the National Suicide Prevention Lifeline where you can find more tools and resources like an online chat feature.

1-800-273-8255
www.suicidepreventionlifeline.org

If you think we're being overly dramatic about this, we're not. Student loan debt in the US now totals over $1.2 trillion, which exceeds total credit card debt. Over 40 million Americans owe on student loans. The class of 2015 graduated with an average debt of over $35,000, the most in history. Loan balances well into six figures are common for graduate students. Roughly 1 in 4 student loan borrowers is currently in either delinquency or default, according to the Consumer Financial Protection Bureau. When you consider the sheer magnitude of student loans in the US today, and how incredibly quickly this debt has grown, it's no surprise that student-loan-related suicide has become a frighteningly real concern.

We're here to talk about the financial imperative of paying off all your debts, but we're very aware that highlighting the importance of repaying these loans, and the advisability of repaying as early as possible, might trigger stressful reactions for many. We'll lay out the cold hard facts, because it's important for you to understand them. But please know that we're sensitive to the difficulties inherent in discussing this subject.

The entire reason that both Amber and I are writing this chapter is to provide the best possible advice for you, and to guide you to your brightest financial future.

Finally, information can be a great weapon against stress. The more you know and understand about your options to deal with your student loan debt, the less power those debts will have over you. Student loan debts can be private, federal, or a combination of both. Privately funded debt from different sources can often be consolidated into a single, lower rate loan. Federal student loan debt comes in many forms, so you'll need to research what all your options are. The Federal Student Aid website is a great place to start. It can be just as important to know whom to avoid. Sadly, the student loan explosion has attracted a swarm of sleazy outfits who prey on student borrowers. To find out who they are, check NerdWallet's Student Loan Watchlist.

Once You Know Better, You Can Do Better

A Note from Amber

I know from personal experience that financial struggles can lead to feelings of stress, hopelessness, depression, and even suicidal thoughts. I reached a point during college when it all felt like it was just too much to bear. My living situation with my roommates was both tumultuous and stressful. I was working way too many hours per week between my job and my internship, and it started to take a toll on my school performance. I attended a college that works on the quarter system, so time seemed to be slipping through my fingers like sand.

As the end of the quarter came and went, so did my possibility of saving my GPA. For the first time in my life, I felt like I was on the brink of losing it all. My grades were so low that I was on the verge of dismissal from the university.

With dismissal would come the loss of both of my jobs. The jobs I had were on campus, and I had to be an enrolled student to keep them. So, when I realized the potential impact of the events ahead of me, I found myself discouraged in a way that I had never before experienced. To make it worse, I did not have an E-Fund. The small balance in my checking account, no more than a few hundred dollars, was all that I had to my name. My situation seemed like it was spinning further and further out of control.

I panicked.

In that moment of weakness and desperation, I convinced myself that my ability to earn money was the only thing I had going for me. If I couldn't make money to care for myself, let alone to make any progress on paying back those crushing loans, then what was the point?

Then I nearly made a really, really bad decision. But I am fortunate enough that I cried myself to sleep that night instead of swallowing those pills.

None of us are exempt from the mind games money situations can play with our heads. Whether you're a student like I was, a professional athlete, a doctor, a dancer, or even a stay-at-home parent, we all can find ourselves in discouraging, stressful, and even tragic financial situations. But we are not defined by our circumstances, no matter how dire they might seem. Circumstances are simply the results of past knowledge and decisions. Going forward, we can create a new reality, if we're willing to be courageous enough to experience the discomfort of growth. Reading this chapter is a great first step in the direction of new possibilities because once you know better, you can do better.

Your personal financial journey is just that: a journey. There will be massive successes, tragic failures, and everything in between. Regardless of what happens along the way, you can still reach your goals. Take the lessons you learn—from successes as well as failures—and apply them as best you can.

This story has a happy ending. After talking with the dean, I was able to stay enrolled. Staying enrolled meant that I could keep my jobs. Bit by bit I began to regain control of my finances. I had to change my major, and it's turned out to be a better fit for me in the long run. By the time I ultimately graduated, I felt I'd learned far more about myself, about life, and yes, about money, than I'd ever expected from my college experience. And that new perspective eventually led me to make a really big decision a few years later.

Net Worthy Nugget #2.7

> The yellow phase is where you methodically build net worth. The sooner you start, and the more you save and invest, the easier it will be for you to achieve financial independence.

If the red phase was a grind, the yellow phase is a glide. The yellow phase is the simplest to describe, because bathtub-filling is your single, primary objective during this entire phase. Your strategy is "earn, save, and invest." You just keep on repeating those steps, over and over, until there's enough water in your bathtub to last you the rest of your life.

So, how long will that take? One of the great things about the yellow phase is that the speed is completely up to you, depending on your own priorities in life. If reaching financial independence as early as possible is a major priority for you, then you take a pedal-to-the-metal approach. That will mean saving and investing the maximum proportion of your earnings that you possibly can, spending only enough today to meet your basic needs. But if you're not in as much of a rush, you can slow down and enjoy the ride by saving and investing relatively less. A slow journey with a nice, comfortable lifestyle, a fast and frugal dash, or somewhere in between? There's no one right answer for everybody. It's up to you, and you can even change speeds during the yellow phase if your priorities in life change. Remember, though, the math behind compound interest strongly favors *early* saving and investing.

The "earn" part of the strategy is often dramatically different for you than it was in the late 20th century, and this is a point that Boomer parents can be slow to appreciate. Then: a single (or very few) employer for most of one's working life, and not much opportunity, or need, for supplemental income. Now: it's time to hustle! Every millennial knows that's not just a sassy dance you do with your friends at the disco on Friday night, it's a major feature of today's employment landscape for young adults. It's about building your skills, network, and opportunities through a diverse combination of work experiences. To fill in the gaps, young adults have proven highly adept at pursuing—or even inventing—side hustles. The single-employer option is much rarer today, and it's sometimes even seen as unattractive due to its limited flexibility.

Regardless of how the "earn" part works for you, it's the "save and invest" aspect that powers your journey through the yellow phase. Chapter 7 is where you'll find every detail you'll need for a safe, dependable, and highly successful long-term investment program.

How long do you stay in the yellow phase? How much water in your bathtub is "enough?" You probably know people who have very specific, quantified retirement-savings goals. That's fine for some people, but most of the time, the end of your yellow phase is like an upward-moving elevator. Each time the door opens, you decide whether to get out on that floor or stay on the elevator and continue upward a while longer. Once you've managed to fill your bathtub to a certain threshold, your financial life becomes a series of "how much more water do I really want to add?" decisions. For simplicity, let's consider just 3 such occasions, which we'll call points A, B and C.

First, you'll reach point A, when you have enough accumulated net worth to provide for a comfortable enough but "no frills" lifestyle. Most people don't choose to stop working when they reach point A, but a few jump at the chance. Others take this as an opportunity to completely change the type of work they do. Point A might be the perfect time to do something that pays less but is more fulfilling. You'll still be increasing your water level, just at a slower rate. But no matter what you choose, just imagine how nice it feels to know—at last—that it's truly a choice. (Trust me, even if you keep working, you'll never think of your boss quite the same way after you've reached point A!)

If you keep on working, eventually you'll reach point B. Here, you've built up enough to stop working and spend the rest of your life at the same level of lifestyle you're currently living. From there, you can choose to get off the elevator at point B, or continue working until you reach point C, where you can enjoy a dream lifestyle—for the rest of your life.

The Net Worth Bathtub
Closeup

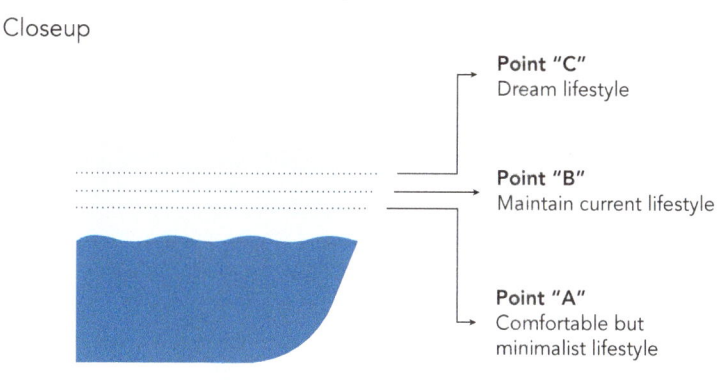

Point "C"
Dream lifestyle

Point "B"
Maintain current lifestyle

Point "A"
Comfortable but minimalist lifestyle

The harsh truth is: most people never even get to point A. It's usually because they waited way too late to get serious about saving and investing. But if you power through the red phase, then start saving and investing early enough, you *will* get to point A and beyond. There's no need to decide ahead of time on whether to step off the elevator at floor A, B, or C. A lot of what you'll need to consider in that decision will depend on what's going on in your life at that time, both inside and outside your working life. Just get aboard the elevator, and get it moving upward. Deciding when to get off is the fun part.

A Hard Perspective on Social Security

A Note from Amber

A close family friend of mine is on the cusp of retirement age and is one of those people who has barely reached point A. Her hope was that Social Security would pull through and provide sufficient support for her. And that was her plan for retirement. Her *entire* plan. She says things like "I've been poor my whole life, what else was I supposed to do?" And I just wonder what is going to happen to other people I know who are approaching her age. Are they just going to try to keep working until their bodies give out? The idea is so stressful and disheartening!

Net Worthy Nugget #2.8

The green phase represents true financial independence! You reach it when you have sufficient net worth to walk away from your primary job, or not. This 21st century definition of financial independence is entirely different from the old idea of "retirement" and should not be confused with it.

The residents of Late 20th CenturyLand rode a very different kind of elevator. Others operated the controls while you were just a passenger along for the ride. The elevator only made one stop, at the floor marked "retirement age." At that point, the doors opened wide and all you heard was "end of the line, everybody out!" That's what the word "retirement" meant: going from full-time work to full-time leisure overnight, usually at a fixed, predetermined age that you didn't have any control over.

The three-phase path we've been describing is *nothing* like that. It's not nearly as simple, and it's not nearly as limiting. Your progress along the path is completely determined by choices that you make yourself. You can achieve financial independence, but only if you choose to, and only if you take the steps necessary to make it happen. It's hard to imagine how today's financial path could be any more different than the old "retirement" game.

And yet—incredibly— the R-word is still alive and well. People keep using it as if we were all still living in that old financial and working-world reality. Financial institutions still advertise, "Come see us about retirement savings plans!" Our vote would be to retire the word "retirement," permanently. But since that's not going to happen, the next best thing is to make sure you understand that traditional retirement is just one of many choices available to you in the green phase. You may or may not choose to retire, but it's incredibly empowering to reach a state where working for an income is truly optional.

What's the most important thing in your life? Where do your most intense, heartfelt passions lie? Whatever your answers to the questions are— or will be in the future—remember this: if you're financially independent, you'll be in a far better position to pursue those dreams and to participate fully in those areas of your life that mean the most to you than if you're still financially dependent.

But, you won't get there automatically. Unlike the 20th century, it only depends a little bit on how much money you make. And, it doesn't depend at all on your age or how many years you've worked for your employer. Instead it all depends on you—on the decisions you make and the actions you take.

Here are two places you *don't* want to end up. You don't want to find yourself midway through your financial life and barely getting started with your long-term investing; you'll have too far to go and not enough time to get there, and your only choices will be very risky ones. Unfortunately, that's where millions of Americans find themselves right now. And, you *really* don't want to be late in your financial life and still struggling with debt or some of the other basics. But yes, there are millions in this category, too.

The earlier you start, the easier it is. If you stick with it, sooner or later, you'll arrive at the green phase. And it's pretty awesome. We'd tell you all about it, but you're going to have to write that part yourself. When you've achieved financial independence, you're free to build the life of your dreams, any way you want.

The Bottom Line

A Note from Amber

Earlier, I explained that my financial crisis in college gave me a new perspective on life, and this in turn led me to make a big career decision. I've become a certified financial educator and money coach. I have the privilege of helping others with the same issues I struggled with, and that gives me a feeling of much greater usefulness in the world than anything else I could have chosen to do. (Especially counting seeds!) That's also why I created my blog, for the simple reason that I wanted to help people feel good about their finances, no matter what their numbers might look like at the moment. I know what can happen when people feel alone, overwhelmed, and unsupported, so I have a special understanding of the importance of this work. It feels more like a calling than a job.

I have a deep, personal understanding that the red phase can be a dark and dangerous place. Getting through it is no joke, and it takes some serious commitment. I'm just inches away from getting out of it now myself, and believe me, once I'm out I never want to slip back into it again. My own red-phase experience has given me compassion for those struggling through it. But it's also the reason I feel a special joy when I'm able to teach, advise, or encourage others to overcome those challenges. Knowledge is power, and I want to be a force in providing people with the power to improve their financial futures. I hope after reading this chapter, you're feeling the power, too. I'll meet you in the green phase!

About the Co-Author

Amber Berry is a millennial who shares her passion for personal finance through her website, feelgoodfinances.com. As a Certified Money Coach and blogger, she enjoys working with women and young adults to help them transform their relationships with money through education and compassion.

"I thoroughly enjoyed co-creating this work to share the knowledge with my fellow millennials in a way that is digestible, compassionate and useful. I think it is important to find new ways to explain information and I hope this book resonates with anyone who needs it. My hope is that anyone who reads this book will realize that financial independence is for everyone!"

Chapter 3

Money Basics

by Chris Smith with Monica Viera

Net Worthy Nugget #3.1

The ability to grow your net worth requires an entirely different skill set from that needed to acquire income. Like any life skill, mastering it requires commitment, time, and practice.

Net Worthy Nugget #3.2

Get organized. There's no substitute for an approach to filing, calendar management, contact list management, and task tracking that's dependable and works for you.

Net Worthy Nugget #3.3

Where to set up your checking and savings accounts? Credit unions and online banks are great choices.

Net Worthy Nugget #3.4

Always use a credit card . . . but never use credit.

Net Worthy Nugget #3.5

Eventually, you'll have 3-5 credit cards. They should all be carefully selected cash-back cards with no (or very low) annual fees.

Net Worthy Nugget #3.6

You have to pay income taxes, so do it smart: Meet all deadlines, pay everything you owe (but not more), and every year get a little smarter about how much you need to pay, and be more efficient in how you go about managing and paying your taxes.

Net Worthy Nugget #3.7

Insurance is an essential tool in dealing with risk. The goal is a "Goldilocks strategy" for deciding how much you need, for how long, and in which major insurance categories. Expect your needs to change as you go through life, often considerably.

Net Worthy Nugget #3.8

Your credit score has always been important in determining whether you're able to borrow money to buy a house and at what interest rate. But whether you end up buying a house or not, credit scores are increasingly being used for other important purposes, too. To build and maintain an excellent score, all you need is a simple strategy of zero debt, zero late payments, regular credit report review, and a low credit utilization rate (the amount you owe on your cards, as a percentage of their limits).

Net Worthy Nugget #3.9

All humans are subject to irrational financial thinking, even (especially?) those who believe they aren't. Irrationality can completely sabotage the best financial plans, so it's in your interest to understand it, recognize it, and take steps to actively combat it.

Net Worthy Nugget #3.10

Virtually every advertiser wants you to believe some version of this big lie: the definition of "saving money" is spending money—but (supposedly) less of it than some so-called "normal" price. Advertisers keep on using this line because it keeps on working. Stop believing it and start seeing through it, every time, starting now.

Net Worthy Nugget #3.11

You'll make wiser long-term decisions, financial and otherwise, if you talk them over with the "future you." Make a habit of it.

Net Worthy Nugget #3.1

The ability to grow your net worth requires an entirely different skill set from that needed to acquire income. Like any life skill, mastering it requires commitment, time, and practice.

Building a strong financial future requires two major life skills: 1) the ability to make consistent money in a profession of your choice and 2) the ability to use that money wisely, safely, and successfully to get on a path to a financially independent future. Everybody is already aware of the importance of the first one. It's a main goal in our educational system. People spend tremendous amounts of time, energy, and money mastering these skills before entering their chosen field—and then even more is required to stay current and continue to grow.

But what about the knowledge required to take care of that income once you've earned it? That skill is every bit as important, but somehow it gets ignored and neglected. The prevailing attitude seems to be: if I just earn enough money, all that "financial stuff" will just more or less take care of itself . . . I hope.

The very fact that you're reading this means you've begun to at least suspect that "hoping for the best" isn't a great strategy for financial success. Good for you, because it's not. We all have that friend who works really hard and is great at what they do but who seems a little lost about where it's all headed financially. They're making money all right, but somehow they still seem to experience more than their share of financial crises. Maybe that friend is even you. Any time they feel stressed about finances, their first reaction is to double down on the first skill—to work even harder, to try to make even more money.

If you're not sure where you're headed, increasing your speed won't help! What you really need is to find a good, sustainable balance between life skills #1 and #2. If you feel unbalanced right now, worry not. You have a lot of company. Most people haven't realized how important life skill #2 is, or if they have, they can't find a solid, practical way to master it.

The point here is to encourage you to make a distinct, deliberate, and very conscious decision to build your personal finance skills. You probably already realize that it won't happen by itself, and that it's going to take some commitment, time, and practice. The good news is that it's not nearly as hard to build this skill as most people think it's going to be. The even better news is that the knowledge outlined in this book can serve as a straightforward, handy way to go about it.

At your job, some amount of competition is probably inevitable. But when it comes to achieving financial independence, the only real competition you have is with yourself. Resolve now to build the skills you need to start mapping out a solid financial foundation. Instead of competing with others, consider working together with friends, colleagues, or family members. It can make the learning more fun, and besides, this is one time when your success doesn't come at the expense of someone else's. But whether you learn solo or with others, resolve to start the journey now.

Net Worthy Nugget #3.2

> Get organized. There's no substitute for an approach to filing, calendar management, contact list management, and task tracking that's dependable and works for you.

It doesn't matter if you have loads of money in your checking account if you're constantly late on your bills because you can't keep track of the due dates. It doesn't matter if a company who claims you owe them money is completely mistaken if you've lost the documents that would have helped you prove your case. Most important of all, it does no good to have a great idea about improving your financial situation if a chaotic organizational environment prevents you from accessing the critical details you need to actually implement that idea.

There's an old saying that 80% of life is just showing up. If that's true, the financial version of it could be that 90% of financial success is knowing where all the records are and when everything is due. Seriously. Strong organizational skills translate very directly into financial empowerment and control.

There's no one right way to build these organizational skills into your life. The best guiding principle is to seek a balance between simplicity and completeness. You might need to experiment a little bit, or ask somebody who seems to have a great system, before you find the approach that works best for you. Here are a few specifics:

1. **Filing:** Commit to having a space, whether it be physical or electronic, to store the important financial information in your life: bills, receipts, checks, payments you've made, insurance policies, past tax returns, and anything else even remotely financial, just in case. You never know

when you may need to access these at some point, and when that happens, quick and easy access can save you money and stress.

2. **Calendar management:** The modern American adult is often overwhelmed by bills. Make sure you know what needs to be paid when. Automate the payments when you can, or track their due dates on a (real or virtual) calendar when you can't. Budgeting and calendar management go hand-in-hand when you're planning your upcoming financial month or year.

3. **Contact list management:** Keep contact information like your bank's customer service number, student loan representative, tax specialist, insurance agent, and more, so that you have always have access to the assistance you need.

4. **Task tracking:** Again, whether it be physically taking down notes on a paper or a whiteboard, or using an app on your phone, keeping track is an essential life skill that will help you prioritize and keep you focused on what needs to get done. The dividing line between the financial and non-financial aspects of your life is blurrier than you may first suspect, so keeping track of all of your important to-do's on a single integrated list is a good move.

Socio-economist Randall Bell, PhD, is the author of *Rich Habits Rich Life: The Four Cornerstones of All Great Pursuits*. He's studied success for 25 years, analyzing the core characteristics that all great achievers have in common. He writes: "Those who maintain both a calendar and to-do list are 289% more likely to be millionaires, as compared with those who have no real set schedule." We're not saying that getting organized alone will guarantee financial independence, but it's worth noting that adopting these few simple disciplines can put the 289% working in your favor, instead of against you.

Five Hours a Month = Peace of Mind

A Note from Monica

Like several other young adults, I found it difficult to keep my finances organized. Back when I was in high school and I had one job and one bank account, it was much easier to stay on top of things. But when I started college, I took out some credit cards and loans, which made staying organized a task in itself.

Simply put, I was ready for that extra money but not the responsibility that came with it. I made excuse after excuse as to why I was too busy to sit down and face all the bills I had to pay off. My reasoning at the time changed almost weekly to serve my current interests (staying as irresponsible and free of added worries for as long as possible). Most of us have that nagging voice in the back our heads alerting us to pay off what we owe, but we're also pros at silencing it. This dangerous game eventually caught up with me, and I learned the hard way that the "freedom" I traded off back in college to ignore paying my bills actually sabotaged my chances of freedom for life after college.

For a few years, because many of bills were sent to a collections agency and my credit score dropped drastically, I couldn't apply for a one-bedroom apartment to live in on my own since most property owners ran a credit check. So, I had to live with my parents for years after college. Although they wanted me to have my freedom, they weren't willing to cosign on any lease for an apartment either, knowing my track record with money.

So, I finally began to face all the bills I had to pay to get myself out of $70,000 in debt, but things got worse before they got better. Despite working full-time, I was still too broke to go out with friends for more than a year because I was still busy playing catch-up. I couldn't believe I had this heavy price to pay simply because I hadn't stayed organized with my finances when I was younger. And I began to feel really overwhelmed and depressed.

A difficult thing about being a modern adult is that there are so many bills (and sometimes loans) we have stay on top of. Even with the management tools that are available to us, it still can take a significant amount of effort to keep ourselves on track. Or so I thought. When I finally came around to my senses, I figured I'd have to start budgeting, task tracking, and managing my contacts. I just didn't know where to start.

Eventually, this is what I came up with. I take a few hours every two weeks to sit down, pay my bills, and do my budgeting. This feels like a good balance for me because I'm always in the know about where my finances stand, but I don't have to micromanage them daily. Each two-week mark is also a good time to reflect and see if I've saved any money and if my current strategies of managing money are working for me.

Instead of using a filing cabinet, I use a binder with pre-printed Excel sheets so I can fill in current numbers. I scan these onto my computer with my phone so I can keep electronic copies, just in case something were to happen to the binder. My binder is thick, but it's divided into sections that basically encompass my entire financial life: I have a calendar of when certain bills are due, a contact list for banks and loan services I've used, copies of bills, and a calendar for my budget.

Now I know it is possible to take charge of my financial life by simply allocating five hours a month to its organization. No longer do I feel an underlying sense of anxiety about the stress of pending loan payments and bills. I see the five hours I take monthly not only as an investment for my future, but as an effective strategy to maintain a sense of sanity in the present. If I would have known earlier that managing my finances would have been so important, I probably would have put much more effort into them earlier in life. This "minor inconvenience" would have saved me from a lot of unnecessary struggle years after.

Net Worthy Nugget #3.3

*Where to set up your checking and savings accounts?
Credit unions and online banks are great choices.*

Sometimes, in order to make the best decision possible, life requires you to part with what's familiar and comfortable. Statistics show that most people still think commercial banks are the best place to put their money, but it could be because they're constantly flooded by ads that assure them that this is the truth. It isn't.

Commercial banks have evolved into a lose-lose proposition, at least for individual consumers like us: you get a very low interest rate on deposits while getting hit with fees left and right. As you may already know, you can expect to be charged a fee whenever you overdraft, use an ATM, fall below a required minimum balance, replace a lost debit card, you name it. With so many possible fees, it's no wonder that more and more people are turning to credit unions or online banks.

If you've used a commercial bank your entire life, it may take some time to get used to something different, but it can save you lots of money down the line. Credit unions have a better customer service reputation compared to commercial banks and are generally open to the public. Like commercial banks, credit unions have physical branches you can go into and conduct your banking in person. Online banks don't have this feature, but the trade-off is that they are open for business 24/7, year-round. Like credit unions, online banks feature much higher interest rates on deposits and extremely low fees.

Don't stick with a commercial bank just because that's what you've always done, or because that's what other people you know do. If you do a little research, you'll find a credit union or online bank—or maybe both—that meets your needs much better.

Net Worthy Nugget #3.4

Always use a credit card . . . but never use credit.

Anytime you have a choice of how to pay—cash, check, a debit card, or a credit card—always choose a credit card. Make it a lifelong habit, and never look back. Here's why:

- Unlike cash, credit cards leave an electronic trail that you can always use to track for budgeting or tax purposes. Debit card transactions at certain places (like gas stations, hotels, and car rentals) tend to charge a higher amount until your transaction is cleared, which can put you at risk for incurring overdraft fees. And checks create an unpredictable timing problem, since the recipient can choose to cash them whenever they'd like.

- Credit cards are instant, convenient, and very widely accepted.

- If your card (or your card-account information) falls into the wrong hands, you're not responsible for any fraudulent charges, as long as you promptly report the loss.

- If you buy a good or service which turns out not to be what was promised or expected, you're in a much stronger position to dispute a credit card transaction. Your credit card provider will work on your behalf to get your money back; if you bought with a debit card, you're on your own.

- Finally, and most importantly, credit cards are the only option that will directly help you improve your credit score if you use them as suggested below.

But what about the dangers of credit cards? What about the super high interest rates? That's where "never use credit" comes in. **Always pay the full balance, every month, on every card, no exceptions**. If you do that, you'll enjoy all the benefits of credit cards, but you'll never pay a penny of interest. Interest is only charged on the balance carried over from the previous month. As long as you always pay the full balance, that carryover will always be zero, so your interest charges will always be zero.

If you pay online, you can even automate this rule by enrolling in the AutoPay (or similarly named) feature. We highly advise you to do that. That way, you never run the risk of forgetting to pay the full balance. Your credit card will access your checking account each month and automatically transfer the amount needed. Now you see the real discipline required here: you've got to keep your monthly spending low enough to be sure you've always got enough in your checking account to cover it.

How to Pay for What You Buy: Step-by-Step Improvement Guide

A Note from Chris

When you started out in life, you didn't even have a bank account in your own name. Now you're aiming for a small collection of cash back credit cards someday. How do you get from point A to point B? Here's the typical sequence, along with the pros and cons of each:

1. **Coins and bills**
   - ⊘ **Pros:** Convenience. There's no authentication required—you hold them, you can spend them. They're widely accepted, no questions asked. It's obvious when you're running low, and it's hard to spend more than you have.

   - ⊗ **Cons:** Cash can generally only be used at physical point of purchase. It leaves no trail, so unless you're willing to manually keep track of paper receipts, it's a nightmare for taxes and budgeting. There's little defense against theft and fraud, and cash can't help your credit history/score.

2. **Debit card**
   A card issued by your bank that enables you to authorize the payment of a purchase directly from your bank account.

   - ⊘ **Pros:** They're convenient and widely accepted. A debit card allows you to spend what's in your checking account, but not more than that. The transaction details are available online.

   - ⊗ **Cons:** They require constant monitoring of checking balance, since attempts to overspend result in overdraft charges. They're subject to "blocks" (gas, rental cars, hotels, for example, temporarily charge the card more than the actual amount spent, which can make balance tracking problematic). You've got limited defense against theft and fraud, and a debit card provides no help with credit history/score.

STOP. Do not proceed past a debit card until you've demonstrated strong financial skills and discipline. The test is: six consecutive months of regular use with zero overdrafts. Once you pass the test, proceed to the highest of #5, #4, or #3, based on your ability to qualify.

3. **Secured credit card**
   If you can't qualify for a full credit card, a secured card is a great transitional step that allows you to build your credit history/score. These are special credit cards that require you to pay an upfront deposit, which then becomes some or all of your credit limit. With responsible use, the credit limit is raised and/or deposit returned. Examples: CapitalOne Secured Mastercard and the Discover It Secured Card. Pay the full balance each and every month.

   ⊘ **Pros:** Your use of a secured card is monitored by the credit bureaus; responsible use establishes history and will build your credit score. These look like and work as conveniently as a normal credit card (merchants can't tell the difference). They offer the same strong protection against theft and fraud as a normal credit card. Transaction details are available online.

   ⊗ **Cons:** Irresponsible use will further damage your already fragile credit. Failure to pay the balance in full in any month will trigger truly astronomical interest charges. Credit limits are typically low at first, so you'll probably need to be using both a debit card and a secured card for some time.

4. **"Average" Cash Back Credit Card**
   A card authorizing you to spend up to a predetermined credit limit, covered by the card issuer, regardless of your bank account balance. Card owner must make minimum monthly payment, with the balance subject to interest. Requires "average" credit score (~630) or better to qualify, pays moderate percentage of cash back (~1.5%). Example: CapitalOne QuicksilverOne ($39 annual fee). Pay the full balance each and every month.

   ⊘ **Pros:** By paying the balance in full each and every month, cash back comes into your financial bathtub, but no interest leaves it—all while you are building up your credit history/score. They're convenient and widely accepted, with strong protection against theft and fraud. Transaction details are available online. They may include special benefits for new/first-year cardholders.

   ⊗ **Cons:** Irresponsible use will further damage your credit. Failure to pay the balance in full in any month will trigger interest charges; it's easy to get in deep trouble fast if you don't stay disciplined.

5. **"Excellent" Cash Back Credit Card**
   Same as #4, but requires "excellent" credit score (~690) or better to qualify, pays substantial percentage of cash back (2%-5%). Examples: Amex Blue Cash, Discover It Cashback Match, Citi Card Double Cash. Pay the full balance each and every month.

   ✓ **Pros:** Same as #4, but the cash-back faucet is turned up substantially higher!

   ✗ **Cons:** Same as #4.

6. **Multiple (3-5) "Excellent" Cash Back Credit Cards**
   What's the strategy? Keep your first card open and active, even if it's only in the "average" category, because credit scores like long, uninterrupted, successful credit card account histories. Don't add more than one new card per year, because credit scores think adding cards too fast looks like a sign of trouble. Mix and match spending among the cards in whatever way is necessary to maximize cash back; just be sure to use each card often enough to prevent it from becoming deactivated (usually one transaction per year is enough). Pay the full balance on each and every card, each and every month.

   ✓ **Pros:** Same as #4, but your utilization rate is so tiny now, you're killing it on your credit score!

   ✗ **Cons:** Same as #4, plus you've got more to manage—why it's so key to get organized first.

How to Pay For What You Buy

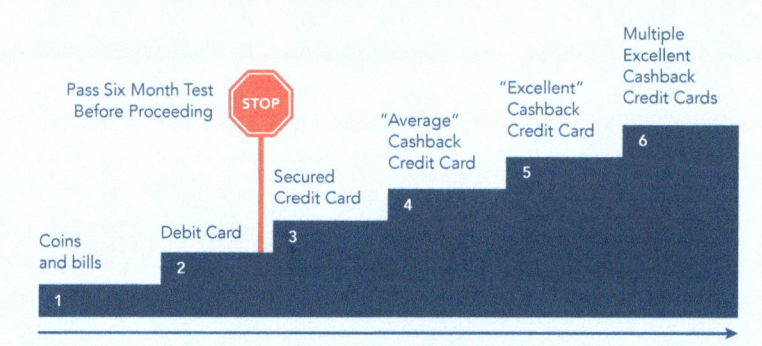

1. Coins and bills
2. Debit Card
3. Secured Credit Card — Pass Six Month Test Before Proceeding (STOP)
4. "Average" Cashback Credit Card
5. "Excellent" Cashback Credit Card
6. Multiple Excellent Cashback Credit Cards

Increasing Credit History and Score
Increasing Financial Skill and Discipline

Net Worthy Nugget #3.5

Eventually, you'll have 3-5 credit cards. They should all be carefully selected cash back cards with no (or very low) annual fees.

It may seem confusing to advise you to sign up for credit cards you don't necessarily need, but there's a science to how this can *increase your credit score*. Each time you add a card, you expand the limit of what your average monthly charges are compared to. Some call this the ultimate credit score hack; whether it's a true hack or not, it's definitely worth taking the time to understand the concept:

Credit Utilization Percentage = Sum of your credit card limits / Sum of your average monthly balances

Let's say you currently have a credit card with a $1,000 limit, and your average monthly spending on that card is $400. This means you're using 40% of your available credit. But if you have two credit cards that each have a $1,000 limit, and you spend $300 on one of them and $100 on the other, this time you're only using 20% of your credit even though you're spending the same amount. By adding the second credit card and doubling the credit available to you, you've lowered your utilization ratio by 20 points—and that increases your credit score.

Although this is a powerful concept, it's crucial that you add the credit cards you accumulate slowly, because it can actually hurt your credit score if you apply for too many cards in a short period of time. Getting a new card every year for three to five consecutive years would be a good way to go about doing this.

Another way to lower your utilization percentage is to ask for a credit limit increase on one or more of your existing cards. It doesn't hurt to ask; making the request has no impact on your credit score. The worst thing that can happen is that you'll be told no, but if your request is approved, that means an instantaneous uptick in your score. Still another way of playing the utilization game is to increase the frequency of your payments. If you pay off the full balance twice a month instead of once, you'll cut your utilization percentage in half. All of these tools taken together—adding credit cards, requesting credit increases, and paying more frequently—work together to substantially reduce your utilization and increase your credit score.

Finally, not all credit cards are created equal; there are some really good ones and some really bad ones out there. It's not a good idea to respond to direct mail credit card offers ("you've been preselected!"), nor is it good to allow yourself to be influenced by advertising. Credit card providers will bombard you with advertisements, assuming you'll be so overwhelmed that you'll just feel "safest" with the most familiar card or bank you've heard of. Don't fall for it. Virtually all credit card offers that come through direct mail are for cards with high annual fees—don't even open them. The same thing is true with cards pushed at you while you're in the middle of making a purchase that offer "instant savings." You may save on that particular purchase, but you'll give it all back and more on the annual fee.

So what kind of credit card are you looking for? You'll zero in on two things. The first is a very low annual fee. Many cards have no annual fee at all, and of course, those are best. The second requirement is to receive cash back as a percentage of what you purchase on the card. The percentages may be small, usually in the 1-2% range, but can be as high as 5-6% for specific categories of spending. Since you'll be using your credit card(s) for virtually all your purchases, the cash back can really add up month after month.

The world of credit cards changes very fast, so up-to-date research is important when looking for a card to add. Our current favorite site to research credit cards is NerdWallet.com. Click on the "Cash Back" symbol, and you'll see a great selection of cash-back cards, most with no (or low) annual fees. Of course, the best cards (the ones with the highest cash back percentages) require the highest credit scores.

The bottom line: decreasing your credit utilization percentage increases your credit score. Paying every card off in full, every month, means you won't pay any interest. Choosing cards with no or small annual fees means that aspect will be painless, too. Add in the cash-back factor, and the net effect is that you're not only increasing your credit score for free, you're actually *bringing money into your bathtub*, at the same time. See why this is a much better way to go than debit cards?

Net Worthy Nugget #3.6

You have to pay income taxes, so do it smart: Meet all deadlines, pay everything you owe (but not more), and every year get a little smarter about how much you need to pay, and be more efficient in how you go about managing and paying your taxes.

Studying the US Federal Income Tax rules of the road isn't necessarily interesting to everyone, but it is absolutely practical for you to know about. Over the course of your entire financial life, taxes will end up being one of your biggest overall expenses. Taking the time to learn some of the basics—or maybe even some of the more advanced aspects—can end up making a big difference. So even if the topic seems intimidating or boring at first, spending some time getting comfortable with the tax basics is well worth it.

Here are four suggestions to help you navigate the world of income taxes:

- **Pay what you owe, in full and on time, every year.** Whether you agree with this politically or not, from a legal standpoint, it's simply not optional. There's a reason behind the old saying, "The only two certainties in life are death and taxes." Failing to pay, for any reason, can get you on the wrong side of the IRS, which can have serious implications. And procrastination just adds stress and pressure to an already challenging situation.

- **Don't pay more than the legal minimum amount you're required to pay.** Two taxpayers in the same financial situation could end up paying very different amounts, and both could be considered in complete compliance. The reason? One of them was likely more familiar with the tax code and was able to take advantage of specific deductions, credits, or other handy aspects. This is perfectly legal and is known as avoiding taxes. On the other hand, intentionally misrepresenting your situation in order to pay less is called evading taxes, and this is a serious criminal offense.

- **Commit yourself to staying up-to-date on the basics.** Ignorance can be expensive. You could end up paying more than you have to when you aren't as familiar with relevant tax documents. You don't have to become an expert on the whole landscape, just on those parts of it that affect you the most.

- **Know when to ask for help, and what kind.** How much help you need depends on how much time and effort you're willing to put into it, but it also depends on how complicated your tax situation is. If you're single, with no dependents, a light income that comes from a single source, few if any deductions, and your tax year is very similar to last year's—you can probably get by on your own just by spending some quality time at good old IRS.gov and carefully following the instructions on your tax form. But as you go through your financial life, it's not unusual for your tax situation to get more complicated. When that happens, it might be time to invest in some well-established, taxpayer friendly software, like TurboTax, H&R Block, or TaxAct. But if your situation has gotten even more complex—or if you don't like the idea of wrestling with tax software any more than the prospect of poring over the IRS website—then it may be time to hire a CPA specializing in income taxes. It's the most expensive kind of help, but if that's what it takes to make sure that you're meeting, but not exceeding, all of your tax obligations, then it's a bargain.

Remember getting organized? If you've taken that goal to heart, finding all the documents and records you need will be a breeze. Disorganized or missing records can quickly turn it into a mountain, but being organized is a surefire way to keep your income tax preparation task molehill-sized.

Net Worthy Nugget #3.7

> Insurance is an essential tool in dealing with risk. The goal is a "Goldilocks strategy" for deciding how much you need, for how long, and in which major insurance categories. Expect your needs to change as you go through life, often considerably.

There's a fairy tale many American children know called "Goldilocks and the Three Bears," where Goldilocks, the little girl, struggles to make decisions because she's looking for something just right. In the story, "right" means centered and balanced. It would be wise for you to be as picky and diligent as Goldilocks when shopping around for insurance plans.

At its core, the insurance decision is a trade-off between the amount in premiums that you're willing to pay versus the amount of risk that you're willing to "bear" (sorry!). It's not wise to shy away from paying a modest premium which will protect you against potentially huge, catastrophic expenses—but sadly, that's what many people are doing by failing to get medical insurance. On the other side of the coin, it's not wise to say yes to every single auto insurance coverage option, at the highest possible coverage amount—over time, the premiums will cost more than the financial risk you're trying to guard against. What you want is not too much risk, nor too much premium expense—like Goldilocks, you're looking for that "just right" happy medium.

It's important to understand that that this "just right" amount isn't something you can calculate or solve for. The trade-off is different for different people—sometimes very different—because people have such different attitudes about risk. Other people in your life, including your insurance agent, may have their own opinions, but it's important for you to strike the balance that's right for you.

When you shop around for insurance, words like "coverage" and "deductible" will be thrown around. Here's what they mean:

Coverage: upper limit of what your insurer is responsible for
Deductible: lower limit of the claim your insurer is responsible for

If you incur a covered expense over the coverage amount or under the deductible, *that money comes out of your pocket.* To avoid this, you can raise your coverage amount and decrease your deductibles, but this will raise the price you pay on premiums.

Most beginners either buy too much or too little insurance, and once they have it they neglect to adjust it as life circumstances change. Always make sure you're up-to-date with your insurance policies, and update them as you move through life.

There's one particular form of insurance that deserves special comment—life insurance. First, the only type of life insurance we recommend is called *term* life insurance. The other type is called permanent (which comes in many varieties, such as universal, whole, or variable), and it is much more expensive than term life insurance. The considerable amount you'd pay for it would be better invested in your long-term investment program (which we'll discuss in Chapter 7). Second, you only need term life insurance for a very specific phase of your life. You don't need it until you have financial dependents, and you no longer need it after your net worth is high enough to provide for your financial dependents in the event of your death by simply providing for them in your will. Finally, it's often tough to beat the term life insurance premium rates that are available through your employer. Be careful, though, because sometimes, leaving such an employer might leave you without life insurance coverage.

Net Worthy Nugget #3.8

> Your credit score has always been important in determining whether you're able to borrow money to buy a house, and at what interest rate. But whether you end up buying a house or not, credit scores are increasingly being used for other important purposes, too. To build and maintain an excellent score, all you need is a simple strategy of zero debt, zero late payments, regular credit report review, and a low credit utilization rate (the amount you owe on your cards, as a percentage of their limits).

Your credit score is a 3-digit number, designed to predict the likelihood that you'll pay back money that you borrow. Although there are multiple types of credit scores available, the one that is most commonly used by lenders is the FICO score; FICO is otherwise known as the Fair Isaac Corporation, which was an early pioneer in the credit scoring field. Your FICO score can range from 300 to 850; the image below breaks down how different scores are interpreted.

Your Credit Score
What your FICO® score means to lenders

<579
Lenders view you as a very risky borrower

670–739
Most lenders consider this a good score

800+
Lenders view you as an exceptional borrower

300 ———————————————————————— 850

580–669
Some lenders will

740–799
Lenders view you as

Your credit score really is important to your financial future. If you're dreaming of buying a house someday, your credit score will determine whether you can get a mortgage and what interest rate you'll be charged. Traditionally, that's been the main importance of credit scores, but now they're now being used for all kinds of other purposes. Car insurance companies are charging higher premiums to people with low credit scores. Landlords, cell phone providers, car rental agencies, and all sorts of other companies are using credit scores as a way to screen out risk; often, those with low scores will be required to pay higher deposits. Lately, even prospective employers are checking out your credit history. When it comes to credit scores, what you don't know really can hurt you.

So, what goes into determining your credit score? Let's start with what *doesn't* affect it, because there are plenty of misconceptions about that. Although it seems counterintuitive, your financial condition—past or present—isn't used in determining your score. Your bank account balances, investments, assets like cars or houses, job titles, or income levels? None of those matter. Neither do your age, marital status, race, gender, or sexual orientation. What does matter is *anything and everything that has to do with your history of debt and repayment*. Since a credit score is a measure of how likely it is that you will repay borrowed money, the best available information about that is how well or not well you've repaid borrowed money in the past. And by the way, if you've never borrowed any money, or if you've done very little of it, it is entirely possible to not even have a credit score yet.

So, if you're ever late on a bill that qualifies as "repayment of debt," such as a car loan or monthly credit card bill, that can have immediate negative implications. But here's a twist that many people aren't aware of. If you're late on a bill that does not fall into the "repayment of debt" category, like, a utility bill for example, that should have no effect on your credit score, right? That's true, but only up to a point. If your utility bill goes unpaid long enough, the utility company will turn your account over to a collections agency. Once that happens, boom! That amount is now instantly reclassified as debt you've failed to repay, and your score takes an instant hit. Establishing a habit of "on time, every time" for every monthly bill is a core habit for financial health in general, and for a strong credit score in particular.

So where does FICO get all the information about your debts and how well you repay them? Collecting all those financial transactions is the job of a special kind of financial company called a credit bureau. In the United States, there are three major ones: Equifax, TransUnion, and Experian. Here's a high-level view of the credit score world: you generate transactions, and those transactions are collected by the three credit bureaus who summarize them into credit reports. The information in the credit reports is then run through FICO's credit scoring algorithms, which then results in your actual 3 digit credit score.

The Credit Score World

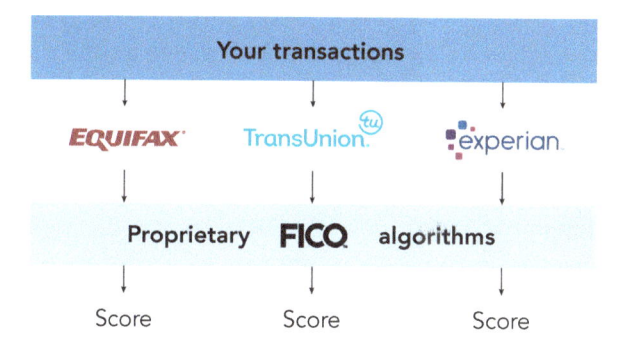

These days, it's getting easier to see your FICO score without having to pay for it. An increasing number of banks and credit card providers are now providing credit scores free for their customers. But be careful if you stumble across an ad promising free credit scores. Be absolutely sure that you're dealing with who you think you are and not a "look-alike" scammer before you provide any confidential account information in search of a score. And even if you are on a legitimate site, beware of offers for very high-priced credit monitoring services that are unnecessary for most people.

Here are four tips designed to get you a strong score, without borrowing money or paying interest:

- **Zero new debt:** Follow the red-phase strategy of paying down all your existing non-mortgage debt to zero, without missing any monthly deadlines along the way. Once you've gotten it to zero, keep it there! You might hear some people recommend that you take on new debt specifically to increase your credit score, but that's like spending a dollar to save a dime. It's the most expensive way to try to improve your score, so we'll focus on other means.

- **Zero late payments:** Pay on time, every month, every bill.

- **Regular credit report review:** When credit reports have errors, it hurts your credit score—and errors occur surprisingly often. When you spot an error, the credit bureau is required by law to work with you to get it corrected. You are entitled by law to get a free copy of your credit report once a year, from each one of the three major credit bureaus. The place to request that—and the only place you should ever go for this—is AnnualCreditReport.com. Use a four-month stagger strategy: request your free report from one the bureaus, wait four months to request one from the second bureau, then another four months for the third, and repeat each year.

- **Minimize your credit utilization score:** As described in Nugget #3.5, divide your average balance by your credit limits, across all your credit cards. The lower this ratio, the higher your credit score. Three ways to lower the score are to add new credit cards (up to an upper limit of 5), request credit limit increases on your current credit cards, and pay the full balance more frequently than monthly.

A Perfect Credit Score? No, Thank You!

A Note from Chris

What if you had to make a choice: the highest possible credit score or the highest possible net worth? Easy question, right? Nugget #1.5 spells out very clearly that net worth is the single most important measure of your financial condition, and Nugget #1.7 goes on to say that accumulating net worth is your single most important financial goal. That doesn't mean you don't want a high credit score, though. You do. But remember that increasing net worth is the goal, and your credit score is simply a tool to help you achieve it.

It's a good thing that question is an easy one to answer, because it's not hypothetical—it's a real choice you'll be faced with repeatedly throughout your financial life. Here's a way to break it down that makes the distinction clear. To get a perfect credit score, you have to do lots of things perfectly well, over a long period of time. These things fall into three categories:

1. **Help your net worth.** Making all your loan and credit card payments on time, for example, helps both your net worth and your credit score. Nothing wrong with shooting for perfection in this category!

2. **No direct effect on your net worth.** Earlier we advised you to apply for credit cards you don't need, and to request credit limit increases you don't need, all to lower your utilization percentage and therefore increase your credit score. This doesn't cost you a dime (as long as the cards you add don't have annual fees), so shoot for perfection here too.

3. **Hurts your net worth.** Two words: *installment loans!* This is debt with a fixed monthly payment, like student loans, vehicle loans, appliance and furniture loans, and the like. You'll increase your credit score by establishing a long history of consistently making installment payments on time. The catch is, each of those payments is costing you interest.

So do as much as you can to maximize your credit score in categories #1 and #2, but category #3 simply isn't worth it. Our red-phase requirement (Nugget #2.4) says to pay off all your non-mortgage debt ASAP and to steer completely clear of it for the rest of your financial life. To be clear: *whatever you do, don't take out a car loan (or any other non-mortgage installment loan) just because it might increase your credit score. The potential increase isn't that great, and it's a dangerous habit to pay interest unnecessarily. Even worse, this line of thinking can lead you to buy things you can't really afford, using the highly dubious rationale that it will increase your credit score. Don't do it!*

Of course, if you are paying off existing installment debt, that's another story. Continue making regular on-time monthly payments on those—you might as well get all the credit score benefit you can from those payments until you're ready to completely pay them off. But as soon as you're in a position to retire an installment loan early, do it without hesitation.

Net worth first, credit score second. Focusing on categories #1 and #2, with a heavy emphasis on lowering your utilization percentage, will get you a terrific score—and that's all you need. Perfect may be possible, but it's not financially wise.

Net Worthy Nugget #3.9

All humans are subject to irrational financial thinking, even (especially?) those who believe they aren't. Irrationality can completely sabotage the best financial plans, so it's in your interest to understand it, recognize it, and take steps to actively combat it.

We all have two sides to our personality: a rational one and an irrational one. And depending on the circumstance, be careful about which side of you is in charge. You'd think that when it comes to making financial decisions, Rational You ought to be completely in charge. But guess what? Irrational You just loves to show up and get involved in your financial business. Now, Irrational You knows better than to be obvious about it, so beware of disguises and sneak attacks. If you think you're completely immune to this, watch out. You're probably *especially* susceptible. Advertisers and retailers are absolute experts on how to draw Irrational You into your financial decision-making processes without you even realizing it. Come to think of it, sometimes other people in our lives—like spouses, partners, or kids—get pretty good at locating our "financially irrational" button, too!

Sometimes it's as simple as a lack of willpower or discipline, or the idea that delayed gratification gets boring after a while. Irrational You may want to cut loose, spend some money, and have some fun. Other times it's more complicated than that. If you're not careful, Irrational You can do serious harm to your financial future in a big hurry. Don't underestimate your susceptibility. A big irrational impulse can undo years of methodical financial progress—but only if you act on it.

Here are your best lines of defense:

- Automate your financial decisions in advance: Pay yourself first, before you even have a chance to be tempted to spend.

- Use your monthly budget, which forces you to compare different spending choices in advance—if you can afford either A or B, but not both, you make a rational decision in advance. Without a budget, you'll buy whichever you see first.

- Be aware of sellers' tactics (like prices that end in 9, time-pressure in the form of sale prices "only good until midnight tonight!," and the use of the magic word "free" in any part of an ad).

- Sleep on big financial decisions if possible—you're far more likely to later regret a rushed financial decision.

- Talk big financial decisions over with people whose opinions you respect, who know you well, and who have your best interests at heart.

- Take a "cooling off period" for windfalls (that is, any unexpected money that comes your way); deposit any windfalls into an inconvenient-to-access account, and let those dollars sit for several months until Irrational You loses interest.

There's an entire rapidly growing field of study called "behavioral economics" that explores the ways in which we wonderfully complicated human beings go about making economic decisions. It turns out that Irrational You is alive and well in each of us, influencing our decisions more than we ever realized. But irrational doesn't necessarily mean random; some of our most irrational behavior is entirely predictable. Check out *Predictably Irrational* by Dan Ariely, or any of the growing number of books and videos on behavioral economics, to learn more.

Net Worthy Nugget #3.10

> Virtually every advertiser wants you to believe some version of this big lie: the definition of "saving money" is spending money—but (supposedly) less of it than some so-called "normal" price. Advertisers keep on using this line because it keeps on working. Stop believing it, and start seeing through it, every time, starting now.

A common theme will pop out at you from almost every advertisement, whether it be a television commercial, a magazine ad, or a pop-up on your browser: "If you buy X, you'll save Y much money!" Most of the time, there's a very specific deadline to meet to realize those savings, just to make sure your irrational self understands the urgency. If you look a little deeper, there's usually a comparison between the price that's being offered today and some reference price—such as the usual price, the competition's price, whatever. The difference between the two, obviously, is what you "save." This bit of reasoning is repeated so often throughout our lives that most of us just accept it as being true.

It's not. The polite phrase for what it is might be "magical thinking." Less polite terms include lie, trick, or scam. And our irrational selves can't get enough of it.

Think about it logically. If the usual price is $10, and you buy at $7, you didn't just save $3. You just *spent* $7. Period.

If you purchase *anything*, money is leaving your bathtub, not coming into it. If you buy two, will you save twice as much? Why not buy a hundred, and really rack up the savings? After pausing to reflect, rationality will return, and you'll realize that the only real definition of "saving money" involves making a deposit in your savings account.

Two Definitions of Savings

Reference Price minus **Offer Price** equals **Savings**

Make a deposit in your savings account!

Don't Be Fooled!

A Note from Chris

When I talk about this fictitious definition of savings in a class or workshop, it often stirs up some debate. The idea that you can save money by spending it is so deeply ingrained in our thinking that it can be hard to let go of.

Yes, of course it's true that lower prices are better than higher ones—but that only results in savings if you were absolutely going to buy that same product or service, at that time, *anyway*. A great price on a pair of shoes doesn't save you a penny if you weren't in the market for a pair of shoes just like the ones on sale, already cranked into your monthly budget in the first place. Advertisers don't want you thinking through it that carefully though, so they'll do their best to dazzle and distract with a huge savings number. The higher the reference price, the bigger the savings—so a common tactic is to fudge the reference price up as high as they think they can get away with. They do it because they know people rarely question it.

But what if you are in the market to buy, and you come across a great price? OK, in that case, the "save by spending" logic might contain a grain of truth, but only under a very specific set of restrictions. Here's an example: Say that you buy a loaf of bread, from the same store, every week, the price is always $2.50, and that's what your normal monthly grocery budget is based on. This week is no exception: You're planning on your usual $2.50 bread purchase, and there is no chance whatever that you'll skip, or buy tortillas instead of bread, or buy your bread at a different store this week. Under these tightly defined circumstances, if you go into that store and they're having a one-time-only sale, for $1.50, on the type of bread that you always buy, then in a certain very narrow sense you can say that you've "saved" a dollar. A very important reason that this example represents savings is that you are the one who's coming up with the reference price of $2.50, so you know it's an accurate basis for comparison.

Never mind that all these restrictive assumptions are rarely met in real life. Advertisers take this teeny tiny grain of truth and blow it up into an entirely fallacious world where any price that's somehow less than an arbitrarily declared benchmark price represents "saved" money, and it's off to the races. Our irrational selves are eager to buy in, because it seems to give us a green light to spend. But that won't be you, now that you understand the truth behind this very common tactic.

If you're still not convinced, take the 10X challenge. The next 10 advertisements you see or hear that promise a specific dollar amount of savings, whether online, in an app, TV, wherever—stop and make a note of it. Once you've gotten to 10, go back through them and see how many of the 10 would truly represent savings —an *improvement* in your bathtub's water level—if you bought. Hmmm . . . zero? Maybe one? Now that you understand the game, you won't look at these savings promises the same way ever again.

Black Friday Magic

A Note from Monica

I used to get excited every year when Black Friday came around. My mother and I made a tradition out of it, waking up super early and eating bagels together before going out and emptying our wallets. The drive back home around noon would be bittersweet. Sure, we got all of our cousins and friends gifts, but just like the year before, we'd spent much more money than we'd intended.

"It's all . . . relative," I joked to my mother the last time we went Black Friday shopping, motioning at the gifts (which were for . . . my relatives). She didn't laugh.

"Do you understand the joke?" I pressed.

"Yes," she said, still tight-lipped.

I stayed quiet. Even though I was being hilarious, at that moment, it just didn't matter because the money we'd lost was no joke.

My mother and I simply weren't immune to those big sale signs that suggested we'd be actually saving money if we bought one thing because we'd get an accompanying product at a discount. Advertisers for Black Friday begin their brainwashing weeks before with seductive ads that many shoppers don't even question.

After the last few Black Friday trips ended with that same gnawing self-questioning ("Do I regret buying this for my cousin? Wasn't it a good deal?"), we buy presents more carefully. We've gotten more careful about getting sucked into whatever marketing that suggests we're "saving" if we're spending money in the first place. Instead, we just look for the gifts we have in mind at the lowest price we can get them. What a concept, right?

Turns out there's no "magic" when it comes to saving money—or regarding the holidays, for that matter. Yes, a few years ago, at the tender age of 22 years old, I experienced a double tragedy. Not only did my mother and I find out we weren't saving money by spending it, but in so doing I found actual proof that Santa Claus doesn't exist after all!

Net Worthy Nugget #3.11

You'll make wiser long-term decisions, financial and otherwise, if you talk them over with the "future you." Make a habit of it.

The earlier you start, and the more consistently you make decisions designed to fill your financial bathtub faster, the easier it is and the faster you'll get there. But especially when you're young, the prospect of eventual financial independence seems a very long way off. Embracing the concept of delayed gratification doesn't come naturally to most of us, and the further away the payoff, the harder it can be to wait it out.

But while you're waiting, try getting to know your future self. Just like you'd get to know a new neighbor or co-worker, the best way to form a connection is to invest a little time into it. Write the future you a letter. Have a conversation—especially if you're in the middle of making a decision with long-term implications—and ask the future you for their perspective. Keep a few pictures of the future you around that you'll encounter on a regular basis. Before you know it, you'll be inseparable.

This may sound like some completely random mind trick, but there's actually a lot of hard science behind it. Psychologists have found that some people have a stronger connection with their future selves than others, and that those people have a much easier time with things like exercising, overcoming bad health-related habits, and—you guessed it—saving money. But if you're one of those people who doesn't have a particularly strong connection with your future self, it turns out that a little bit of practice goes a long way, especially if it involves visualization.

Face-aging software is all over the web these days, and now you know how to put it to good use. A phone app like Aging Booth (free for both iPhone and Android) can take a selfie and turn it into an unnervingly vivid portrait of the future you. It's one thing to try to convince well-meaning parents or friends that some YOLO-based adventuring is more important than saving for the future, but it's quite another to make that case to your future self while looking them in the eyes. Once you get to know the person whose pockets (and bathtub) your short-term spending comes out of, the concept of delayed gratification becomes much more personal, and much more motivating.

Your new friend—your future self—is a great resource for financial decision-making, and they can also add a valuable perspective to almost any kind of long-term decision, including non-financial ones. If you're interested in learning more about the science behind your connection with the future you, watch Hal Herschfield's excellent TED Talk on the subject ("How can we help our future selves?" on YouTube), or check out the book *The Marshmallow Test: Why Self Control is the Engine of Success* by Walter Mischel. Your future self will thank you for it!

About the Co-Author

Monica Viera is best known for her YA novel, Crazy Meeting You Here. She also writes for *The Female Insider*, *Tiny Buddha*, and *Cough Country*. She likes jazz, punk, and fiscal responsibility (in that order).

"When working on this book, the information about credit (credit reports, credit scores, credit cards) especially resonated with me. I got into a challenging debt situation myself. If I'd known then what I know now, it didn't have to be that way. If you're a young adult, I hope you'll take this information to heart, and apply it in your life for your own empowerment."

Chapter 4

Budgeting and Your Magic Number

by Chris Smith with Nick Matiash

Net Worthy Nugget #4.1
Wisely and carefully managing how much you spend is a bedrock principle of building net worth. And budgeting is your main tool for doing so.

Net Worthy Nugget #4.2
Budgeting is a monthly process with four vital steps: plan, spend, compare, and learn.

Net Worthy Nugget #4.3
Today's powerful tools make budgeting simpler, faster, and more comprehensive than ever before.

Net Worthy Nugget #4.4
Your monthly savings goal is super important. You'll arrive at this specific, quantitative goal after careful thought and consideration, and you'll only change it on rare occasions. It's called your "magic number."

Net Worthy Nugget #4.5
"Paying yourself first" means capturing your savings as soon as your paycheck hits your checking account, and immediately applying them to your top financial priorities. It means you'll spend what's left over after saving (which guarantees you'll build net worth), instead of saving what's left over after spending (which never works).

Net Worthy Nugget #4.6
One-time windfalls represent special opportunities to accelerate your progress, and you should consider them carefully. Before deciding what to do with a windfall, impose a cooling-off period.

Net Worthy Nugget #4.7
A pay raise is another special opportunity to accelerate your progress. Decide how to handle such an increase consciously and deliberately. Consider this strategy for building net worth: a little for now, the rest for the future.

Net Worthy Nugget #4.8

Supplemental income—whether active or passive—can also be used to accelerate your progress, potentially tremendously. Recent economic trends (the sharing economy and peer-to-peer transactions, for example) have created an explosion of supplemental income opportunities.

Net Worthy Nugget #4.9

Learn the difference between streams (regular, ongoing expenses) and pops (one-time expenses). Financial beginners fear the pops most, but streams are sneaky-dangerous and can do incredible damage in the long run. The best budgeters have very few streams and watch them like a hawk—so should you.

Net Worthy Nugget #4.10

Beware of teaser rates! Retailers like cable/satellite TV providers and cell phone carriers use these to get their foot in the door; by the time these rates expire, you've become hooked on the worst kind of huge expense stream. Stop falling for the teaser rate game, every time, starting now.

Net Worthy Nugget #4.11

If you can't afford to pay the full price up-front, you can't afford it. Buying furniture, appliances, or mattresses on a "rent with option to buy" or "no interest until next year" basis is still borrowing, whether it seems like it or not—and usually on very unfriendly terms.

Net Worthy Nugget #4.1

Wisely and carefully managing how much you spend is a bedrock principle of building net worth. And budgeting is your main tool for doing so.

Let's say you wanted to lose some weight. How would you go about doing it? Would you come up with a plan, keep track of what you ate and how you exercised? Or would you just wing it and hope for the best? Chances are you'd choose the former plan. What about if you wanted to pursue your dream career? Would you get the right education, find the right path to get you there, and then execute accordingly? Or would you choose to wander through adulthood aimlessly and hope your dream opportunity will fall into your lap? Again, you're probably going to opt for the plan with an itemized what-to-do list. If you're smart enough to dive into this chapter, I'd bet you're smart enough to choose a proven plan over guesswork with your life's important decisions.

Meet your formal plan for your financial life: The Budget. Just like losing weight and pursuing a career, your finances need a game plan. You can't expect optimal financial success if you're not aware of where your money is going. You may get lucky from time to time, the same way you may lose a pound here or there without a purposeful diet and exercise regimen. But if you're looking to take the guesswork out of your success, creating a budget for yourself is essential.

In creating a budget, *you* are in control of what happens to your money. You are no longer left standing, jaw on the floor, when your bank account "somehow" has $0 in it. The proactive measure of the budget increases your awareness of the flow of your money and also gives you more control over where that money goes. Do you know how much money you spend a month on cups of coffee? Do you know how much you spend on going out to lunch during the workweek? If you don't, your budget will shine a nasty spotlight on some of these bad money habits. You can then use this information to make better choices with your money—choices that will lead to your ultimate financial success.

Nick's Net Worthy Notes #4.1

A Note from Nick

Budgeting was never something I was interested in. I earned money and spent money, but I never gave much thought to where it was all going. It never hurt my financial situation, but it certainly didn't help me. It wasn't until I got married that being more conscious with my money became important. My mom gave me a book about money years ago, which had since collected a couple inches of dust, so I finally decided to open it up and give it a read. The book was *The Total Money Makeover* by Dave Ramsey. While reading it, I realized how important it was to keep an eye on where my money went. My wife and I sat down and started looking at our spending habits and tried to craft a budget. It was eye-opening to see how some of our simple purchases added up: $40 a month at the coffee shop, a bottle of wine every week or so made for $50 at the liquor store. The list went on and on. It wasn't until we saw how our money was being spent that we could fix it. We've been budgeting for a year now and our financial future looks MUCH brighter. We've paid off both of our cars, and with the extra money we're saving on car payments we have our sights set on saving up for our first house! We are no longer slaves to our expenditures, but we now control how our money is spent. It has brought incredible peace of mind to both of us.

Net Worthy Nugget #4.2

Budgeting is a monthly process with four vital steps:
plan, spend, compare, and learn.

Now that you know why to budget your money, let's talk about how. It's a four-step, cyclical process that should be done monthly for best results.

The Monthly Budgeting Cycle

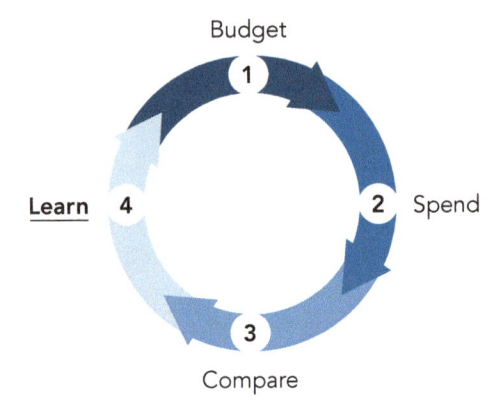

Budget (1) → Spend (2) → Compare (3) → Learn (4) → [cycle]

- **Plan/Budget:** Before the month begins, make a specific plan for where you want your money to go. Decide how much you'd like to save per month, then divvy up your total spending limit into categories, with a limit for each category. Some of these might be: Mortgage/Rent, Car, Insurance, Groceries, and the like.

- **Spend:** Put your plan into action! As you go through the month, stick to your spending limits as best you can. You made your budget for a reason, so keep yourself in check.

- **Compare:** You created your spending plan and executed it for a month. Now that the month is over, it's time to compare your *intended* spending with your actual spending. The numbers will not lie, so don't try to make them. If you spent more than you wanted to in certain areas of your budget, be honest with yourself about it. It's the only way you can improve your skills.

- **Learn:** This is easily the most important part of the process, as is brings you full circle. Once you have planned, spent, and compared, take the time to learn about yourself and your habits. If you're spending too much money eating out at restaurants, don't ignore it. See it for what it is, and adjust your spending habits. This works both ways.

If you realize your budget was unrealistically low for gas or groceries, don't get frustrated, just make the proper adjustments in your future budgets.

When you master the art of budgeting, you'll realize two main benefits. First, you'll have much more control over the total amount you spend each month. As the frequency of financial red alerts caused by overspending goes down, your financial confidence and peace of mind go up. Second, it's very empowering to actively decide, in advance, what you're going to spend your money on. This is called intentional spending, and it means that at the end of the month, you'll be much happier with what your dollars bought than if you just randomly went through the month with no particular priorities or plan.

It's going to take a few months to perfect the process, but it will be worth it. The longer you keep this process in play, the less time you'll have to spend on it. In the beginning, the comparing and learning periods of the cycle will unearth some problems that need fixing. The more often you do it, though, the smoother the process gets. Stick to it and you're sure to find success.

Nick's Net Worthy Notes #4.2

A Note from Nick

I promise I'll be quick here—and try not to lecture—but if you're not doing Step 4 of this process, you're wasting your time. Well, not entirely. It's not a waste of time to plan a budget and spend accordingly, but it's not optimized if you don't learn from your spending habits. When we made our first budget, we allotted far too little for groceries. For those first few months we would casually remark, "Oh shoot, we're over the grocery limit again," without making any changes. It caused some tension in our home because we felt like we couldn't keep it under the cap we'd created. It wasn't until a few months later that we made the adjustment. Instead of trying to force ourselves to spend less on groceries (which we were keeping tight as it was), we decreased another area of spending to make room for a surplus in the grocery part of the budget. Learn from your budget mistakes, and adjust accordingly!

Net Worthy Nugget #4.3

Today's powerful tools make budgeting simpler, faster, and more comprehensive than ever before.

But, wait! Most people aren't big math fans, and I'll bet you aren't either. You don't want to spend the time adding up all of your income, dividing it into monthly paychecks, and then subtracting away all of your expenses. Don't hit the panic button just yet. Nowadays, there are tons of interactive budgeting tools that can assist you in the process.

Two such products worth mentioning are mint.com and YNAB.com (YNAB stands for You Need A Budget). Both are programs you can find online that also feature companion smartphone apps. The beauty of these two tools is that they prevent any number-fudging on your part. You link your bank accounts, credit card accounts, and any outstanding loan accounts (car, mortgage, and so on) right into your secure mint or YNAB account. Within each program, your accounts are updated live. If you spend $20 on a haircut, since your accounts are linked to mint or YNAB, you'll see that expense be deducted from your budget within a couple of hours. You will never get the chance to "round down" on the price you paid for anything, because everything is synced right to your phone or computer.

There are some differences between these two, though; for one thing, mint is free and YNAB is not. There is good reason for this. At their core, they both serve the same purpose: syncing your accounts to give you live updates of your budget. In comparison to YNAB, though, mint is much more self-serve. You have all the information you need at your fingertips, but it's up to you to decide how your budget is allocated. YNAB provides a more educational approach. It actually shows you what a good budget might look like and helps you modify yours to fit your needs. Along with the educational approach, YNAB assists you in meeting your long-term savings goals as quickly as possible. For example, if you want to save for a wedding, a car, or a house, YNAB's service will cater to that savings plan.

There are more than just these two tools; new ones are hitting the market all the time. Explore the internet and your app options and see what you find. These two are our favorites within their respective categories (self-serve vs. educational), but budgeting tends be a very personal process, so you might find something else that fits you and your financial personality perfectly.

Nick's Net Worthy Notes #4.3

A Note from Nick

I am a mint user myself (mainly because it's free! One less thing to work into the budget). It's amazing how it links your accounts right into the app or website, and you can see your spending in real time. It even has status bars that show you how close or far away you are from reaching your limits. It's been a great tool for my wife and I as we've taken control of our finances.

Net Worthy Nugget #4.4

Your monthly savings goal is super important. You'll arrive at this specific, quantitative goal after careful thought and consideration, and you'll only change it on rare occasions. It's called your "magic number."

How often do you daydream about the day you no longer have to work for money? That landmark day when you get to live outside of the walls of your occupation and do the things you really want to do? What you're dreaming about is financial independence. If you no longer depend on your job or your paycheck to live your life, you've made it. But here's the problem: "Financial independence" is an ambiguous term that is hard for most to grasp. How do you get there? What steps do you need to take? How long until you arrive?

It all starts here, with your "magic number." Your magic number is the percentage amount you choose to save each month so that 10, 20, or 30 years down the road, you have stockpiled a load of cash to live off of. You can get to that stockpile fast or slow, but you won't get there at all if you don't have a magic number.

First, the *bare minimum* magic number you should shoot for is 10% of your income. That may seem daunting if you have been saving 0% of your income and now we're asking you to push it to 10%. It will seem even more daunting when we clarify that the 10% is applied to your gross income, not your take home pay. The thing is, it's better to fight that fear now and find a way to save than to push your 10% savings goal down the line. You'll see it here and in every other finance book you'll ever read: the single most important thing you can do improve your chances of achieving financial independence is to start saving early. Do it, and do it now.

Your magic number percentage is like a speedometer, showing you how fast you're moving toward financial independence. If you stay saving at 10%, you'll be saving slowly and methodically. As long as you've started early enough in your life, there's nothing wrong with that. But what if you cranked up your savings to 20%? Could you do 30%? Why not 50%? With every percentage point you increase your savings, the faster you'll move toward your goal of financial independence. Picture your saving and spending habits as a gas and a brake pedal, respectively. If you choose to save more, you're pushing the gas pedal to the floor, cranking up your speed towards financial independence. If you choose to spend more, you're taking your foot off the gas and firmly planting it on the brake. They are polar opposites and need to be seen as such.

Remember, the goal is to fill up your financial bathtub to an adequate level. The higher your magic number, the faster you'll get there. This is a firm decision you need to make and then stick to it. Don't set a low savings goal (5-6%) and say to yourself, "I'll throw extra money at my savings when money's not as tight." You probably never will. Our tendency is to spend what we have. Instead of falling for this natural human temptation, choose your savings goal first, then let the rest of your budget fall into place.

Nick's Net Worthy Notes #4.4

A Note from Nick

Confession: my savings number is 6%. That's how much of my paycheck goes to my 403b before taxes are taken out. I am a teacher in New York state, though, so (as of right now) we have a pension I also pay into for my retirement. With those combined, I'm probably close to a 10% savings number per month, but I'd still like it to be higher. More on this after Nugget #4.7.

Net Worthy Nugget #4.5

"Paying yourself first" means capturing your savings as soon as your paycheck hits your checking account, and immediately applying them to your top financial priorities. It means you'll *spend what's left over after saving* (which guarantees you'll build net worth), instead of *saving what's left over after spending* (which never works).

"Put that cookie down, you'll spoil your supper," I would hear my grandma say as I reached for a cookie before dinner. The sweet old woman wanted me to enjoy a cookie, but not until I ate my dinner. Dinner was important. It provided the nutrients the dessert was surely lacking. That's why I had to wait until after dinner to have a cookie (or ice cream, cake, or all of the above).

We have to eat dinner first, taking in all the important macro and micro nutrients, before we can think about having some dessert. If you try to eat dessert first, you may not leave yourself enough room to eat your whole dinner that will provide all of the healthy nutrients your body needs. Think of your savings plan (your magic number) as dinner and your budget and expenditures as the dessert.

Why must the savings come first? Because if you wait until you've spent all of your money elsewhere (for good reason or not) you may not leave enough room to meet your magic number of savings for the month. If you're not hitting your magic number consistently and building up substantial savings over time, you're going to be left with less money than you'd hoped for when it's time to cash in that savings plan. It's best to address the savings first, then use whatever room is left in your budget to take care of bills, expenditures, and luxuries.

It also takes the human element out of your savings plan. By putting aside your magic number at the beginning of the month, you've created a savings habit. Now it's not a matter of "should I save or should I not?" The decision is already made, and the savings start piling up. If you put off that decision until after your money is spent, you are treading in unsafe waters. You are now leaving it up to your willpower to stash your leftover cash for savings or spend it as a reward for being a good boy or good girl during the month.

Don't spoil your savings. Decide to save first, then spend your money after. Just like saving dessert for after dinner, the spending will be much sweeter knowing that you've taken care of business beforehand.

Net Worthy Nugget #4.6

One-time windfalls represent special opportunities to accelerate your progress, and you should consider them carefully. Before deciding what to do with a windfall, impose a cooling-off period.

When asked, Siri says a windfall is "any type of usually high or abundant income that is sudden or unexpected." Visions of lottery winners and beneficiaries of large estates quickly come to mind. Of course those are windfalls. But don't think you need to receive upward of one million or even one thousand dollars to experience a windfall. It's simply when you come into some money you didn't think you'd have. It could be someone paying you back money that you lent years ago, or a larger-than-usual tax return.

Your first instinct will likely be to spend that load of cash you've come across. Slow down. Think back to the image of your financial bathtub. A windfall of any size could positively impact how quickly you fill that tub. If you take that money and quickly spend it, it's as if you took gallons and gallons of water and poured it directly down the drain. Those gallons are now gone forever, but it's even worse than that. You've also given up the opportunity to turbocharge those gallons through the enormous power of compound interest. A large windfall, turbocharged by an enormous power—that's a king-sized double whammy to miss out on. Sure, you may buy something you'll enjoy for a year or two. But wouldn't you rather have the freedom to walk away from your job . . . a year or two sooner?

In Chapter 3, we talked about the irrational financial impulses that all of us are subject to. It turns out that nothing activates those irrational impulses as quickly and powerfully as a windfall. There's a reason lottery winners are far more likely to ultimately declare bankruptcy than the losers. It's true! Look it up.)

Q: What's the smartest thing to do with a windfall?
A:

That's not a misprint. The smartest thing to do with a windfall is *nothing at all*. Implement a "cooling-off period" to let your irrational financial impulses calm down. Those impulses are famous for being compelling, but the one thing they're not is patient. So, put that windfall into a separate bank account, one that's a little bit inconvenient to access, for at least 6 months before deciding what to do with it. (Wait even longer for a truly large windfall.) Your irrational mind is like a dog chasing squirrels, and after some time, it will have completely forgotten about the windfall. Meanwhile, your rational mind is getting more and more used to seeing that water in your bathtub, available for turbocharging. After six months, what had been a major test of willpower has now been magically transformed into a no-brainer.

Net Worthy Nugget #4.7

> A pay raise is another special opportunity to accelerate your progress. Decide how to handle such an increase consciously and deliberately. Consider this strategy for building net worth: a little for now, the rest for the future.

A pay raise can be as tempting as a windfall to pour down the metaphorical drain. It's more money than you used to have, and this time you've actually earned the increase in cash flow. You may feel entitled to reward yourself for the bump in pay. Not so fast. You may not recognize it immediately as such, but every pay raise represents a very special kind of decision opportunity—a true inflection point on your journey to financial freedom.

Just like saving your windfall income, making the decision to save any pay raises allows you to *increase your savings without decreasing your spending*. Your standard of living will remain constant because you would still be living off of what your old paycheck gave you.

It's a win-win situation. You continue to live your life without having to cut expenses, and you get to throw even more money on top of your heaping stack of savings. When making money decisions, it's best to play the long game. What's more important: spending the extra 2-5% of your paycheck on something trivial you'll stop using after a year? Or padding your savings account to make your financial independence come sooner than expected? Of course it's the latter. Now imagine what would happen if you chose to save every dollar of every pay increase you earned for *an entire decade* of your financial life. Your lifestyle stays constant, no extra sacrifices, but your magic number keeps escalating, and before long you're screaming toward financial independence at warp speed. If that's a little too extreme for you, choose to divide every pay increase into two pieces. You spend some of it now, guilt-free, and put the rest into your bathtub. You'll still be accelerating toward financial independence very quickly, if not at quite a blistering pace. Choose accordingly. Oh—and congrats on your raise!

Nick's Net Worthy Notes #4.7

A Note from Nick

Earlier I mentioned that I send 6% of my paycheck directly to my 403b before taxes are taken out. One strategy I have started to practice since doing the research to help Chris write this chapter is upping that percentage of savings with the raise I get every year. I have a standing appointment with my financial advisor at the beginning of every school year to increase my percentage of savings by 2%. That way each raise helps contribute to my overall savings, and I don't feel the decrease in income because my weekly paycheck will stay about the same. I'm filling up my financial bathtub without depriving myself of spending money. My standard of living won't change from year to year, but my savings will, which is incredible.

Net Worthy Nugget #4.8

Supplemental income—whether active or passive—can also be used to accelerate your progress, potentially tremendously. Recent economic trends (the sharing economy and peer-to-peer transactions, for example) have created an explosion of supplemental income opportunities.

We've travelled through many nuggets together in this chapter, so it's time to level with you. As noted at the beginning, this chapter is co-authored by Chris Smith and Nicholas Matiash. The two of us connected to put this together for you and to help raise your financial awareness, as well as give you tools to put these finance principles into action. Here's the thing, though: we're not both financial gurus. Chris provides the wisdom from his life and career in finance, and I, Nicholas (you can call me Nick, we're friends now) am the wordsmith helping him hone his message. I've practiced some of these tools of budgeting in my own life, so I do have experience with it. In the end, it is a combination of both of our backgrounds that brings you everything on the pages of this chapter.

I tell you this because writing this chapter is supplemental income for me. I don't write for a living; this is just something I enjoy doing outside of my career that provides some extra cash. In today's economy, there are so many ways you can make some money on the side. You could be a freelance writer, an affiliate marketer if you have a decent social media following, or play in a cover band on the weekends to pad your pockets. The list of what you could do to make some extra cash is long, but we're more interested in what you do with that extra money.

Don't try to make more money so you can have shinier toys in the here and now. Use that extra cash flow to supplement your long-term savings. Any money I make from this or any other freelance writing project is thrown right into savings. It is extra money to serve my ultimate financial goals, not to be used to finance some short-term, short-sighted purchase that will satisfy me only temporarily. Again, finances are a long game to play. Play it well.

Nick's Net Worthy Notes #4.8

A Note from Nick

True to my words written here, the money I earned while writing this chapter and other things I've worked on has been leveraged toward paying off debt and saving some money. My wife and I both do some freelance work outside of our careers and have used that money to change our financial outlook. We used to spend the extra money on vacations and objects. Sure, the vacations were great, but using the money to build a more financially independent future is much more rewarding. Now we've put it to work for us, and it has paid huge dividends!

Net Worthy Nugget #4.9

Learn the difference between *streams* (regular, ongoing expenses) and pops (one-time expenses). Financial beginners fear the pops most, but streams are sneaky-dangerous and can do incredible damage in the long run. The best budgeters have very few streams and watch them like a hawk—so should you.

If you're having financial problems, what worries you more: your car needing a new transmission or your car payment? Your big family vacation expense or the cup of coffee you buy every day from Starbucks? Within each question you've just read, I've provided an example of a pop and a stream.

A pop is a one-time expense that probably is quite large in proportion to the rest of your budget. It could be that new transmission or that family vacation. Whether it's something fun (vacation) or not so fun (transmission), you're going to throw a lot of money at it all at once. It might not be something you've planned ahead for (well, OK, you probably planned your vacation), so the element of surprise may add to the feeling that it's wrecking your budget.

A stream, however, is the smaller, consistent spending you probably don't sweat too much *because you've gotten used to it*. It could be your car payment or your daily coffee purchase. Think about all of the things you pay for monthly. This could be your rent, your electric bill, or your car insurance. Without fail, these expenses come out of your bank account every month. Some streams are necessary expenses, like the ones just listed, and others are not. The streams you don't even think about can be especially dangerous:

- The cup of coffee you grab on your way to work

- The 3-5 times a week you grab lunch while at work instead of packing your own

- Going out for drinks every weekend

The list can get lengthy, but I'll stop there. There are tons of things you spend money on without much conscious thought. They seem so minuscule in the moment that you hardly flinch when you decide to pay for them. But let's put some numbers on some of the examples provided.

- One cup of coffee every workday: 1 cup × $3 per cup × 5 days = $15 a week. $15 × 4 weeks = $60 a month. And that's being conservative.

- Lunch 3 days a week: 1 Lunch × $10 per lunch × 3 days = $30 a week. $30 × 4 weeks = $120 a month. If you knew this is what your lunches added up to, would you choose to bring lunch more often? We hope so.

The point is, knowing the difference between pops and streams is crucial to your overall understanding of your budget. And now that you know the difference, you can get to work identifying each of your streams and roughly quantifying each one. You'll see that there are a few streams you can't do much about, at least not quickly. In order to keep a roof over your head, you have to pay your rent or your mortgage. But once you've identified what your streams are, you'll quickly realize that some could be cut down to size, while others can be eliminated altogether, with little or no real sacrifice. We are all creatures of habit, and our financial lives are no exception. Take notice and be aware—it's more in your control than you think.

Nick's Net Worthy Notes #4.9

A Note from Nick

The streams got us good for a VERY long time. Cups of coffee every week. Nights out on the town. A bottle of wine here and there. Altogether, I'd say our streams were costing us upward of $200 a month. That's pretty much a car payment! Once we saw how they added up, it was much easier to control our habits. Give yourself the awareness necessary to make quality changes in your budget. It took us a while to see how the streams were destroying our monthly income.

Net Worthy Nugget #4.10

Beware of teaser rates! Retailers like cable/satellite TV providers, and cell phone carriers use these to get their foot in the door; by the time these rates expire, you've become hooked on the worst kind of huge expense stream. Stop falling for the teaser rate game, every time, starting now.

"Enjoy cable TV at just $29.99 a month, starting today!"

Sounds like a great deal, doesn't it? Don't be a sucker. I'm allowed to say that because I have lived the life of a sucker on more than one occasion. First, make sure you read the fine print when you sign a long-term contract with a cable TV provider, satellite TV provider, or some other deal that locks you in for a year or two. What they are presenting to you in the big bold numbers and letters are what we like to call teaser rates. There's a reason they make the "$29.99 a month" in size 72 font, then write "after one year of service, your monthly bill will double" in size 4 font. They are drawing you in with the large print and then sucking your budget dry with the fine print once you've gotten comfortable with their service.

So, what can you do to avoid the eventual uptick in price? Once you see your bill increase, call their customer service people and start complaining. They will tell you "it's the contract that you signed, sir" or "there's nothing I can do about it, ma'am." The key is to remain calm and polite—but also very firm and clear that you're not happy with the rate increase, and you'll definitely cancel the contract and leave the company's service if something isn't done about it, today. What no huge company will tell you is that is much more difficult (and much more expensive) for them to try and secure a new customer than it would be to pacify the customer who's already paying them. So, if you politely persist, you will eventually be transferred to a magical extension called the Customer Retention Department. Begin smiling now, because your whole purpose in calling in the first place was to get transferred. You see, this department is a whole roomful of friendly folks whose sole purpose is to keep you on board with their service—and they're *fully authorized to make almost any deal they deem necessary to keep you*. Including—you guessed it!—extending your teaser rates for a while longer. So, what do you do when those extended teaser rates expire? Ah, you're catching on. That's right, just call back again!

There's also another option to consider. If you want to get into *really* serious cost savings, consider cutting the cord. Get rid of it entirely. The big players used to have a hammerlock on this kind of entertainment, but not anymore. Today, there are many services that can be used to supplement your TV viewing experience at much cheaper rates. Instead of having cable or a satellite dish, consider using the service of Netflix (between $10 and $15 a month depending on your plan), Hulu (basic packages start at $7.99 a month, but adding on other features like Showtime and commercial-free can run you up to $21.99 a month), or Sling TV ($20 a month, with a little more for larger packages). If you had all three of those services in their basic form, you'd be spending around $40 a month. No doubt that's less than any cable bill you've ever had. All of these services just need a Wi-Fi connection.

But do they really replace your beloved TV? Netflix has a gigantic library of pre-aired shows and movies to choose from at your leisure. There's no live TV here, but there's classic shows and movies that never get old at your fingertips. Hulu has an enormous library of TV shows and movies as well, with the added benefit of airing shows that are currently on the air. If your favorite show airs on cable TV on Monday night, Hulu will have it ready to watch on Tuesday morning. Sling TV offers the closest thing to a cable TV experience. Through Sling TV, you can watch live TV from 10-20 channels. If you want more channels than that, you simply pay $5 more and add on certain packages. You can watch the game on ESPN knowing it's only costing you $20 a month while your friend across town watches the same game while racking up a $100+ cable bill.

Here's a back-to-the-future angle on cord cutting: antenna reception. Antenna technology has come a long way over the past decade, and it's worth a little research to find out how many channels you can pull in where you live, completely free. If you live in or near an urban area, an inexpensive indoor set-top antenna will do the trick. More elaborate attic or rooftop models can dramatically increase your range and choices. How-to guides are all over the web; two of our favorite sites are AntennaWeb's info on cord-cutting and Grounded Reason.

Both cutting the cord and fighting for your teaser rates are great ways to reduce some of those streams that affect your budget. By the way, cell phone data plans work almost the same way—the few biggest, best-known carriers are masters at teaser rates, but there are some much less expensive alternatives, and more emerging all the time. Take a serious look at services you're using monthly and think about whether you want to keep transferring water from your bathtub to the cable or satellite TV company's or the cell phone carrier's. C'mon, those bathtubs are full enough already! Choices like these can make a large difference over the course of a year or two. Do yourself the favor and research what changes you can make today.

Nick's Net Worthy Notes #4.10

A Note from Nick

My wife and I are proud users of Netflix and Hulu. We don't have cable in our apartment, and frankly, we don't miss it. We watch any current shows on Hulu (shows are uploaded within 24 hours of airing on TV) and watch reruns of some of our favorites like *Friends* and *The Office* on Netflix. At first, I objected to the idea, because I'd be missing out on all the sports channels! What I've realized since then is that I don't miss it all that much. Major sporting events are aired on the basic cable channels like ABC, CBS, or NBC, which anyone with a TV and a cable connection can see. Anything else can be live streamed on a laptop for the most part. Cutting the cord has saved us much more than it's taken from us. I definitely recommend it!

Believe It—Budgets Make You Happy!

A Note from Chris

By happy, you might think I mean you'll be pleased that your financial situation looks like it's improving at last. Or that I'm talking about the peace of mind that comes from finally moving beyond the high-stress monthly scramble to somehow make ends meet. And yes, it's true that those kinds of happiness await you if you commit to making budgeting a consistent monthly habit.

But I'm not just talking about simple financial happiness. I'm talking about something much deeper. Budgets are the gateway to depths-of-your-soul, one-with-the-universe, peace-and-serenity happiness.

Budgets, really?

Let's break the things you spend money on into three basic categories—A, B, and C priorities. The A priorities are the things you're most passionate about, which reflect your deepest values in life. B priorities are important too, just not quite as much. But C priorities are on the other end of the scale—money you spend almost mindlessly, either for instant gratification, or by pure, rarely examined habit.

This one-two punch that the C's pack—instant gratification purchases that seem small but add up, and streaming habits—are perfect examples of your irrational self getting its way without your rational mind paying much attention. So, C spending seems to just happen by itself, before you even know it. But spending on A's *rarely* happens by itself; it usually takes some reflection, thought, and planning. If you don't have a plan for the month—if you just go from day to day reacting to what comes up—you're very likely to end up with C heavy spending, like the "No Budget" graph. You'll say things like, "All the money's gone, but I don't really even know where it all went."

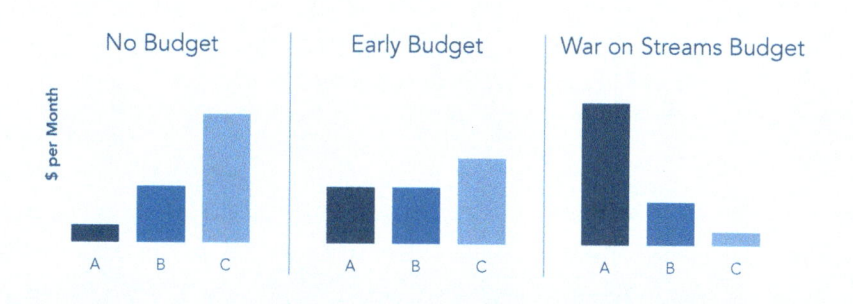

Once you begin budgeting, your financial decision-making is transformed in a subtle but profound way. Instead of your decisions being made one at a time as they happen to come up during the month, they're made in advance, *in comparison to other things you might spend your money on*. It's one thing to ask, "Should I buy this new jacket, yes or no?" But you move to a much higher plane when you ask, "What's more important to me this month, a new jacket or that class I've been hoping to attend?" This kind of comparative decision-making, early in your budgeting journey, will quickly result in fewer dollars going toward C's, and more toward A's. See? You're getting happier already!

Once you've built up your budgeting skills and experience, you'll be ready to declare an all-out war on your spending streams. Get ready for an even bigger jump in happiness. It can take some time to make fundamental changes in big streams like your transportation habits or your living situation, but those are the ones that can deliver huge savings. You can use those savings to increase your magic number, or you can pump up your spending on A's, as shown in the graph—your choice.

There's a special kind of happiness that comes from knowing your financial resources are closely aligned with your deepest life priorities. Without a budget, your spending is random and unfocused; you look back at a month or a year feeling unsatisfied, wondering where it all went. With a budget, you can adopt a lifelong habit of focused, intentional spending on the things that matter the most to you. Now that's happy!

Net Worthy Nugget #4.11

If you can't afford to pay the full price up-front, you can't afford it. Buying furniture, appliances, or mattresses on a "rent with option to buy" or "no interest until next year" basis is still borrowing, whether it seems like it or not—and usually on very unfriendly terms.

This nugget reflects the same ideology as the previous one. Just like teaser rates, financing your furniture or appliances has a "too good to be true" vibe to it. They will lure you in with low monthly payments or 0% interest. But the devil is in the details! The same size 4 font fine print, which is almost impossible to interpret even if you can manage to read it, tells the real story. Be late on any payment—even if just by a tiny bit—and you will see your payments balloon to a number that will make you cry. The instantaneous hit to your credit score will make you cry even more. What you first thought was a dreamy deal for a new couch turns into a nightmare.

There's only one surefire way to avoid being duped by this game of contracts and legalese: don't play it. Instead, save up and pay in full the day you walk in the store. Aside from running the risk of huge payments and penalties for not getting it paid off in time, you may be able to save some money up-front. If you have the money to pay cash for something at the point of sale, you have the power of negotiation in your corner. Let's say you want to buy a refrigerator that's priced at $1,000. The commissioned salesperson would much rather make a sale for $850 or $900 than let you walk by being stubborn at $1,000.

You may think you have the discipline to pay it off before your teaser rate or 0% interest runs out, but the risk is not worth the reward. Since you can most likely negotiate a lower price by saving up and paying up-front, financing your large purchase will still cost you more money over time.That's before we even consider the crazy increase in interest and price if you aren't able to make it happen during your given time window. Play it smart and pay up-front. Trying to use their system to your advantage is a dangerous play. Remember, it's their system for a reason.

Net Worthy Nugget #4.12

> Your biggest opportunities to cut spending may be "hidden luxuries"— items that previous generations may have considered necessities or entitlements which today are neither. Examples include people with significant debt and less-than-average income choosing to rent living spaces solo, own cars solo, or live in the highest cost-of-living areas.

Of course, we all want to listen to our parents and those from their generation. They've accumulated lots of valuable life experience, and they probably have a lot of wisdom to share when it comes to big money decisions. But it's also true that times are changing much faster now than they ever did. Smart and savvy money decisions 5 years ago, let alone 25 years ago, may not be good moves at all today.

Depending on your location, certain necessities of the olden days have become luxuries at best. Do you live in a big city and own a car? Why? With Uber, Lyft, and other driving services, you can save a good amount of money on transportation. This doesn't even just apply to people living in big cities. Uber has spread like wildfire and is available all over the country (go to uber.com/cities to find if it's near you). This would erase your car payment and car insurance, which would most likely mean an extra $300-$500 a month back in your pocket. Of course, Uber is still not free. Let's say you conservatively spend $250 on Uber rides a month. That's still a net savings over the course of the month, and you never have to find a parking spot again!

Speaking of living in big cities, do you absolutely need to live in the Big Apple? Or LA? Or San Francisco? In most cities, the cost of living has gone from steep to astronomical. If you work in the city, it doesn't automatically mean that you have to live there. Explore surrounding neighborhoods and suburbs that can provide a close commute while saving you hundreds of dollars a month.

While we're on the subject of housing, why not find a roommate? Or several? You can take your house, apartment, or condo you love and split the rent and utilities down the middle. This concept is universal to anyone trying to save a few dollars. If you own your own home and have a spare bedroom, see if a friend or relative wants to rent it out. You're allowed to have a roommate after college. Especially if you're saving yourself some money.

Just like using a cable or satellite TV provider isn't as necessary as it once was, owning a car, living alone, and living in high-cost areas shouldn't be assumed as norms in our society. Don't be afraid to challenge the status quo to save yourself a buck or two. Thinking outside the box can go a long way toward your financial success.

The Bottom Line

A Note from Nick

Budgeting has changed the future outlook for my wife and I on so many levels. Before we started doing it, we spent freely and felt we really needed anything we bought. Budgeting has allowed us to rein in our spending habits and be more intentional about how we spend. It took a while, but we have started to see a clear divide between our needs and wants. This has also made us appreciate the things we have and the things we purchase in a more meaningful way, since we are using everything more intentionally. The cherry on top of it all has been how we've paid off both of our cars in one year's time (wiping out $500 in car payments per month). This extra money has allowed us to accelerate our search for our first house. With our first house in our sights, starting a family together is not too far behind, and we couldn't be more excited. All of this started with getting control of our spending habits.

Money is not the root of all evil, but if you don't know how you're spending it, it may feel that way. It may feel like you're losing your spending freedom by putting restrictions on what you buy, but it's actually quite the opposite. By creating a budget, my wife and I have created more financial freedom than we had before. Things we thought to be years in the distance have come to us faster because we were spending more responsibly. Start budgeting today—you won't regret it!

About the Co-Author

Nick Matiash leads a double life: he's a high school math teacher by day, and a men's life coach by night. His website is entitled Moving Past Mediocre (movingpastmediocre.com), where he shares all the tools and methods that he's found useful in living the best life possible.

"Money and money habits are definitely useful in living the best life possible, which is why I loved helping to write this book so much. One of my favorite quotes is, 'If you fail to plan, you plan to fail.' Making sure you have a plan for your money and being conscious of where it goes is crucial to living a great life. Money isn't everything, but having peace of mind about your financial situation is one of the greatest gifts you can give yourself as an adult."

Chapter 5

Cars

by Chris Smith with Samantha Poelstra

Net Worthy Nugget #5.1

Today's young adults are buying cars later in life, and for different reasons, than previous generations. More than ever, it's wise to carefully consider alternatives before deciding to buy.

Net Worthy Nugget #5.2

The key to wisely buying a car is to focus on minimizing net price (initial purchase price minus anticipated resale price).

Net Worthy Nugget #5.3

Never buy a new car.

Net Worthy Nugget #5.4

Set your sights on the most economical category of vehicle that will meet your needs for the foreseeable future. Then seek out well-known makes and models within that category with the highest mpg and the best reputation for durability, dependability, and safety.

Net Worthy Nugget #5.5

Maximize your chances of buying a resale winner car by sticking to seven well-established rules of thumb.

Net Worthy Nugget #5.6

Never borrow money to buy a car.

Net Worthy Nugget #5.7

You can buy from a private party or a car dealership, and you can represent yourself or engage some professional help. The best choice for you depends on your individual situation, experience, and confidence. Whichever route you choose, research is vital.

Net Worthy Nugget #5.8

Minimizing miles driven will minimize almost every category of automotive expense.

Net Worthy Nugget #5.1

Today's young adults are buying cars later in life, and for different reasons, than previous generations. More than ever, it's wise to carefully consider alternatives before deciding to buy.

For previous generations, owning a car or any vehicle was a symbol of freedom. Buying a car said, "I'm ready for this adulthood thing," in a way that few other things could. Millennials inherited a different world, one of private smartphones and social media, entirely new personal transportation options (like Uber, Lyft, and Zipcar), new technologies that promise to change the world every few months, and a consumer culture that relies on the next best thing. When it comes to cars, millennials have been fashionably late to the ownership party compared to previous generations, but when they arrive, they're buying brand new cars and taking on loans to pay for them. Both are huge mistakes.

Much of American life is credit-oriented and involves borrowing. It feels normal to borrow. We need loans to pay for college. We need credit cards to build credit so that we can eventually get loans to buy other commodities—like cars, houses, and more college. We are told upfront that buying new is saving us money because of green technology or an amazing mpg, or because this model helps give back in some way. Marketers know that millennials care about how businesses impact the social world we live in. Millennials want their consumption to matter. Often, these are just tactics that marketers use to hoodwink younger consumers into agreeing to loans that do nothing but suck future finances dry right now, before anyone feels the loss. Do you hear that? That's the sound of thousands of dollars flying out the passenger side door of that shiny new vehicle you just drove off the lot.

You can avoid these potholes! First of all, be sure of your decision to buy a car. Are your reasons solid and practical, or are you falling for advertising pressure—that seductive message that you "deserve" one or that you "need" that new car to show you know what you're doing? Take a serious look at all the many transportation options available to you. If you have decided that buying a car is right for you, do your future self a favor and buy wisely using the tips in this chapter. After all, the long-term financial impact will be enormous.

Using the right tools now can make buying a car much less of a burden and can get this car-ownership party on the road! Buying smart is easier now than it has ever been thanks to an explosion of car-related information available online. But it's still true that the moment you sign on the dotted line of an automobile title, you immediately obligate yourself to a host of costs that come attached to the price tag. With a few targeted hours of research, you can easily narrow your focus down to which kind of vehicle is right for your needs, your current budget, and your future financial well-being.

Samantha's Scion: Good Move or Bad Move?

A Note from Samantha

Hi, I'm this chapter's co-author, Samantha, a nineties kid from Montana who bought her first car a few years ago. Here, we will explore my story—the choices I made while buying my car and the many decisions I will make differently when I purchase my next one. I'm no car expert, but I know now that to purchase a car wisely you don't have to be.

A few years ago, I bought a 2008 Toyota Scion XD, with 18,000 miles on it, for $11,000. Using the concrete tools we'll discuss within this chapter, we'll learn together whether my Scion purchase was a smart one. What does your gut tell you?

Net Worthy Nugget #5.2

The key to wisely buying a car is to focus on minimizing net price (initial purchase price minus anticipated resale price).

Before we get all practical and tactical—and we will—we should get one very important idea straight. Buying a car is different from buying a pair of shoes or a burrito or almost anything else you'd buy. That difference is: you're probably going to resell that car someday. But when you're in the throes of car hunting, resale many years in the future is probably the furthest thing from your mind. How can it make sense to think about selling something you haven't even bought yet?

This is step one of making your wisest purchase. Make the mental shift of thinking in terms of net price. Net price is the amount it costs to buy your vehicle minus the predicted value of the car when you sell it in the future. You want a car that you can sell for a price as close to the one you paid as you can get it. Over the course of your car-buying life, this one concept can easily end up improving your future self's net worth by many tens if not hundreds of thousands of dollars. No joke. You'll be amazed at what a big difference it makes in how you go about the process of buying—and what you ultimately end up selecting.

A common first reaction is, "What? I have no idea when I'm going to sell, how much I'll drive it before then, or what's going to happen to the economy. How am I supposed to know what I'll be able to sell a car for, years from now?" Well, you can't, at least not exactly. But it's amazing how much you can predict with just a bit of targeted research if you know what to look for.

Unless you're a vintage car collector, your car is going to depreciate while you own it. It will lose value. Focusing on net price means understanding the most important factors that determine how fast it's going to depreciate or lose its value. Most people are surprised to learn that two cars of the same make, model, and year can have very different depreciation profiles ahead of them— and this part of a car's financial future is remarkably predictable in advance. An even bigger surprise may be how vastly different the financial scenarios are when comparing a fast-depreciating car to a slow one.

Net price thinking is exactly what the automotive industry doesn't want you to practice. The main financial aspect of buying your car they want you to think about is savings! Just like we discussed in Chapter 3, their definition of saving money is a very peculiar one, which somehow involves you transferring huge amounts from your financial bathtub into theirs. (Imagine how much you'd save if you bought two cars! There's an idea for them—a bundle.) Even though you're wise to that now, most people aren't. Sellers want you examining the initial price so deeply that you forget to wonder whether that car will be worth anything close to that initial price a few years from now.

Most people have a very narrow idea of what it means to be financially smart when it comes to buying a car, and it all centers around getting a "good deal." You want a good deal, too, but your definition is built on the net price, not just the initial price. Now that you understand that, your odds of successfully finding a good deal are about to go way up.

Net Worthy Nugget #5.3

Never buy a new car.

Imagine you are sitting in the driver's seat of your brand-new car, for which you just paid $20,000. The odometer reads zero, and the sun is shining through your flawless windshield. The radio is blasting your favorite song as you pull out of the dealer's lot, but as you glide down the road you begin having second thoughts. "That other make was a nicer color," you think. "Maybe I should buy that one instead." So you drive back to the lot to swap your purchase. Upon your arrival, the dealer looks you in the eye and says, "Look, buddy, you wanna trade in a used car worth $16,000 in exchange for a new car worth $20,000? Sorry, but no deal." You look at the odometer and it reads: one mile. Sadly, you are the sucker who just paid $4,000 to drive a brand-new car one single mile. Your net worth just went down by $4,000—literally, immediately, and irreversibly. (Hope your mile was a scenic one, at least.) Now, this specific scenario isn't one most people experience. But the financial loss, those thousands of dollars down the drain, happens to everyone who buys a new car instead of a used one.

Where did that $4,000 actually go? It was part of the $20,000 you originally paid, but more to the point: it was an immediate transfer of wealth from your financial bathtub straight into the dealer's—part of which was then also shared with the car's manufacturer. Now you know why the automotive industry spends billions of dollars each year promoting the thrill, prestige, and yes, even the smell, of driving a new car.

Here's the deal with depreciation on cars: the newer the car, the faster it depreciates. And the very first mile on a brand-new car is the all-time, undisputed, undefeated world champion of depreciation.

Take a look at this graph:

Depreciation Rate of a Typical Car
As percentage of MSRP

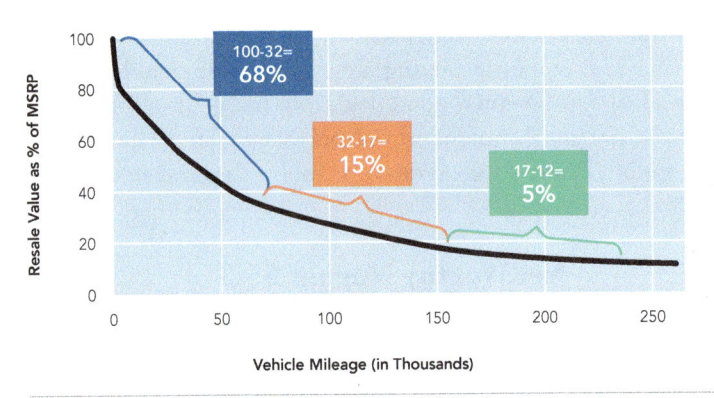

[Graph: Resale Value as % of MSRP vs. Vehicle Mileage (in Thousands). Brackets show: 100-32= **68%**, 32-17= **15%**, 17-12= **5%**]

*KBB data, composite makes/models, 15,000 miles/year and "good" (54%) condition

The graph bases everything off "MSRP," or manufacturer's suggested retail price. When you buy a new car from a dealer, though, most of the time you'll pay less than the full MSRP—because of the "door-busting inventory clearance blowout," "red hot Rocktober sales-a-thon," or whatever.

The falling slope represents the resale value of a typical car. As you can see, the slope is steepest within the first 75,000 miles driven, and after that it slows a bit. This means that if you buy a car with more miles on it to begin with, when you go to resell it will retain more of its value relative to what you paid for it.

Let's say you buy a brand-new car, own it for 5 years, and drive it an average of 15,000 miles per year (which is, incidentally, about how many miles the average US driver puts on their car each year). That adds up to 75,000 miles, which is the width of the first bracket. How much can you expect to sell your 5-year-old car for at that point? Check your airbags, because you're about to run into a financial roadblock. As shown on the graph, you'll only get back 32% of what you paid for it. Ouch! Remember, net price is the price you pay for the car initially, minus the anticipated price you'll get back when you resell it. The net price of a brand-new car is staggering.

But now let's consider the same car from the point of view of the person buying it at the 5-year mark. To keep it simple, buyer #2 also owns the car for 5 years and drives it an identical 15,000 miles per year. That's the second bracket above. Buyer #2's net price is less than a quarter of what buyer #1's was because buyer #2 bought it for a fraction of its original price—and it's the same car! What's going on here? Buyer #1 bought into the advertising hype and just couldn't wait to breathe in that new car smell. Buyer #1 gets the smell (for a few weeks anyway), but along with it comes a huge portion of the car's depreciation. Buyer #2 gets the same car but smiles a lot more knowing that they are off the hook for most of the depreciation.

The trend continues for buyer #3, shown by the nextbracket. By this time, the car is admittedly closing in on senior citizen status and is unlikely to impress any potential dates. But buyer #3's financial bathtub is a lot fuller, freeing up money they could spend on travel, investing, or whatever they desire.

The difference between being the first or second owner isn't a few percentage points—it's many, many thousands of dollars. Car dealers will quickly point out that new cars come with various warranties, get better gas mileage, and are more reliable. All that may well be true (although maybe not by the amounts claimed), but those operational savings are drops in the bucket compared to the enormous differences in depreciation. It's like spending a dollar to save a dime (heard that one before?). Let somebody else pay that depreciation bill. You'd rather put your money into things that appreciate—like a house (Chapter 6) or your long-term investment portfolio (Chapter 7).

Keep in mind that the graph shows a typical car. We just saw that you can dramatically improve your financial experience by choosing to buy older cars. And there are even more ways to improve your experience. Not all makes and models, not all model years, and not all individual cars follow this typical curve. Some depreciate much faster and some much slower. With a little research, it's remarkably easy to identify the winners. Read on, because that's our next stop.

Not Brand New . . .
But Still Pretty New
A Note from Samantha

So how is my Scion looking so far? It's a good news, bad news scenario. The good news is, I managed to miss out on that financially devastating first mile! But looking at the graph, 18,000 miles is still pretty new, which implies I bought my Scion while the car was still in a pretty steep part of the depreciation curve. Not terrible, but not great—so far, a solid "meh." It would have been smart for me to find out how other Scion XD's from 2008 depreciated and perhaps find a different make or model with a better net price before I signed the dotted line.

Net Worthy Nugget #5.4

Set your sights on the most economical category of vehicle that will meet your needs for the foreseeable future. Then seek out well-known makes and models within that category with the highest mpg and the best reputation for durability, dependability, and safety.

What's a "category of vehicle?" Mid-size pickup truck. Sports car. Full-size SUV. Those are examples of categories. So, the first part of the nugget is simply encouraging you to put some serious, practical thought into selecting a category that makes financial sense for you. If you're early in your financial life, still in the red phase with a lot of bathtub-filling in front of you—a low-mpg sports car or a high-end luxury car are examples of categories to avoid. You'll be spending far more to get from point A to point B than you need. Your goal is basic transportation. Car advertisers want to convince you that your goal is something far more ego-driven and nebulous. We suggest that a great response would be, "I don't fall for cheap advertising gimmicks." Your choice of category is an excellent opportunity to demonstrate you've adulted your way beyond advertising and have fully entered the esteemed grounds of enlightened, mature, and financially wise territory. If only everything in life were this easy.

To get you started thinking about categories, look at the chart below. See why it's so important to start out with a practical, economical choice? The differences in price are enormous:

Huge Price Variability Among Categories
Average price paid for new cars, 2017

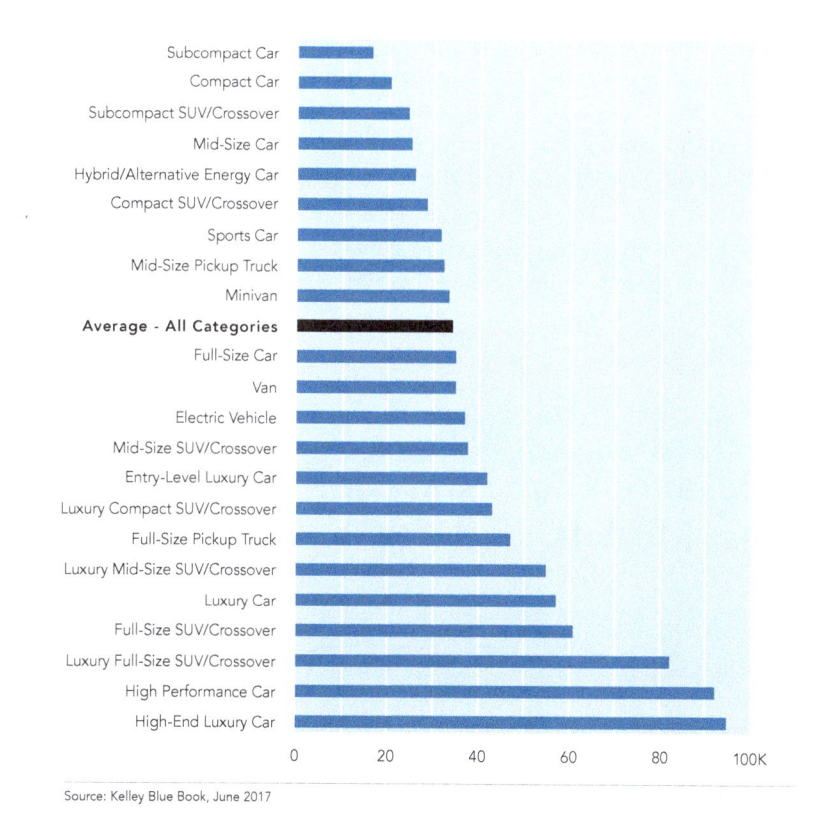

Category	Price (K)
Subcompact Car	
Compact Car	
Subcompact SUV/Crossover	
Mid-Size Car	
Hybrid/Alternative Energy Car	
Compact SUV/Crossover	
Sports Car	
Mid-Size Pickup Truck	
Minivan	
Average - All Categories	
Full-Size Car	
Van	
Electric Vehicle	
Mid-Size SUV/Crossover	
Entry-Level Luxury Car	
Luxury Compact SUV/Crossover	
Full-Size Pickup Truck	
Luxury Mid-Size SUV/Crossover	
Luxury Car	
Full-Size SUV/Crossover	
Luxury Full-Size SUV/Crossover	
High Performance Car	
High-End Luxury Car	

Source: Kelley Blue Book, June 2017

What about hybrids, electric cars, and other alternatives to traditional internal combustion engines? You'll want to do lots of research if this appeals to you. Gas and other repair and maintenance savings are simple to quantify; the social responsibility aspect is up to you to determine how to value. But as with all cars, it pays to think hard about net price—and this is where it gets tricky. Nontraditional technologies are much more difficult to predict when it comes to future resale value. Any time big technological advances are involved, early adopters often pay a steep premium, which won't come back on resale. Competing battery technologies suggest that eventually only one will prevail; if you own a car with the losing technology, you'll take a sharp resale hit. In short, alternative technologies are inherently financially riskier due to the greater uncertainty of resale. If you choose to go this route anyway, try to minimize financial risk in other ways to the greatest extent that you can.

So now that you've selected a category, the next step is make and model. The wording in the nugget looks deceptively simple. You're probably thinking, "Well, duh! Why would I look for a vehicle that isn't dependable or safe?" The answer is, you wouldn't, but you could still fall prey to a great sales pitch. We've discussed the wealth of information on cars available online, but the vexing truth is that there's a fine line between consumer information and automotive industry PR—and it's sometimes hard to tell which side of the line any particular website is on. Prepare to be shocked, but . . . it's even possible that some customer reviews are fake. So it pays to be smart with research. Confirming conclusions from multiple sources is one good practice. Relying on sites known to be objective, independent, and credible is even better.

Car Research Tips: Categories, Makes, Models, and Years

A Note from Chris

The internet has completely revolutionized buying a used car. Sellers used to have a vast information advantage, and if the seller was a car dealer, it was even worse. Today, the playing field has been leveled; with a little bit of focused research, it's possible to find out almost anything you need to know to help you in your car buying decision—but it helps to know where to look. Since we're aiming to zero in on categories, makes and models, here are some tips on where to start your research in those areas:

- **General Automotive Trends:** Cars have drawn huge attention from traditional media for a long time, and there's a lot to be learned from sources like the websites Car and Driver and Motor Trend. Consumer

Reports has a had a longstanding focus on used cars as well. Be aware that cruising around these kinds of sites will subject you to ads and articles featuring choices way outside your price range. Stay focused!

- **Safety/Reliability/Quality:** The National Highway Traffic Safety Administration website (www.nhtsa.gov) is a wealth of safety information and features an easy-to-understand 5-star rating system for specific makes, models, and years. A relatively new resource is CarComplaints.com, which clearly outlines which makes and models are the most problematic, and why. It's also a great way to learn about the surprising difference in quality and reliability from one model year to the next. Here's an example showing Honda Accords: You might get a "good deal" on a 2003 or a 2008 Accord, but it might be a net price problem—because you may have to give a good deal when you resell. (You can click on those specific years to find out exactly what kinds of problems caused those complaints.)

Honda Accord
Model year comparison

Here are total complaints by model year for the Honda Accord.

The 2008 Honda Accord has the most overall complaints, and the most-reported problem is also with the 2008 Accord for premature brake wear.

Worst Model Year:
2003
Worst Complaint: Transmission Failure

Year	Complaints
2017	45
2016	135
2015	112
2014	239
2013	458
2012	216
2011	189
2010	464
2009	947
2008	2,441
2007	282
2006	192
2005	295
2004	612
2003	1,672

Source: Carcomplaints.com

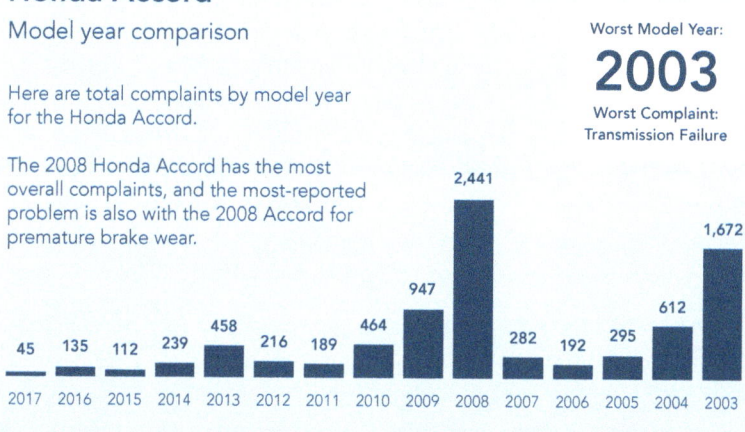

- **Forums:** Independent, brand-specific forums are indispensable to your research. These are online communities of owners who discuss everything from recalls to styling to transmissions. Sometimes a well-posed question from a newbie can flush out incredibly valuable and specific advice from a passionate, highly knowledgeable community. An example of this kind of site, to stay with the Honda example, is the

Unofficial Honda Forum (www.hondaforum.com); virtually every well-known make has a forum of some kind like this. Most are independently operated, but you'll see dealers and even employees of the manufacturer participating, too. As long as it's transparent, it's actually good to have their participation. In general, be wary of forums run/moderated in ways that are tilted to serve the interests of the industry rather than the consumer. Finally, Reddit has dozens of make/model specific subreddits; here's the Accord again, as an example: www.reddit.com/r/accord/.

- **Price:** The two "old reliables" for price info are Kelly Blue Book and the NADA (National Automotive Dealer's Association) Guides.

So, look for a car that is safe, reliable, and has great gas mileage (mpg). Why the focus on mpg? It's simple: gas is your biggest operating expense, by far. The difference between 23 mpg and 27 mpg may not sound like much. But if you drive 15,000 miles per year, for 5 years (like our graph above), those 4 extra miles per gallon will save you a cool thousand bucks. Mpg adds up!

A final note on makes and models: as you go through your research, you'll find that it's super easy to get tons of information on Honda Accords and Toyota Corollas, and it's much harder to research Saturn Skys. Rule of thumb: the makes and models that are most popular in the United States year after year, with the most commonly chosen options and extras, will always depreciate much more slowly than average. Makes and models that are aimed at small niche markets, or whose sales have been declining, or have been discontinued altogether, are resale nightmares. The boring truth is: stick with what's best known, because it will always be easy to find lots of buyers when the time comes.

An Untimely Demise

A Note from Samantha

I've got some bad news about my Scion, folks. My Scion XD was the first model of XD put out by Toyota, and it didn't last long on the market. It was discontinued in 2014, just shortly after I bought it! When I looked around, I didn't think to look up its relevance on the market historically, so when I go to resell, chances are there won't be many people looking for my make and model. To make it worse, The Independent Car and Driver website rates the Scion XD a lousy 1.5 stars out of 5. And CarComplaints.com shows me that the 2008 model has the most complaints of any year and a number of recalls I wasn't even aware of. Time to go to my mechanic . . . the car I'm driving might not even be safe to drive!

However, I did a good job selecting a make and model that fit my lifestyle. I often transport large canvases because I love to make artwork, and the Scion's backseats fold down, revealing all the space I need to haul materials. I can sleep in the car when I go camping, and the mpg is great for cross-country road trips to see my family. But unfortunately, I didn't look at the whole picture, and instead I was sold on what I thought was the only car for me when there is a whole category of compact vehicles built for adventuring (Subaru anyone?) that I could have tapped into.

Net Worthy Nugget #5.5

Maximize your chances of buying a resale winner car by sticking to seven well-established rules of thumb.

So you've zeroed in on the category that makes most sense for your needs. Then, you narrowed it down to a few makes and models based on focused, intelligent research. Now, you're starting to look at listings for (gulp!) actual, specific, individual cars. At first, you're excited to finally be engaged in the "let's choose one and buy it!" part of the process. But that soon devolves into an advanced case of information overload. Tons and tons of listings, each containing detail after detail. Is there some smart way to go about picking the few resale winners out of this giant junkyard? Follow these simple rules of thumb, and save yourself the years-long headache:

1. **Many years old, but very few miles per year:** Do you know what a Grand-car is? These are used cars being sold by grandparents, retirees, or other well-seasoned folks who have had a car for several years but haven't driven it long distances during those years. Cars that have done way more sitting than driving. A Grand-car has experienced massive depreciation financially speaking, but underneath that well-depreciated hood is an almost new engine, just yearning to be put to good use. Boom! That's what you're looking for. A Grand-car will be delighted to give you the best years of its life, and for only a fraction of its original price. And when you're ready to sell it, you'll get back an amount almost embarrassingly close to what you paid. That's net-price gold right there.

   How old is a Grand-car? Three years is the bare minimum, but five years and older is prime Grand-age. As for mileage, you won't stand for any car that's been driven more than 15,000 miles per year. But to get into to truly great resale territory, be even pickier and limit your search to cars with 12,000 miles per year. Believe me, with those criteria, the haystack just got much smaller. Here's a handy-dandy tool that summarizes this for all you visual learners out there. (See image opposite).

2. **Title status = "clean":** Every car has a title, a legal document that establishes who legally owns it. And every title has a status. There are some title status codes, like "rebuilt" or "salvage," that might get your attention because you can often buy those for a rock-bottom price. Eventually, though, you'll find out that this cuts both ways: the only way you'll be able to sell such a car is by giving somebody else an equally great deal. None of that for you. Whether it's called clean, clear, or normal in your state, that's what

Used Car Age and Mileage
Pick a winning combination!

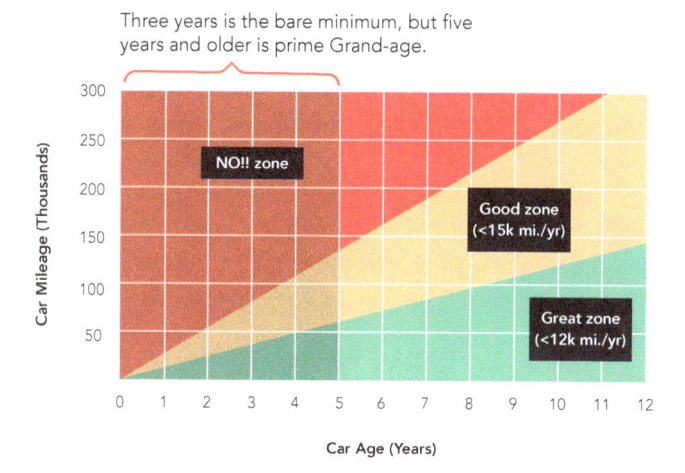

Three years is the bare minimum, but five years and older is prime Grand-age.

[Chart: Car Mileage (Thousands) vs Car Age (Years), showing NO!! zone, Good zone (<15k mi./yr), and Great zone (<12k mi./yr)]

you want, and you'll walk away from anything else, no exceptions. The car may look, drive, and inspect just fine, but if the title isn't clean, you don't care, because it'll just be too hard to resell.

3. **Few (or one) previous owners:** It's theoretically possible for an 8-year-old car to have had 5 different owners, each one of whom meticulously followed the manufacturer's service schedule and won blue ribbons for safe driving. But try convincing future buyers of that. You want a short, simple, and easy-to-understand chain of ownership. Exactly one previous owner is as short and simple as it gets. Two or three is as far as you want to push it.

4. **A nonviolent past:** Future buyers won't care whose fault it was; a car that's been in an accident is worth less. Even if repairs have made the car as good as new, no mechanic can fix the financial damage. You want cars that have been lucky (or inactive) enough to have avoided any kind of damage, especially collision-related. A fender bender or two is as far as you'll bend; anything more than that, walk away.

Wait a minute—how do you find out all this information about a used car? And, even if the seller volunteers this information, how do you know if it's true? Easy answer: you request a Carfax report. Carfax has truly revolutionized this aspect of the used car marketplace, and you wouldn't dream of buying a car without it. All you need is that vehicle's VIN (Vehicle Identification Number) or license plate. Just enter it into Carfax and that car's history is no longer a mystery. You'll have to pay for the report, but it's not expensive, and the information it provides is vital. By the way, if the seller "helpfully" offers to provide the Carfax report for you, saving you the expense? Thanks, but no thanks. Requesting an original report yourself is the only way to be sure you're getting the truth.

5. **Better safe than sorry:** A car with a sketchy reputation for safety is going to be hard to sell, so it's vital to avoid buying one in the first place. Don't trust informal channels like social chatter or well-intentioned advice from friends and family, because those won't sway future buyers. Instead, consult the NHTSA website. If you want 5-star resale value, take 5 minutes to check the make, model, and year you're considering has a 5-star safety rating. You might consider a 4-star model if everything else looks solid, but 3 or less is out of the question.

6. **Stick with "always popular" makes, models, and options:** Nothing expresses your personality like the car you drive, so you want one as wonderfully unique as you are, right? Absolutely not. This kind of subjective, style-driven approach is exactly how the automotive industry wants you to think, but that's in their best interest—not yours. Rule of thumb: the makes and models that are most popular in the United States year after year, with the most commonly chosen options and extras, will always depreciate much more slowly than average. Makes and models that are aimed at small niche markets, or whose sales have been declining, or that have been discontinued altogether, are resale nightmares. Sticking with what's best known makes it easy to find lots of buyers when the time comes. Honda Accords, Ford F-150s, and Toyota Camrys meet

this test. Honda Ridgelines, Ford GTs, and Toyota Scion SDs do not. We're not saying these latter choices are bad vehicles—we're saying they're resale risks.

Popularity can vary considerably by region. Imports tend to sell better on the coasts than in the country's heartland. Rural areas favor pickup trucks over sports cars; expect the reverse in urban locations. This isn't the kind of test where you can go to a website and look up a popularity score. But if I'd have taken the time to ask anybody who knew anything about cars whether Scion XDs were an example of "most popular in the US year after year," I could have avoided a financially sad story. And if you can't think of someone to ask, the auto mechanic you'll meet in next paragraph is a great place to start.

7. **Pre-purchase Inspection (PPI):** As a used car buyer, your new favorite three letters are P, P, and I. Any reputable independent mechanic will provide a PPI, and they might even provide it extra quickly for you if they think there's a chance you'll end up using them for service afterwards. The key is that the mechanic providing the PPI is someone that you choose; they must be completely separate from and unaffiliated with the seller. You'll pay for the PPI yourself, whether you end up making an offer or not. Ideally, it's someone that you've done business with before and trust. Either way, though, it's crucial. A PPI can tell you what kind of work has already been done, what's likely to be upcoming, and most importantly, whether the seller has been forthcoming with you.

All of these tests are featured in the Car Resale Winner Calculator in the Net Worthy Navigator App. For example, as you look at a used car listing, just enter the car's model year and mileage, and the app will tell you whether you're looking at a Great Zone Grand-car, or a No Zone resale loser.

The High Price of Obsolescence

A Note from Samantha

When it came to the PPI, I (luckily) knew what I was doing and had it checked out. It came with a clean title and a non-violent past fit for a pacifist. I purchased my Scion from its only previous owner when it was five years old. That means that at 18,000 miles, the previous owner had only driven it 3,600 miles per year! Golden! My Scion lived in the green zone of that graph when I bought it.

But here comes the bad news. My Scion's green zone status isn't nearly enough to offset the sad financial effects of its being a discontinued model. The numbers don't lie; Kelley Blue Book suggests that if I sell my car now, I can get around $6,000 for it, which leaves me with a net price of 55%. That's not good!

Bottom line on net price:

> Sam's original purchase price: $11,000
> Anticipated resale price (now): $6,000
> Net price: $5,000 (45% of purchase price)
> Net Worthy rating: Better than a new car, but worse than average for used

OK, so we now know that the 2008 Scion XD probably should not have been the car I bought back on that fateful day in 2012, because of its high net price, but hindsight is 20/20. Because of how few miles I have driven it (it's now only at 33,000 miles after five years of use) and the regular care my mechanic provides, at least when I go to resell I'll have a car that's still in the green zone and comes with a comprehensive list of regular health checkups—both could help offset the fact that the model is discontinued.

Net Worthy Nugget #5.6

Never borrow money to buy a car.

If you've read the earlier chapters, then this nugget comes as no surprise. If you're in the red phase of your financial life, which is likely, then adding a hefty, new non-mortgage debt will keep you there even longer. If you've managed to break out of the red phase and into the yellow, well, a car loan will plop you right back into red again. In either case, your journey towards financial independence goes into full reverse as soon as you agree to borrow. That goes for leases, any of the various "0% interest until" schemes, bank or credit union loans, and easy dealer financing—you're not interested in any of that. Instead, you'll pay the full amount, at the time of the sale, shake hands with the seller, and drive away in a safe, dependable, well-chosen used car with killer resale value—that you now own free and clear. Once you've experienced that feeling, you'll never settle for any other way of going about it.

What About Car Loans?

It makes **no sense** to borrow money to buy a depreciating asset	**Awesome feeling** to drive away in a car you own free and clear!

We understand that this advice can be very challenging to follow, especially if your need for a car has come up suddenly—if you're starting a new job requiring a commute, for example. If you can find creative ways to get by while you save, though, you'll thank yourself in the long run. Here are six reasons to avoid borrowing:

- **You'll pay more for the car.** Money talks. Paying up front, in full, gives you bargaining leverage. They want your money, and they want it now!

- **You'll pay interest, and it's not tax deductible.** How much interest? On average, around $4K over the full life of the loan, for a new car. Straight out of your bathtub, into the bank's or dealer's. If you'd invest that money instead, the amount you'd earn eventually approaches what it would take to go and buy a used car with cash. This isn't a student loan or a mortgage, where the IRS cuts you some slack on the interest portion; instead, this is the cold, cruel world of consumer financing, and you're on your own. And what about those "zero interest" financing offers? Better check the fine print. The 0% looks nice, but it's only there to hide nasty, very consumer-unfriendly language that no bank or credit union would ever use.

- **Miss a payment or two, and the car can be repossessed.** You're already out all the money you've put into the loan so far—now there's not even a car to show for it. Oh, and your credit score's trashed, too.

- **High risk of going upside down.** Upside down means that the car is worth less on the open market than the balance on your loan, and that's a financially vulnerable position to be in. If you decide—or get forced by circumstances—to sell before you'd planned, you end up eating the difference.

- **You may not be able to pay off early without a penalty.** Many auto loans, especially when written by a car dealer, are written with fine print prepayment terms very unfriendly to the borrower. If you want to pay off the loan early, you may still owe the full amount of future scheduled interest anyway.

- **Your emergency fund will have to be bigger.** Your E-Fund requirement is 4, 6, or 9 month's average expenses. If your average expenses include a $450/month car payment, the math becomes much more challenging. It's disheartening, but it makes perfect sense; if you're hit with an unexpected financial emergency at the same time you owe a large debt, you're at even more risk than you otherwise would be.

Bottom line: it makes no financial sense whatsoever to borrow money to buy a depreciating asset that's going to cost you plenty to own on top of that. None. Your very best approach is the one that's easy to understand but hard to do: save up for it.

If You Absolutely Have to Borrow for a Car, Here's How

A Note from Chris

When you saw this nugget for the first time, you might not have liked it. It's harsh. It's clear cut. Six short words, starting with "never." Not much wiggle room there.

I wrote it that way on purpose, because I know that lots of people really want to buy a car, sooner rather than later, and wiggle room is exactly what they'd be looking for. If you really want something but can't afford to buy it yet, a very big-ticket item like a car is the last thing you ought to make an exception for.

But I also know that there's a difference between wanting a car and needing one—some people truly need a car sooner than they can save all the way up to buy one. If you've given it serious thought and that's where you find yourself, then you'll want to move ahead as safely as you can. Here's how.

- Hold out as long as you can. It won't be comfortable or convenient, but every month you can delay buying is another month you can save, ultimately reducing the amount you'll need to borrow.

- Prearrange financing with your bank or credit union before you begin looking at cars, to make sure you can pay the loan off early without penalty. Under no circumstances arrange financing with a car dealer.

- Limit your search to the lowest-priced cars that will meet your needs, even if you've qualified for more. Be sure to follow the seven rules in Nugget #5.5; the fact that you're borrowing doesn't change the importance of a resale winner.

- Your goal is to borrow the smallest amount that you can, which you can do by paying as much of the car's price as you can from your own savings first, before accessing the prearranged funding from your bank or credit union. Be sure to leave at least one month's expenses in your E-fund, though.

- Continue saving as much as you can. If you can save up enough to pay the loan off early, do it!

- Promise yourself that's the last car loan of your life. After you've paid off the loan, keep driving the paid-off car while continuing to save, and don't replace that car until you've saved up enough to buy its replacement in cash.

Net Worthy Nugget #5.7

You can buy from a private party or a car dealership, and you can represent yourself or engage some professional help. The best choice for you depends on your individual situation, experience, and confidence. Whichever route you choose, research is vital.

We've reached a fork in the road. Now that you've settled on a category of car and are armed with resale winner tips from Nugget #5.5, the next question is—where do you go to buy? And do you represent yourself or bring in some outside expertise? The used car market is in the midst of an internet-driven extreme makeover. The traditional dealer-based approach is still stubbornly hanging on, but a variety of other alternatives have also emerged. Each of these has its pros and cons, which you'll need to weigh for yourself. Above all else, the guiding principle here is research, research, research.

Here are your main choices:

- **Do it yourself—private party seller:** That's right, a peer-to-peer transaction between you and a private seller. If you live in a big enough metropolitan area, you might find all the listings you need on Craigslist. Or you can broaden your search area using a site like Autotrader.com. The advantage of a private party sale is that you're cutting out the middleman's markups as well as the notorious pitfalls of dealer negotiation, while getting a potentially great price. Here's the catch: sometimes, private party sellers are honest people who simply prefer not to trade in their cars to a dealer. But sometimes private party sellers are selling cars that have problems that a dealer would spot, and they're hoping you won't. It's up to you, your automotive research skills, your PPI mechanic, and your gut feel at reading the seller's intentions, to tell one from the other. And if you're concerned about meeting a complete stranger in an unfamiliar place to see a car, many police departments are now providing Internet Purchase Safe Zones near their stations.

- **Do it yourself—car dealer:** Although this choice is tempting because it seems so simple, you should only go this route if you're highly knowledgeable about dealer selling practices or have the help of a friend or family member who is. You'll protect yourself with research every step of the way. For starters, you're only willing to consider buying from the small subset of car dealers who have excellent reputations for solid pricing and trustworthy used car sales practices. How do you find that out? Check out DealerRater.com, an independent source of customer reviews and ratings. And, review the dealer's inventory online and already have your resale-winner car picked out ahead of time, before you even set foot on the dealer's lot. Even then, the full-blown dealer negotiation process awaits you, so beware of traps and pitfalls. If you know someone who's knowledgeable about the games dealers play, bring them along.

- **Hire a car broker:** These come in all varieties, but the type you're looking for will charge a fixed fee, determined up-front, for their services, and will work exclusively in your best interest, independent of any tie to dealerships. The fee might range from a few hundred dollars up to a thousand, depending on the price range of your target car. A broker might be an independent agent, a small company, or an online service. They're often former salespeople or dealership managers, so they know the game inside and out. If your mental image of negotiating with a car dealer is something like the gunfight at the OK Corral, hire your own gunfighter! After much careful research, or course. If you go this route, be sure to instruct your broker about your insistence on all the resale winner criteria in Nugget #5.5 above.

- **Use a car-buying service:** Did you know that AAA or Costco—or even some banks or credit unions—will do car buying on your behalf? It's true, and it's an interesting option. Compared to car brokers, the fee is usually much smaller. That's because these services are usually not independent; often, they have prearranged pricing with local dealers. If they're transparent about that though, this can be good for everybody concerned. You're unlikely to get an eye-popping bargain, but if your goal is to simply get a fair and square price, all while bypassing the worst parts of the dreaded negotiation process, this can be an attractive way to go.

Here is what you won't do, under any circumstances: go to a dealer without a very specific, pre-researched car (or two) in mind. After all, they're pulling out all the stops and spending big advertising bucks just to get you to wander in and say, "Hey, show me what you've got!" Once you do that, you're one step closer to forgetting all about net price and buying into their seductive but highly dubious definition of "saving money." Don't fall for it. Just remember to stick closely to the principles we've described in these nuggets and arm yourself heavily with research, and you're sure to make a wise choice.

What About Selling A Car?

A Note from Chris

We've gone to great lengths to show you how to find those resale winner needles in the used car haystack, and we've talked about the various ways to buy. But what about selling? Here are three points to keep in mind:

- Never trade your car in to a dealer. By now you know better than to believe the advertised promise that a dealer will pay "top dollar" or "craaaaazy prices" for your car. Instead, you'll get a much better price if you sell your car, on your own, to a private party. This is a peer-to-peer transaction with no middlemen. List your car on Craigslist, AutoTrader, or any of the many sites featuring used car listings.

- Adopt a "no negotiation" policy. Most people selling a car for the first time are nervous about negotiating with strangers, who may be more familiar with the process. Especially because car sales are among the biggest transactions you'll ever make, it's natural to worry about making a mistake or being taken by a smooth-talking operator. The truth is, the buyer is often just as apprehensive about the process as you are. How about making it clear, right from the start, that your price is going to be set by Kelley Blue Book, to the dollar. It's like saying, "I don't want to overcharge or undercharge, I simply want a fair price." Most buyers are relieved to hear that and are happy to agree. Then, it's a simple matter for the buyer to decide if the car meets their needs or not, and if so, you'll have a deal—simple and fair.

- Maybe it's better to never sell your car. There are two main alternatives: buy a Grand-car and resell it while it still has some decent resale value, or buy a Grand-car and drive it until it dies (or becomes more expensive to repair than the value of the future miles such a repair would enable). Both are great ways to go, and debating which is best can be an exercise in uncertainty because it involves making an educated guess about how many more miles you can coax out of that car before it finally becomes economically unrepairable. I recommend the buy-and-resell strategy for most people and the drive-it-until-it-dies approach only for people who are quite knowledgeable about cars and repairs or know someone who can reliably help them.

Net Worthy Nugget #5.8

Minimizing miles driven will minimize almost every category of automotive expense.

The net worthy approach to buying a car is very different than what most Americans have been taught. But there's another powerful financial principle when it comes to cars that you already know perfectly well: drive your car as little as possible. If you keep miles to a minimum, here's how you'll save:

- Your depreciation rate will be slower, making your net price higher.

- You'll spend less on gas and oil.

- You never miss any of your car's recommended service intervals, but you'll stretch out the timing of when you hit them.

- You'll pay less for parking. Oh, and statistically speaking, traffic tickets, too.

- If you drive less than 10,000 miles per year, you might be able to save by opting for per-mile car insurance.

Earlier, we said the average American car is driven about 15,000 miles per year. If that's you, but you can manage to reduce your miles driven by a third to 10,000 miles per year, how much would that save you? Depending on how you went about it, somewhere between $700 and $1100 per year. Keep that up over a few consecutive years, and you've saved enough to pay for your next used car.

How do you cut down on miles? You already know. Carpool. Public transportation. Batch up and organize your errands. Research and buy online instead of in person, when it makes sense. Track your miles for a month, and you might be surprised by your habits. Minimizing miles makes your financial bathtub and your planet happier at the same time. What could be more perfect?

The Big Finish

A Note from Samantha

Well, friends, here we are at the finish. Though I am sad to report that Sam from 2012 made an unwise decision buying her Scion because its net price is so tragic, she did a few things right by intuition! I am not in debt over my car, which is a huge freedom in itself. When I go to resell, I won't be tied to a loan with an interest-fueled balance thousands of dollars higher than what I'll be able to sell for.

I did a few other things right too. I bought a used car, but mainly because the purchase price was more affordable than a new car would have been. And I bought a green zone Grand-car, which should have been net price gold. So it wasn't the Scion's age and mileage that doomed the net price; it was the fact that Toyota discontinued the Scion XD, pure and simple. In fact, if I'd have bought a Scion XD in the red age/mileage zone, my net price would have been even more tragic!

When I sell within the next couple of years, I am confident I can pick a resale winner that fits me and my lifestyle without emptying my financial bathtub. These nuggets have changed the way I approach my car in every aspect, whether that's more confidence in my own car-scouting ability or my diligence to take good care of my Scion now so that I can get the most value out of it later!

I hope you're feeling as ready to get behind the wheel and make informed decisions about your next car purchase as I am. Ultimately, though we can't control systemic challenges like the health of the economy, armed with this kind of knowledge, I believe we can all break through the financial barriers to car ownership and come out on top without a debt-ridden roundhouse kick to our future financial gut. See you out on the resale-winner speedway, folks.

About the Co-Author

A firm believer in education and an advocate for a digitally literate world, **Samantha Poelstra** writes and edits content for a variety of businesses and implements high level search engine optimization strategies to help those who ought to be seen on search get the spotlight they deserve. She grew up in a family that survived on coupons and church-supplied casseroles, so she's all about helping others accrue wealth on their own terms so they can better assist the communities they're a part of.

"Financial knowledge is usually passed down generationally in families who already have the knowledge, so creating resources like this book is one way to share the wealth, so to speak. It should be required reading for all!"

This page intentionally left blank

Chapter 6

Houses

by Chris Smith with Dion Beary

Net Worthy Nugget #6.1
From a pure financial standpoint, it's almost always better to buy than to rent.

Net Worthy Nugget #6.2
Buying a house is a very big decision; don't do it unless you can commit to staying in that house for at least 5 years.

Net Worthy Nugget #6.3
Once you enter the yellow phase of your financial life, put yourself into one of three categories when it comes to buying a house: as soon as possible, maybe someday, or probably never.

Net Worthy Nugget #6.4
Your approach to renting (before you buy or if you choose not to) should always be: as cheaply as you safely and comfortably can.

Net Worthy Nugget #6.5
The geographic aspect of buying (which region of the country, which state and city) is more critical than ever—make it a deliberate, conscious choice.

Net Worthy Nugget #6.6
If you decide to buy, there are 5 significant financial readiness tests you'll need to pass.

Net Worthy Nugget #6.7

Set a target price to yield just enough house to meet your needs for the foreseeable future, but no more than that.

Net Worthy Nugget #6.8

The most important financial criterion in selecting a house is resale value.

Net Worthy Nugget #6.9

The type of mortgage you want is a 30-year, fixed-rate, with at least 20% down.

Net Worthy Nugget #6.10

Once you've successfully bought your house, responsibly maintain and care for it, be very selective about remodels and improvements, and never take out a home equity loan.

Net Worthy Nugget #6.1

From a pure financial standpoint, it's almost always better to buy than to rent.

Buying a house is a huge part of the American Dream. That's because a house isn't just four walls and a roof. It represents comfort, safety, and ownership. It's a place to potentially raise a family and build memories that will last not just your lifetime, but your children's lifetimes as well.

Just for those soft benefits alone, buying a house would be worth it, but the pragmatic, financial benefits to home ownership make the case even more solid.

The saying is so basic, even financial novices know it by heart: "It is always better to buy than to rent." But is this advice really as true as people say it is? After all, renting can look pretty attractive for busy millennials trying to kickstart their careers and social lives. There are no lawns to mow, no multi-decade commitments to sign, and if anything breaks, you can call someone who'll come and fix it for you.

But the numbers don't lie. Buying will *almost* always be a better financial decision in the long run. But why?

Let's think about your financial bathtub. Month after month, you send your rent payment down the financial drain, never to be seen again. The property owner's bathtub is getting filled up with water coming directly out of yours. Consider that housing is the single biggest category in most people's monthly spending. That means that if you rent, a major part of the time and energy that you put into earning your income is going toward ensuring a bright financial future for . . . your landlord. Ouch.

Down the Drain

A Note from Dion

For fun, and to torture myself, I decided to roughly calculate how much in rent I've paid over the past five years since I graduated college.

- Ten months in a lower-income neighborhood right after college: $3,500.

- Two years in a slightly nicer neighborhood: $16,200.

- Two years in the nicest neighborhood in my city: $22,656.

That's more than $42,000! The city I live is close to the US average when it comes to rental prices, so it's not like I was getting gouged. But the point is, that money is out of my bathtub forever.

Buying a house is different. It's totally possible you could end up paying $42,000 over five years for a mortgage, but the difference is the money doesn't simply flow out of your bathtub. Money will also eventually flow in, usually much more than the amount that's flowed out, because you own the house.

You see, real estate typically appreciates. That means it becomes more valuable as time goes on. Even though this technically isn't "interest," you can think of it just like compounding interest in a bank account because the effect is the same over time. The landlords and owners of apartment complexes use this compounding interest effect as the justification to increase the price of rent every year. Living expenses will already be the single biggest category in your monthly budget, and compounding interest in rent makes it more expensive each year.

Now, if you own a home, compounding interest becomes your friend. Your home becomes worth more while your mortgage stays the same, meaning the value of your purchase becomes better every year. If that isn't enough to convince you, a couple of major tax benefits sweeten the deal.

The first big tax break for homeowners is called the mortgage interest tax deduction. Each year, homeowners can deduct the interest they've paid on their mortgage, as long as they live in that property as their primary residence. There are limits to how much you can deduct depending on your filing status, but these limits are so high that very few people will ever approach them. That relief at tax time is sure to feel amazing.

A second tax benefit of homeownership isn't quite as well known. It's called the capital gains exclusion. Normally, if you suddenly gained $250,000, Uncle Sam would want his cut. However, when you sell your primary residence after living in it for at least two years, you don't have to pay taxes on the profit (again, within some very high limits). You can even subtract the cost of the improvements you made to the residence when calculating the size of the capital gain.

But let's not think too much about a house as an investment for flipping. Maybe one day you'll become a real estate mogul and purchase houses to flip them or rent them out, but that's a different conversation. Right now, let's talk purely about a house as a residence.

Net Worthy Nugget #6.2

Buying a house is a very big decision;
don't do it unless you can commit to staying
in that house for at least 5 years.

You've probably noticed by now that we're very careful to always include the word "almost" when we're talking about how it's cheaper to buy a house than to rent. That's because there are a few big things you need to make sure you've got in place before you buy.

Now, here's something frustrating: renting is cheaper than buying *in the short term*. Think about it.

Let's imagine buying vs. renting as a race between two people. The "winner" is the one who ends up making the smartest financial decision. That'll be the person who has the most money in their bathtub.

On the first day of the financial transaction, the renter jumps out to an early and impressive lead. The renter paid $1,000 for their first month's rent, while the homebuyer paid a $50,000 down payment, plus the first month's mortgage of $1,150. The renter so far looks like they're sitting pretty. But this turtle race is just getting started.

The renter keeps shelling out (sorry, turtle pun) rent payments month after month, and every time the lease expires, that rent payment is likely to go up. That's it—the full extent of the renter's financial picture is money going out of the bathtub, at an increasing rate, for life.

The buyer's financial picture is a little more complicated. Sure, the buyer makes mortgage payments each month. But in the background, the value of the house that buyer lives in keeps consistently creeping up. At the same time, with each payment, the buyer's percentage share of ownership creeps up, too. These two effects combine to give the buyer a positive and growing equity position in the house. That equity position won't be converted into hard cash until the house is resold; but it's real nonetheless and eventually becomes an important component of the buyer's net worth. Sooner or later, the positive effect of that equity position allows the buyer to pull ahead of the renter in our hypothetical race.

It may take just a few years, or it may take 10 or more, but that fateful day is called the "breakeven point." And once the buyer pulls ahead, the race is all but over—it's extremely likely that the buyer will just keep on extending the lead, further and further each year. By the time the buyer has been in the house for a few decades, the lead can be well into the six-figure range. Finally, the buyer makes the last mortgage payment and owns the house outright. At this point, the renter looks back at his or her early lead like a cruel joke.

The breakeven point is such an important part of buying a house that the *New York Times* produced an incredibly popular calculator to help potential homebuyers weigh the financial effects of buying vs. renting. Search "rent or buy New York Times" to check it out.

But getting to the breakeven point is easier said than done, especially for millennials. It's not like it was when your parents were younger, when they stayed in one job for decades. Career paths just don't work like that anymore.

According to Forbes, renting is more popular now than at any point in the past 5 years. But why, if we're so sure buying is the better financial move, do so many people still rent? It's because job hunting as a lifestyle requires increased mobility, making many people hesitant to get "tied down" to a 30-year mortgage. And those people are making the correct financial decision for them.

Ask yourself these three questions before you buy:

- Are you ready to stay where you are for the next five years?

- Are you ready to make a house your chief financial priority?

- Are you ready to invest a great deal of time, energy, and money into one thing?

Buying a house is a high-stakes responsibility. It will become one of your chief priorities in life, higher than following that amazing new job lead across the country or following that amazing boyfriend or girlfriend who just found theirs.

If you're not in the position to say for sure that you can stay put long enough to reach that breakeven point, or say for sure that you're ready for this kind of financial commitment, renting is the smarter option.

Net Worthy Nugget #6.3

> Once you enter the yellow phase of your financial life, put yourself into one of three categories when it comes to buying a house: as soon as possible, maybe someday, or probably never.

It's time to set aside the fantasies and hypothetical scenarios and get down to reality. Is this house stuff going to happen or what?

Let's take all you've learned so far and make a decision. Where is your head right now when it comes to buying a house? You'll fall into one of three categories. Each seems pretty simple at first, but each comes with its own set of complications and guidelines that'll help you increase your net worth. Like all the advice in this section, the most important thing you should be doing is thinking critically and considering all the variables.

- **"I want to buy a house as soon as possible."** Good for you! You've got a lot to do now to get prepared. You'll need to save up for a down payment, work on increasing your credit score and income, and decide which city and region you'd like to buy in. We'll go over a lot more of what you've got to accomplish in later sections.

- **"I want to buy someday, but not in the foreseeable future."** Good for you too! You may want the house just as badly as people who choose the first statement, but maybe you realize you have other financial needs that require tending to first, like paying off debt or creating a foundation for your career. We recommend that you start saving for your down payment right away, but other than that, there's no need to take any additional financial steps immediately. That way, when you're ready to buy, you'll have a head start.

- **"I never want to buy a house."** Good for you as well! Buying a house is not a wise financial move if you're only doing it because you feel like you're supposed to do it. If a six-figure purchase doesn't figure into your life goals, then don't bother. There are plenty of other long-term investments you can make. Although most people use home buying as a step toward financial independence, it's not a requirement.

Even if you're not buying a home right now (or ever), we've still got some great advice for you on renting.

Net Worthy Nugget #6.4

Your approach to renting (before you buy, or if you choose not to) should always be: as cheaply as you safely and comfortably can.

Let's take a second to talk specifically to the non-buyers. Those of you who, for financial or personal reasons, have decided that buying a house just isn't for you—or at the very least, isn't for you right now.

The Baby Boomers in your life won't want to hear it. They'll try to convince you that you'll grow out of it eventually. But if you don't have the money to afford it or the desire to be tethered to it, buying a house isn't half as smart as renting.

Not all rentals are created equal. There are good ways to rent and not-so-good ways to rent. Just like anything else, you need to consider your options and come to a decision that's both comfortable on your conscience and on your wallet.

Chapter 4 on budgeting talks about streams and pops—steady spending versus one-time, rarer expenses. Rent payments are a stream, and for most people who rent, this is the single biggest stream in their entire financial picture. Within every rental agreement are tons of little mini-streams that vary in size. For example, an apartment complex without laundry on-site is going to be less expensive than one with a laundry facility. The additional cost in rent for the on-site laundry is a mini-stream. If the complex provides in-unit washers and dryers, that's an even bigger mini-stream. Each one of these mini-streams adds more to your rent, but you usually can't tell by how much—they're bundled in.

When you start adding up the basic rent for your living space, and then bundle in one mini-stream after another, the combined outward effect on your bathtub can become absolutely huge. We could go as far as to call these SUPERSTREAMS. Like all streams, it's very easy to underestimate the long term-effect, because your attention is on the relatively small monthly price tag. But if you live in a nice, superstreamed-up rental for three years, you're paying that monthly price tag 36 times over. It adds up fast.

As fewer people are buying houses, more apartment complexes are being built. They're being stuffed to the gills with fancy amenities. A local webzine recently listed some of the craziest amenities they found being advertised. Examples include:

- A two-story fitness center

- Courtesy bicycles

- Electric car charging stations

- Complimentary on-site yoga classes

- Dog wash station

- Xbox game room with 3D TV

Whether you use any of these amenities or not, you're paying for them in your rent. Can you imagine? The guy who owns the gas-guzzling SUV helps pay for electric car charging stations. The woman with her own fancy commute bike pays for the courtesy bikes, too. We're not saying all amenities are bad. We are saying that it's very easy to overestimate how much value you'll get out of any one of them when you're reading the slick rental brochure or getting the sales pitch while walking through the nicest unit in the complex. Take a very hard, realistic view of how much you'll really use courtesy bicycles or yoga classes, because you'll pay for them whether you use them or not, month after month. See the superstreams for what they are, and make a wise, responsible choice and not an impulsive one.

Renters often fall into a very common trap, so beware. It goes like this: "I really wanted to buy, but it looks like that's not financially realistic. I'll go ahead and rent, but I'm disappointed. But hey, as long as the immediate pressure to save up for a house is off the table, I might as well make up for my disappointment by living somewhere really nice—after all, now I can afford it."

If you catch yourself thinking like this, stop and reconsider—that's the trap. Every dollar you pay in rent more than you really have to delays your financial independence a little bit more. And because streams have a way of adding up to sneaky-big totals, you might be seriously underestimating just how much of a delay you're really signing up for.

How to Save Too Much Money on Rent

A Note from Dion

Now, don't think you have to run out and find the cheapest rent available in your city. Be realistic. The balancing act between safety and frugality is a financial decision as well. Saving lots of money on rent by living next to a toxic waste dump is probably going a little too far if you won't be able to enjoy your financial independence in good health. Likewise, spending a little more in the stream for living in a safer neighborhood could be worth it to avoid the pop of burglary.

I was robbed once, and it ended up costing me hundreds of dollars. I lost my television, gaming consoles, and laptop. To add insult to injury, the police found the perpetrator and found my stuff in his residence, but because I didn't have serial numbers, a jury of my peers decided they weren't CSI'd enough to rule in my favor. The robber actually got to keep my things. (Learn from my mistake and write down or snap pictures of all your serial numbers!)

The extra stream I pay to live in one of my city's safer neighborhoods was, for me, very much worth it to avoid those unexpected expenses of getting robbed. Someone else may opt, perhaps out of necessity, for a different direction. What's important is that you make a financially conscious decision that factors in your ultimate goal: financial freedom.

Net Worthy Nugget #6.5

> The geographic aspect of buying (which region of the country, which state and city) is more critical than ever—make it a deliberate, conscious choice.

Location. Location. Location. Now more than ever, the geographic location of your potential home should be a major factor as you begin to search for what to buy. Most people are sensitive to locations within their general city or region, but why stop there? Let's think about location on an even larger scale, city to city, state to state.

According to an article by the *Economist*, the average cost of a home relative to income hasn't changed all that much in the last generation. In 1990, the average house cost about 2.8 times the median income. The number had risen only slightly to 3.3 in 2015. But this trend doesn't tell the entire story.

Truthfully, houses in high-cost-of-buying cities have ballooned in price well beyond the national average. For example, in San Francisco, the average cost of a house increased from 6.1 times the median income to a whopping 9.1. Similar increases can be found in places like New York, Washington DC, and Boston.

But the news isn't all bad. Home prices are dropping in the Rust Belt—places like Ohio, Pennsylvania, and Michigan. Emerging markets like Orlando, Seattle, and Portland, are seeing big increases, but from a lower beginning point than the original high-cost-of-buying cities.

Because of this variance, the overall average may not have changed very much, but the fringes are getting further apart. The luxury of living in a high-cost area is going to be a bigger stream than it has been before, because the distance between high and average is getting wider.

If you live in a high-cost area and you're looking to buy a house, give the thought of moving to another city some serious consideration. The thought of moving from a San Francisco or a Boston to a Jacksonville, Florida, or a Salt Lake City, Utah, may cause some of you some distress, but from a strictly financial standpoint, the idea of moving is worth a onceover.

Now, we're not saying *never* choose to live in one of these super expensive cities. You might have some compelling, or even nonnegotiable reasons for doing so. Just make a conscious, eyes-wide-open decision based on what makes you comfortable, what you do for work, and what your financial position is. If you go about the buying process without even considering some less expensive cities or regions, you're not doing yourself any favors. This house is going to be your top financial priority for the next 30 years. Why make that decision without considering all the options?

Don't just choose the option that is easiest for you, either, or the one that is the least scary. Sit down, list out your pros and cons, and be honest about what's in front of you. Is your love of Times Square worth adding five additional years to your breakeven point? It just might be! But if you don't ask yourself, you'll never know how much unnecessary money you could be spending—or saving.

Your Best Financial Future? Location, Location, Location

A Note from Chris

There's no doubt about it: moving is a pain. And moving to a place far from where you've ever lived before is an even bigger pain. It forces you to rebuild everything from scratch, from your circle of friends, to your health care network, and everything in between. So why would you ever move if you didn't have to?

Here's one way to think about it: you can make one potentially very disruptive and inconvenient move now, in exchange for a favorable real estate and job picture for decades to come, or you can keep on fighting the same old battles that come along with the status quo, indefinitely.

If you were going to plant a tree, you wouldn't just immediately decide on placing it right outside your front door because that's most convenient. You'd want the tree to grow strong and tall, and to thrive for a lifetime, so you'd put some thought and research into finding just the right spot. You'd check out everything you could about soil, sunshine, moisture, and anything else you could think of, because you know that once the tree puts down roots, it will be hard to ever move. Far easier to get it right now, than to have to deal with a bad placement later.

Here's some data designed to get you thinking. The length of each bar represents the median price of single-family homes sold in late 2016, in each of

House Prices and Job Prospects
Selected US cities

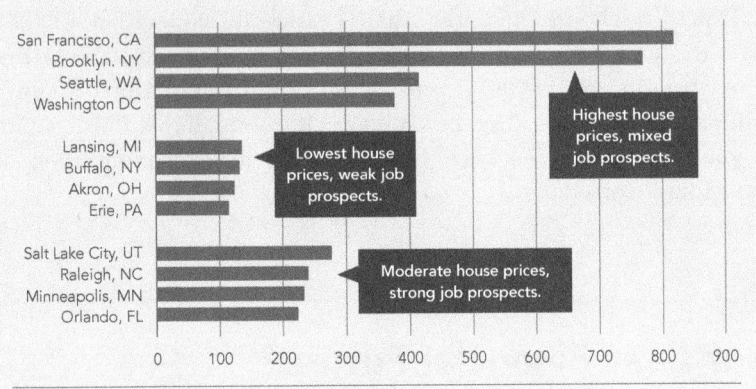

San Francisco, CA
Brooklyn, NY
Seattle, WA
Washington DC

Lansing, MI
Buffalo, NY
Akron, OH
Erie, PA

Salt Lake City, UT
Raleigh, NC
Minneapolis, MN
Orlando, FL

0   100   200   300   400   500   600   700   800   900

Highest house prices, mixed job prospects.

Lowest house prices, weak job prospects.

Moderate house prices, strong job prospects.

House Prices: Medium price for single family home, Q4 2016 Natl Assn of Realtors Brooklyn sourced separately:
Job Prospects: 2017 Study by Wallet Hub

the cities shown. Imagine yourself suddenly transplanted to San Francisco. What would your job prospects be like? What kind of living situation would you end up in? What would the general cost of living do to your monthly budget? Now go through the same thought process, but imagine yourself in Erie. Now, Raleigh. See what I mean? Your financial and career future is likely to be vastly different depending on where you launch it. Where will you plant your tree?

Net Worthy Nugget #6.6

If you decide to buy, there are 5 significant financial readiness tests you'll need to pass.

Now that you've decided buying a house is for you, and you know where you want to buy it, we can get into some of the nitty-gritty financial aspects. Being emotionally ready to buy a house and being financially ready are two very different things. Jumping the gun on buying a house can put you in a financial hole that will take years to climb your way out of, so be careful not to let the allure of homeownership distract you from the reality of your financial situation.

But how do you know for sure that you're ready? The housing bubble crash of the mid-2000s showed us the danger of eager banks and buyers too quick to give and get loans. This was a stark reminder that you can't always trust a bank to advise you on whether you can really afford a home. Luckily, you can give yourself some commonsense tests to evaluate your readiness. Until you can answer yes to all of these questions, you're not quite ready for your home purchase.

1. **Is my emergency fund in good enough shape?** Your E-Fund is your last line of defense against any unforeseen financial setbacks that you might encounter. As we outlined in Chapter 2, the bare minimum you should have available is one month's expenses; ultimately, to leave the red phase, you'll need 4, 6, or 9 months depending on your risk profile. If you don't have that one-month bare minimum, stop the house-buying process right now until you do. In an ideal world, you'd save up 27% of the selling price (shocking, we know, and more on that below) *on top of* a fully stocked E-Fund. If you're able to afford that, fantastic—that's what you should do. But realistically, very few people are able to that, so here's your rule:

   Always maintain a bare minimum of one month's expenses all the way through the entire house-buying process.

   The 27% rule is a huge stretch for most people. And even though buying a house isn't an emergency, it's a very wise long-term financial move. So go ahead and take any E-Fund dollars in excess of one month's expenses, and reassign those dollars into your house fund. Yes, it's an exception, but it's the one circumstance where it's financially justified. Besides, it's temporary. Once you've successfully bought your house and moved in, your next priority will be to replenish your E-Fund back to its full level.

2. **Is my credit score high enough?** If you've followed the credit advice given so far, you're sure to have seen an increase in your FICO score from the last time you checked it. Hooray for progress! But how high is high enough to buy a house? The primary rule is: you do not want a subprime loan under any circumstances.

They're too expensive, and the fine print is very buyer unfriendly. So you don't want to simply achieve the lowest score that will allow you to qualify for any old mortgage; you're shooting for something high enough to completely escape subprime territory. There's no one magic number that will guarantee this; economic conditions affecting credit go through tightening and loosening cycles all the time, banks differ from one another, and so do different cities and regions. All that said, if you're in the 660-670 territory or above, the odds are excellent that you'll be good to go. If you're below that, it's time for some focused attention on improving your score.

3. **Do I have enough saved up?** You should have 27% of the selling price of your house saved up before you buy. That may come as tough news to some people. The 27% accounts for 20% for a down payment, 5% for closing costs, and 2% for other move-in costs. For example, if $250,000 is your price range, that means your required savings is $67,500. Gulp. When I was working on buying just last year, I was talking to leasing agents and realtors and heard numbers as small as 3% for how much I should save up. Remember that these people have a financial interest in you buying a home, whether it's the best decision for you or not.

4. **Is my income high enough for my local housing market?** To do this, start by looking up a few houses in the area you'd like to buy. Don't start looking at specifics like bathroom placements and flooring quite yet. Just find houses that fulfill your bare minimum requirements. Find five for sale and calculate their average price. Now take your annual income (gross income, before any withholding and deductions) and multiply that by 3.4. That tells you what price you can comfortably afford. If that number is lower than the average cost of your bare minimum houses, it's best to continue renting until you can improve your income.

Note: That 3.4 multiple we just recommended for calculating will change slightly from year to year, as interest rates do. We're using 3.4 at the time of publication, when the US average for 30-year fixed rate mortgages is 4.2%. If rates are closer to 5.0% by the time you read this, use a lower multiple of 3.2.

5. **Can I afford monthly mortgage payments and still be able to save?** To calculate the monthly fixed costs of your home purchase, use a PITI calculator to add up the principal, interest, property taxes, and homeowner's insurance into one monthly payment. Then, make some hypothetical adjustments to your current monthly budget. Obviously, you can remove rent, but you'll need to add utility expenses currently covered by your landlord or apartment complex. Add a cost for home maintenance your landlord handles now, something like 0.5%-2% of the house's value per year, and then one-twelfth of that per month. Does your budget still allow you to save ideally your full magic number percentage, but a bare minimum of 10%, of everything you earn per month? If so, you're ready to buy a house.

The Net Worthy Navigator App can help you easily apply these five test to your current financial situation. For example, you won't have to search around for a PITI calculator; there's one built right into the "5 House Purchase Readiness Tests" tool in the app. Remember, real estate professionals and mortgage lenders may have their opinions about what's safe for you, but they're not in your shoes. Having the app in hand throughout the process will keep you firmly locked in to what's really in your best financial interest.

These tests might seem strict, but when you can answer yes to each of them, you can proceed with confidence, knowing that you're on solid ground.

Example: Income Reality Check in Charlotte

A Note from Dion

Let's look at an example to make this simpler. Let's say I'm looking for a house with at least three bedrooms, within 15 minutes of uptown (in Charlotte, we call our downtown "uptown" because it's at the top of a hill), but far enough outside of uptown that I can have a yard. I'd use Zillow or look up five houses that have JUST this bare minimum. I also love hardwood floors, exposed brick, sunrooms, and wraparound porches, but I'm only looking at bare minimum for now.

We'll say the average cost is $200,000. Using some simple math and the magic 3.4X multiple, if I make $59,000 a year or more, I'm good to go. But if I make $40,000, it's time to keep renting until I can increase my income. I could try to do that by changing jobs, getting a raise in my current one, or by adding to my base salary with side hustles: more freelancing and the like.

Remember, the multiple is designed to be on the safe-and-sane side, to allow my transition to home ownership to be reasonably smooth and comfortable. It will definitely be easy to find real estate professionals who think I'm being too conservative, and they'll encourage me to stretch beyond that, and buy something more expensive, or make a smaller down payment. To them, my stretch is a bigger commission. To me, it's adopting a "food optional" lifestyle. No, thanks.

Net Worthy Nugget #6.7

Set a target price to yield just enough house to meet your needs for the foreseeable future, but no more than that.

Now that we know you're in a great position to buy, we can get into the nuts and bolts of how to choose your house. For most homebuyers, this is the most fun part of the process. Daydreaming about dinner parties or quiet Sunday afternoons in your new home can get really exciting. As always, we're here to throw just a little bit of cold water on that. Sorry! It's our job to make sure your purchase is not just one you're happy with, but one that grows your net worth.

Let's dispel a major myth right now. You may have heard lenders or real estate agents tell you that you should buy the "most" house that you can afford. If you can live with a three-bedroom, but can afford the four-bedroom with the bonus room, they'd encourage you to take the more expensive one. They'll phrase this as being in your best financial interest, but ask yourself who really benefits more from you buying the more expensive house? That's right: the lender/agent. The more home you buy, the higher their commission will be. The most expensive purchase is the one that is best for THEIR financial future, not yours.

Instead, aim for the least amount of home that will fill your needs for the foreseeable future. Don't get confused between the amount you can afford and the amount you *qualify* for. The total amount you qualify for is the riskiest amount the bank will give you. Why go for the riskiest amount when you can dial it back a little and stay much safer?

If you qualify for a $400,000 house, but a $300,000 house will meet your needs for the foreseeable future, you should buy the $300,000 house and invest the difference in other areas. (Chapter 7 addresses just which investment areas yield a much stronger positive impact on your finances than the all-too-common advice to "buy more house".) Research clearly shows that this method consistently delivers higher returns. In addition, it gives you a much more diversified investment. That's a way safer use of your money than putting it all into an undiversified house. Anything can happen to a housing market (a big local employer goes under), or to a neighborhood (zoning laws change in ways that badly hurt your resale), or even to an individual house (neighbors move in that nobody wants to move in next to). If you put the entire $400,000 into your house, you could find your return on that investment turning out to be far less than you expected it to be—it could even go negative. A house is an inherently riskier investment than the kind of diversified investment that we'll cover in the next chapter.

Dream House or Wake-Up Call?

A Note from Chris

Remember earlier when Dion shared some of the aspects of the home he was dreaming of? A view of the city skyline, big backyard, wrap-around porch, exposed brick, and a sunroom? Especially when you're considering your very first home purchase, it's very natural to get lulled into dreaming about all the wonderful, idyllic features that you'd love to wake up to every day. I know I did.

It's called the "Dream House" syndrome, and it's often thought of as an essential ingredient of the so-called American Dream. Be careful, though. The Dream House syndrome may be new to you, but real estate professionals know all about it. To them, a list of clients all in the tight grip of the Dream House syndrome would be a dream come true.

Here's where the saying "You can have anything you want, but you can't have everything you want" comes into play. Your financial life is all about prioritization. Buying your first house may well be the first time that the highest priorities in your financial life are seriously challenged. It's a very good idea to see that challenge coming, and to be prepared for it when it does.

If a real estate agent tries to get you to open up about the house you're dreaming of, that doesn't make them evil. They're just doing their job; they need to find out all they can about what you do and don't want, and how badly, so they can help you find just that. And it's your job to give them clear and unambiguous direction when it comes to a dream house vs. a financially pragmatic house.

A dream house isn't necessarily a bad idea. But here's an acid test question I recommend you ask yourself: which *one* thing do you want the most—the fastest possible path to financial independence, or the house of your dreams? I strongly advise against selecting "a little of each" as your answer—when it comes to money, compromising is a poor substitute for prioritizing. Pick *one*, embrace it, and don't look back.

My advice? For your very first house, set your sights very squarely on the financially pragmatic end of the spectrum. Make a clear-eyed, deliberate decision to prioritize the dream of overall financial independence over views, horse stables, heliports, or whatever it is that represents your dreamiest house. For one thing, your idea of what makes a house dreamy may change a lot more easily than you can change houses. It'll be a lot easier to explore more and bigger house dreams *after* you've achieved financial independence.

Bottom line: if you've got a bad case of house dreams, better sleep on it before going house hunting.

Net Worthy Nugget #6.8

The most important financial criterion in selecting a house is resale value.

In thinking about a house as a part of your larger financial position, we need to talk about resale value. It is the single most important financial criteria you should be looking at when choosing a house. This is how you get your money back from the huge purchase you're about to make. It's what makes buying such a better choice than renting.

The Stunning Power of One Extra Percentage Point

A Note from Chris

Before going on, let's zero in on something vitally important about how the math of house buying works. Way back in Chapter 1, one of the very first things we talked about was the immense power of compound interest. When it comes to houses, the way compound interest comes into play is reflected in the rate at which your resale value grows. Now, consider that this compound interest rate is applied (a) to what is probably the single highest dollar value item that you own, (b) for a period of many years. This is like compound interest on steroids, and the upshot is that even tiny differences in resale rates can eventually have huge differences in your ultimate net worth.

Example: Let's say you buy a $250K house in a community where the average rate of appreciation is 5% per year. What will that house sell for in 20 years? Prepare to be shocked—again—by the power of compound interest. That house will sell for $663K: a giant gain of $413K, much more than double what you originally paid for it! Go, compound interest!

It gets better. What if you are a very smart buyer, and you manage to find a house in the community that will appreciate just a little bit faster than average? What if you find one that's a resale winner, that will appreciate by 6% instead of 5%? In 20 years, that house will resell for more than $800K! That one extra percentage point—appreciating by 6% instead of 5%—puts almost $140K extra into your bathtub 20 years later. And 30 years later, instead of 20? That extra point now adds over $355K in value, over a third of a million dollars, to your net worth.

If you can manage to pick out the resale winner that will lock in just one extra percentage point per year, you can shave not just months, but years off the time it will take you reach financial independence.

Now, when it came to cars, there was a simple, specific formula to follow to pick out the resale winners. Houses don't quite work the same way. There are some general rules, but fluctuation, chance, and purely local factors and quirks always play a significant role. *The best way to find a resale winner is to work with an experienced agent who's been in the market for a long time and knows what to look for.* We're talking 10+ years of experience here. Then, once you've found that agent, make sure that they fully understand, right from the start, that you are trusting them to limit their search to *resale winners only.*

Your agent is likely to tell you that the key to resale is location, location, location, and they're right. But there are very few universal rules about what makes a great resale location; instead, *local* rules are what matters. The recipe for a resale winning location in Boise is likely to be entirely different than the recipe in Tampa. Local employment trends, local zoning laws, local public transportation options and plans, local school districts—factors like these are what's vital to understand. That's why an agent with lots of local experience is so valuable. There are a few *general* principles about winning the resale game, though, and it's in your interest to know a little bit about those. Here's a quick rundown:

- **Go in with broad horizons.** We've talked about this a little before when it comes to location and the dangers of a dream house, but it's even more important when thinking about resale value. You need to *think like the masses.* The home that's perfect for you might not necessarily be the one with the best resale value. Does my love for exposed brick help or hinder my ultimate goal of resale? The distinctive, unique features you've dreamed about in your home since you were a little kid aren't necessarily bad. However, if they aren't *common*, they could alienate too many future potential buyers. So think like the masses for your first house; save the unique, distinctive and personalized for a future house.

- **Don't go too old or too new.** We can call this the Goldilocks strategy: not too old, not too new, but just right. If your target house were a human, you'd want one older than preschool age, but not quite to retirement age. New houses are typically in new developments, or surrounded by other new houses. One of the basics of economics is supply and demand, and it applies to houses as well. If there are a bunch of new houses in your neighborhood, this simultaneous influx of supply means it's likely these will appreciate more slowly than the surrounding average, not more quickly or more at all. For older houses, the amount of work you'd have to put into it to make it a valuable resale property is a lot to tackle for a first-time homebuyer. Try your best to strike in the middle. Your experienced agent can help you here.

- **Beware of bargains**. If the goal is ultimately resale, you might think a deeply discounted house is a no-brainer, right? Not necessarily. Obviously, a low price is attractive, but just like with any purchase, you have to ask yourself if it's too good to be true. A discounted price indicates that the seller is anticipating having difficulty selling the house, or has already had difficulty selling it. Whatever that difficulty is, *you might encounter that same difficulty when trying to resell the house later on*. It could be anything from a neighborhood in decline to a particular quirk about the location. Your agent, the one who's known the local area for at least a decade, will be able to give you some insight on the price discount and whether it's worth the risk.

Net Worthy Nugget #6.9

The type of mortgage you want is a 30-year, fixed-rate, with at least 20% down.

Qualifying for a 30-year, fixed-rate mortgage can be challenging enough; adding in the 20% down payment requirement raises the stakes even more. Striving toward this is likely to be a period of intense focus on improving your income, saving up the down payment, and shoring up your credit status; for many house buyers, its the single biggest sustained effort they've ever undertaken in their financial lives. It's natural to question whether there's an easier alternative. Even though there certainly are easier ways to go, which mortgage professionals are likely to point out to you, we still stick firmly to our recommendation. This is the safest way to buy a house and will put you in the best financial position going forward.

Let's start with the 30-year part. If you qualify for a 30-year loan, you may very well also qualify for shorter terms, like 15 years. The offer will definitely sound tempting. Since a 15-year mortgage will have you to full ownership in half the time, you might guess that it would require double the monthly payment size. Not so! This is one of those cases where compound interest is working for you, so the principal and interest payments on a 15-year mortgage are only about 55% higher than a 30-year mortgage. But even if you qualify for something shorter, we still recommend sticking with the 30-year option.

Here's why: paying off your mortgage 15 years earlier is only one way you could use that extra 55% payment each month. Even though increasing your home equity faster is a really good idea, there's another one that's even better: long-term investing; we'll cover why thoroughly in Chapter 7. The type of long-term investing that we'll describe will earn a higher return on average than the typical US house will, and more importantly, it's a much *safer* way to invest. The investment plan that we'll outline is very diversified, featuring thousands of stocks, in many different industries, in many different countries. Deepening your investment in a single house, in a single neighborhood, in a single city is the exact opposite of diversified. If you qualify for a 15-year mortgage and can afford the higher payments, say no thank you, and put that extra 55% into a safer, higher-returning long-term investment portfolio.

What about the 20% down payment? We touched on this earlier, but let's dig a little deeper. It's possible to qualify for mortgages with as little as 3% down in some cases. As always, keep in mind that what is *possible* isn't always what's *best*. Buying a house as part of a larger goal of financial independence requires that you make the decision in certain ways that minimize risk and maximize reward. Low down payments make the purchase of a house significantly riskier and more expensive in the long run.

To explain why this is, we first have to explain the purpose of down payments. Let's imagine that for some reason your house doesn't appreciate. Perhaps the market suffers a major drop and you end up in negative equity, owing more for your house than it's worth. This is rare, but it does happen. In that case, you're considered *upside down*, or *underwater*. Losing money in this kind of situation is often called "taking a bath."

Now, imagine that for some reason you can't make your monthly payments while you're underwater. The lender has the legal right to repossess the house from you. They'll remove you from the house, and you'll forfeit your ownership and therefore the right to any proceeds at all from the sale of the house. This is called foreclosure. You've taken a bath because you're out the down payment, closing costs, and any monthly payments you've made, with absolutely nothing to show for it. Now the lender has the right to sell the house, but if the house is still worth less than the loan balance that will now never be paid off, they're taking a bath, too. It's a lose-lose.

The down payment provides a cushion for the lender to be sure their potential losses in the case of a foreclosure are minimized. The larger the down payment, the smaller your loan balance. The smaller the loan balance, the less chance the lender ends up underwater.

The benefits of a larger down payment are similar for you. Suppose you have to sell the house sooner than you thought. A career opportunity for you or your spouse could take you across the country, or sudden additions to the family could require a larger house. If you're underwater when something like that happens, you'll take a bath on the sale of your house. Large down payments help keep your head above water. In that case, if you have to move unexpectedly, you'll miss out on future appreciation, but at least you won't be taking a bath.

Net Worthy Nugget #6.10

> Once you've successfully bought your house, responsibly maintain and care for it, be very selective about remodels and improvements, and never take out a home equity loan.

When you've purchased your home, the next step is putting in improvements. You might be thinking, "Yes! Now I finally get to get lost in my dreams and turn my house into my childhood fantasies!" Not so fast. Let's stay focused on making this a great financial move first and a dream house second. When it comes to remodeling and improvements, you need to be incredibly selective about what you do.

Like everything else with your house, look at improvements from the perspective of their potential return on investment. Remodeling can get really expensive. Improvements that don't add to the overall value of your home just take money out of your bathtub. Later, you want to sell this house for more than what you paid for it. If you put in an improvement that makes your house *harder* to sell, you're losing money in two different ways: first on the improvement, then on the resale.

For example, one of Dion's personal house fantasies is an enclosed pool area. If Dion bought a $200,000 house in a family-oriented neighborhood without an HOA and built a pool area in his backyard, it could cost $150,000. Suddenly, he has a home in a family neighborhood without a backyard, attempting to charge buyers close to double what homes in the neighborhood typically cost. He's just paid a huge amount of money to reduce his resale value. He's very likely to take a bath here. He wasn't thinking like the masses.

However, some kinds of improvements really can be a net financial positive. Fresh coats of paint in neutral colors, small bathroom and kitchen improvements, and landscaping all add value to a home. Again, think like the masses. Things you love that make your house more unique will generally make it harder to sell. Make improvements that almost everyone would agree on.

But never take out a loan to make improvements to your home. The goal is stay out of the red phase. That's the whole reason you bought the house, so why go right back into adding debt by taking out a loan to improve your house?

Overall, improvements and remodeling can be a great way to add value to your home, but if you do it haphazardly, you'll increase your chances of taking a bath. Do local research, spend as little as possible, and stay focused on resale value as you plan improvements.

How to Be "Not Ready" the Right Way

A Note from Dion

My attempt at buying a house recently was a lesson in patience, perspective, and making sure you've got the correct motivations in everything you do. You might've noticed that several times during this chapter, I talked about the dangers of the dream house. That's because I made the mistake of getting swept up in the fantasies, and reality is not a pleasant wall to crash into.

I started my journey firmly in the "maybe someday" phase we mentioned in Nugget #6.3. After taking care of my family for a year and a half, I was preparing for the next phase of my financial life. Homeownership was starting to appear more appealing. However, I knew I wasn't ready. I had some credit card debt to pay off and had just changed careers, placing me back into an entry-level salary.

But then plans changed. As is often the case with me, it had to do with a girl. She was a few years older than me and further along in her financial journey. She made more, had more saved, had a higher credit score, and was more sure our city was her home for life. I liked her, so I tried my best to keep up, and we decided to buy a home together.

Despite the fact we hadn't saved enough or tackled enough credit issues to really get started, we actually put together a pretty decent plan. I'd live with her for six months while she covered our expenses, and I'd save each of my checks for our down payment. During that time, we planned to passively look at neighborhoods and models to begin developing our idea of what we wanted to buy. That's where things got complicated.

We toured a home in an up-and-coming neighborhood, and somehow, we became obsessed with it. Maybe it was because the wooded area near the backyard reminded me of the woods near the house I grew up in. Maybe it was because there was no homeowner's association to stop her from building a stone deck exactly like the kind built by her father, who'd passed away the previous year. Maybe it was the real estate agent who ensured us all types of assistance and special loans would enable us to leapfrog the hard work of getting ready to buy.

Our plan to scrimp and save and pay down debt and improve credit scores went out the window. Our only concern was buying *this* house, and buying it now. We went from lender to lender trying to get approved for a loan, having conversations repeated verbatim about our financial woes. Slowly, resentment began to set in. We started having fights about whether dogs should be allowed on the living room furniture we didn't yet own for the house we couldn't even afford.

Unfortunately, this ended exactly like you'd expect. Now, not only do I not have that house, I don't have that girlfriend either.

But I do have a great lesson. You see, I'm still not ready to buy, but now I'm not ready in the right way. I've got grit, focus, and a recognition of the importance of making a plan and sticking to it.

The pragmatic tools in this chapter are important: how much to save, what to spend, and so on. But even more important are the mental and emotional lessons. Don't get caught up in fantasies. Don't try to ditch out on the hard part. Don't abandon your plan.

It's OK to be not ready to buy a house. Just make sure you're ready to take the long way to your home. Taking shortcuts will just leave you coming up short.

About the Co-Author

Dion Beary is a writer living in Charlotte, North Carolina. He enjoys writing about ecommerce, finances, and millennials. He is obsessed with Chuck Taylor sneakers, craft beer, and the Carolina Panthers.

"I'm so excited to be able to contribute to such an awesome topic. Even though it was difficult in spots to be vulnerable and share my experiences, I can already tell a ton of people my age are going to be helped by the information throughout this book. From deeper explanations of common advice to new strategies I never even thought of, I've already gained so much knowledge from this project that I'm going to immediately recommend it to all my friends. Dive in and have fun!"

Chapter 7

Long-Term Investing

by Chris Smith with Colby Howard

Net Worthy Nugget #7.1
Long-term investing is by far the simplest, safest, and most common way of building net worth to achieve financial independence in today's financial world.

Net Worthy Nugget #7.2
Forget any preconceptions based on short-term investing that you may have previously picked up. Long-term and short-term investing are entirely different—different strategies, different mindset, different objectives.

Net Worthy Nugget #7.3
Long-term investment in the stock market (done in the way advised here) has consistently yielded at least the 6% real return described in The Million Dollar Plan. This is precisely how you turbocharge your savings—by tapping into the immense power of compound interest over a long period of time.

Net Worthy Nugget #7.4
As much of your long-term investing as possible should be done within tax-advantaged investment accounts such as 401(k)/TSP-type plans and IRAs.

Net Worthy Nugget #7.5
If you work for an employer who offers a 401(k)/TSP-type plan program with an employer match, it's a super high priority to take advantage of the match as completely, and as early, as possible. That's free money!

Net Worthy Nugget #7.6
Target-date funds are an excellent choice for you to begin methodically building net worth early in your financial life. These funds offer the safety of extreme diversity and the convenience of automatic adjustments.

Net Worthy Nugget #7.7

"Traditional" and "Roth" accounts offer two very different types of tax breaks, for IRA and (some) 401(k)/TSP-type plan accounts. If you have a choice, the earlier you are in your financial life, the more it is likely to be in your interest to lean toward Roth.

Net Worthy Nugget #7.8

Small savings in investment fees make a startlingly big long-term difference. Minimizing fees will be your main criterion in selecting an IRA and may cause you to favor investing in your IRA over your 401(k)/TSP-type plan, at certain times.

Net Worthy Nugget #7.9

Once you've established your tax-advantaged accounts and selected a target-date fund, you just keep on accumulating shares (always buying and holding, never selling) into those accounts. You do this on a fixed, regular timetable (like every payday), over and over, throughout the yellow phase of your financial life.

Net Worthy Nugget #7.10

Automate the long-term investment process, through preauthorized payroll deductions and similar means, to the greatest extent possible.

Net Worthy Nugget #7.11

You are a disciplined long-term investor, and you're going to stick with this plan no matter what. The stock market is famously cyclical, and market ups and downs—big ones—are absolutely inevitable. But you don't care. You just continue to methodically sock away shares of your target-date fund, whether the market is going up, down, or sideways.

Net Worthy Nugget #7.12

Most people should be able to get their long-term investment program off the ground without paying for specialized professional help, but there are certain circumstances where such help is highly advised.

Net Worthy Nugget #7.1

Long-term investing is by far the simplest, safest, and most common way of building net worth to achieve financial independence in today's financial world.

Whether you have any interest in the stock market or not, odds are, you haven't escaped headlines that read "Stock Market Tumbles" or "Trump Bump Leads to New Highs." At times, it sounds like being in the stock market is a sucker's game, something you want no part in, and at others, you have this gnawing feeling that maybe you're missing out on a way to grow your money. But those headlines are almost always a distraction from the larger point about the stock market and the main point of this chapter: wisely investing your savings is by far the simplest, safest and most common way of achieving long-term financial independence.

You may have friends who are incredibly interested in the stock market and then those who know very little about it and want nothing to do with it. Great news: no matter where you are in the spectrum, this time-proven advice will be helpful. People who trade stocks on the side are often neglecting the safe, reliable long-term approach, and those who avoid the stock market are quite literally avoiding the most powerful and effective means of saving for their future.

Is it possible to achieve financial independence without long-term investing? Definitely. But it will require plenty of risk, expertise, or luck—and maybe all three. The odds will be against you. But with the long-term investment program that we'll describe here, the odds will be very much *with* you. There's a reason why this kind of program is the most common path to financial independence: it works.

You are now in the driver's seat of your money's future value, and far too few millennials are taking full advantage of that control. As we learned in Chapter 2, the days of very long career stints with a single employer, ending with a cushy pension at 65, have gone the way of dial-up internet and VCRs. The idea of your employer investing your money for you so it's ready and waiting on a predetermined retirement date is gone. Right now, you can decide the timing, the speed, and the amounts of money going toward your financial independence. That control is an immense opportunity to be aware of how smart choices now can lead to meaningful wealth in the long-term.

But you have to know how to do it! Learning how to save and invest for the long-term is much simpler than it sounds—just don't let preconceived notions get in the way. If you're thinking, "I don't plan on needing my 401k when I'm older, I'm going to have a great startup idea and strike it rich," or you're questioning, "Why would I risk my savings in the stock market when it goes up and down so wildly?" then let the next couple pages prove to you that long-term investing is the most effective, safest way to ensure your future is secure, no matter what happens over the course of your career.

An Old Friend with a Valuable Perspective

A Note from Colby

Each person reading this chapter comes from a specific, individual background. Factors such as age, geography, income bracket, and family situation all play into how you'll react to being told for the millionth time "you should totally save!" I graduated college and moved to New York City. Some friends came with me, and others are in Charlotte, Houston, San Francisco, Denver, and Atlanta. I have friends in finance, the military, engineering, marketing, and accounting. We all make vastly different amounts and have vastly different monthly spending needs.

Living in Manhattan, I'm hard-pressed to find a room in an apartment for less than $1,200 a month or a drink at a bar for less than $7. Baseline living expenses and casual weekend activities with friends add up quickly and dramatically. My friends in other cities and suburbs, meanwhile, have already bought a house, spending less on their monthly mortgage payments than I do in rent. It's because of these disparities in costs of living that comparing salaries is such a fraught enterprise. My friends may make less than I do, but in actuality they "accumulate" more due to much lower rents and food prices.

I bring this up because hearing the suggestion that you should remove a specific amount, like 10% of your income, affects each of us differently. No matter where we work, we're surrounded by friends old and new. We have work, and we have life. We have the very normal desire to enjoy ourselves in the process of building a career.

If suddenly doing those things is put into question because some chapter says "think about the future," you may not be too thrilled with the prospect.

If you've read the other chapters, however, you're now a very savvy thinker about each dollar that goes in and out of your wallet. You have a framework of how to measure and change your daily expenses. It's these small changes that will allow you to build the foundation for a wealthy future without sacrificing any of life's meaningful activities and adventures.

When I had just graduated college, I was lucky enough to have someone explain the power of long-term thinking. She used the metaphor of your future self talking to your current self. (Sound familiar? That's the same idea we talked about in Chapter 3.) Your future self is like a trusted old friend, one who brings a valuable perspective worth considering. You in 40 years would know that deciding to spend $2 instead of $4 on coffee every day, and then investing that $2, would mean an additional $100,000 in savings. With each of your days' simple living expenses, ask yourself "what would my future self think about this?" Sometimes you'll change your decision and go with the cheaper coffee; other times, you'll feel sure that your future self would be A-OK with the costly but necessary trip to your best friend's wedding. The wedding, the coffee, and the 6% can all coexist, no matter what your income and geography. It's up to you to decide what's truly valuable in your life. All we are trying to do is advise you that what is small now can be very big in the future, and such a prospect should be on your list of "truly valuables".

Net Worthy Nugget #7.2

Forget any preconceptions based on short-term investing that you may have previously picked up. Long-term and short-term investing are entirely different—different strategies, different mindset, different objectives.

When we say long-term investing, we're talking about a time horizon that could be 40 years down the road. It's hard to even visualize such a far-out point in time, but think instead of 40 years as over 2,000 weeks. You can start to see how powerful it can be. Imagine doing something once a week, like a dance class, or like learning a new language. Now imagine how advanced your skills would be after 2,000 weeks of practice. That consistency would get you close to the fabled "10,000 hours" needed for mastery.

Now take that mindset and apply it to your savings. A small amount of your paycheck, consistently applied, adds up to a relatively huge sum over 2,000+ weeks. Take into account that the stock market returns *on average* 6% a year (after taking inflation into account) and you're multiplying your money over and over and over again. "Compound interest" is a term that we heard in math class at some point, and all it really means is that your money grows, and grows more on top of that growth. Each time you invest a little more, you're giving your money the opportunity to grow a little more. And if it can grow over 40 years, you can start to see the awesome potential.

If you were to take a dollar out, however, you lose that dollar of course—but you also lose all the growth that dollar would have provided. The minute you decide to shuffle money in and out is the minute you can no longer say that you're invested in the long-term. In fact, you are now a perfect target for those headlines we talked about in the beginning. Financial media is built upon short-term "advice." Buy Apple! Sell Chipotle! Sell Apple! Buy Chipotle! Each headline is accompanied by another one giving the exact opposite advice as the websites urge you to click on the one you want to believe. No matter which you click, they make a little more money in selling advertising.

The easiest thing to think right now is "but Apple has done really well over the past 10 years, I could have made a lot of money if I had invested in it." That is undeniably true. But are you a full-time investor? There are people who dedicate their lives to investing and often they win just as much as they lose. Just like someone off the street couldn't just walk in and do your job, you shouldn't try to do theirs unless you're willing to put in the same amount of time. Gamble your savings on a company just because you bought an iPhone and liked it? Think about using that reasoning on your boss. "Why is this a good idea?" "Because I have a good feeling about it." They'd send you out of the room to get research!

Is short- and intermediate-term investing inherently bad? Of course not. Screwdrivers and saws are both excellent tools—but they're poor substitutes for one another. Which one is "best" depends on what job you're trying to do. Well, trying to safely navigate a 30- or 40-year course to financial independence through a series of short- and intermediate-term investment decisions is like trying to cut a board in half with a screwdriver—it's going to be an exercise in frustration. Long-term investing is the right tool for a long-term endeavor. You have the opportunity to gain 6% on your money, year after year, with little time or energy required. This will free you up to put that much more time and energy into being great at your job, which will accelerate your progress towards financial independence even more.

Side note: If short-term stock picking is interesting to you, by all means spend the time and invest the money. Just don't consider that as a substitute for, or an alternative to, a long-term investing program. Go ahead and go for it, but only after two stipulations are met: 1) your long-term investing retirement plan is already well underway and independently funded, and 2) you're investing in small enough amounts that losing all of it wouldn't materially change your life.

Net Worthy Nugget #7.3

> Long-term investment in the stock market (done in the way advised here) has consistently yielded *at least* the 6% real return described in The Million Dollar Plan. This is precisely *how* you turbocharge your savings—by tapping into the immense power of compound interest over a long period of time.

The 6% real return we've mentioned a couple times now—where does that come from? If you look at the stock market over time, you will see big swings both up and down. But draw a straight line from beginning to end and you'll see a 10% return each year on average.

The graph shows just how different short-term and long-term investing really are. It shows that if you held 500 major US stocks (this is a well-known stock index, called the S&P 500) for just one year, almost anything can happen. Based on the actual historical performance of the S&P 500, holding for a year might have gained you a whopping 57%. But you might also have lost

How Risky Are Stocks?*
It depends on how long you hold them!

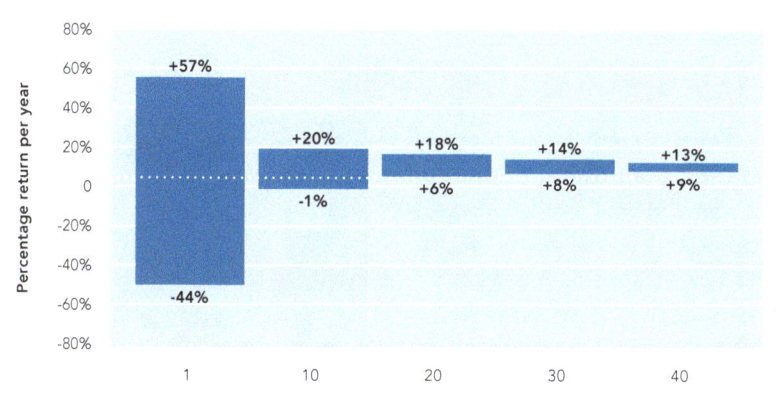

```
80%
60%   +57%
40%
20%         +20%   +18%   +14%   +13%
 0   ........-1%....+6%....+8%....+9%...
-20%
-40%
-60%  -44%
-80%
       1    10    20     30     40
```
Percentage return per year

Number of years held before selling

*Based on actual performance of the S&P 500 over the past 100 years

almost half (-44%) of your money. Now matter how confident the experts in the financial media try to sound, the truth is nobody knows for sure ahead of time if the coming year is going to be a big winner, a big loser, or anywhere in between.

But now look how a little bit of *time* really calms things down. This is the whole key to understanding long-term investing: It's almost impossible to predict what the stock market will do over the next year, but it's remarkably easy to predict what it will do over the next 30 or 40 years. *If you hold a broad mix of stocks long enough, the inevitable ups and downs of the market will cancel each other out, and you're left with the underlying long-term trend.*

What is that underlying long-term trend? Historically, it's been between 9% and 13% growth per year; that's why we feel that using 10% as the rule of thumb is on the conservative side. Remember, that's based on actual historical market values. If you're thinking that things are likely to be tougher in the future than in the past 100 years, remember that this history includes the recent Great Recession, the even more tragic Great Depression, world wars, the cold war, and all kinds of other dicey, dangerous scenarios. The safest assumption is that we're headed for a wide variety of good and bad economic times, just like in the past. And it's still true that nobody knows ahead of time exactly when or how they'll unfold.

What's the Difference Between the Stock Market and a Baby?

A Note from Chris

I've shown the graph above to thousands of people to help explain that the longer you hold a widely-diversified investment, the less risk you're taking. Quantitative thinkers love numbers, and visual learners love pictures; so if you're a quantitatively oriented visual learner (like me, if you hadn't already guessed), that graph is just about a dream come true. I've seen people stare at it in silent fascination, for minutes at a time, then look up and say, "I get this now. This changes everything I ever thought about investing." Sometimes a picture really is worth a thousand words.

But I also know that lots of people are neither quants nor visual learners, and that highly intelligent people come in many varieties. Is there some other way to make the point just as vividly, without such a nerd-oriented approach? Sure there is.

Try this: Besides being the cutest baby ever, this happens to be my grandson Kierian. Let me pose two very specific questions about him to make a point. Where will Kierian be, and what will he be doing, 2 or 3 years from now? I may not know exactly, but relatively speaking, I've got a very, very good idea. That's because I know his parents, their personal and job situations, and their plans over the next few years. But where will Kierian be, and what will he be doing, 30 or 40 years from now? *Who knows*! He could be almost anywhere—Mars, maybe?—doing almost anything!

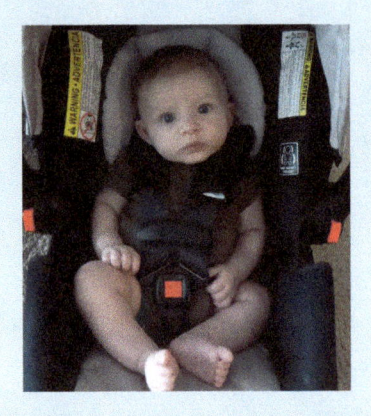

Now here's the part that's critical to understand: *The stock market is the exact opposite* of Kierian. Almost anything could happen in the stock market over next 2 or 3 years; I have no idea whether it will be up or down from today, let alone by how much. Of course, it's not too hard to find experts willing to make a prediction, and they can each sound incredibly convincing—even when their predictions are wildly different from one another's. The problem is, their track records over any long period of time are no better than random chance.

But we have a very, very good idea where the stock market will be 30 or 40 years from now—and it's really good news. A dollar invested today will be worth about $17 in 30 years and roughly $45 in 40 years! The astounding power of compound interest is what makes those eye-popping results possible. Granted, there's a little bit of plus-or-minus on the exact time it will take to reach those levels, because we can't predict exactly when the occasional bubble pops will come along to temporarily slow things down. But it's a sure thing that those levels will be reached in approximately those time frames. For us to confidently build a plan for financial independence via long term investing, *that's all we need to know.*

The dotted line on the graph is inflation (inflation is the reason candy bars that used to cost a nickel now cost a dollar—prices and wages go up over time), which has averaged about 3-4% per year over the past few decades. Now you see where the 6% that we used in Chapter 1, and that we've been referring to here, comes from. If you hold for a long enough time, your average return will be in the 10% range, minus 4% for inflation, leaving 6%. When calculated this way, the 6% value is referred to as the "real" return on investment.

Ready to really see this concept in action? Invest $200 a month for the next 40 years and you'd have almost $400,000. If you were to wait and start in 5 years, you'd have only $300,000 or so. You can start to see the big differences caused by small changes.

We bring up waiting because short-term investors will tell you timing is everything. Invest at the wrong time, they say, and you could lose it all. However, don't let their short-sighted advice cause you to wait a second longer getting started in your long-term endeavor. If you look at the stock market over time you will see a steady march upward, with drops (otherwise known as "bubble pops") sprinkled throughout. For the people investing short-term during these drops, it must feel like the end of the world. For long-term investors, it's as if nothing ever happened. These long-term investors know that stocks go up and stocks go down in a predictable cycle. They don't know when the market will go up or down exactly, and they don't need to, because when they think in 40 year terms, they know the 6% gain will hold. Doesn't that sound like a much less stressful way to live life? Your adherence to long-term investing allows you freedom to focus on everything else that matters to you.

Avoiding this short-term stress over the next 40 years hinges on not checking the dollar amount in your long-term investment account. If you're not going to sell, then why bother checking? All that matters is the number of shares you're accumulating. If you think of it that way, every year is a good year for your long-term investment portfolio; because you finish every year with more shares than you started with.

The Investor with a One-Track Mind

A Note from Colby

I remember being on a commuter train in 2011, at a time when the stock market was experiencing a sharp setback. Ahead of me was a family filling in a four-seat cluster. The father was on his iPad looking at what seemed to be a financial app, judging by the charts and percentages. He was scrolling up and down longingly, but his gaze never left the one large number in red that hovered in the top right corner. The scrolling had caught my attention and I couldn't help but take a quick closer look. What I saw explained everything. That number was ($282,000), in red and parenthesized because it was negative. It meant that his account was $282,000 less than the sum of all the money he'd put in thus far. Surrounded by his wife and young kids, this guy was fixated on what the recent stock market drop had done to his retirement savings. I'm positive this was not the first time he'd opened the app, and it's very likely this torturous set of events happened on a daily basis.

What can we learn from this poor guy's situation? Well, there are some positives and negatives to take away here. The positive is that the "loss" was only on paper (or his screen), meaning he hadn't sold his shares yet and guaranteed that $282,000 loss. With the benefit of hindsight, we know that if he'd simply stayed invested and rode out the short-term storm, he'd make back that entire loss and more over the coming years. But the negative is, every time he checked, he was subjecting himself to the temptation of selling, to "cut his losses"— which would have been the worst possible move. I'll never know if he ended up hanging on, or if he gave in and sold. But one thing I do know is he was *driving himself crazy!* Remember this the next time you have an urge to check the short-term ups and downs in your retirement account. It doesn't do you any good!

Net Worthy Nugget #7.4

As much of your long-term investing as possible should be done within tax-advantaged investment accounts such as 401(k)/TSP-type plans and IRAs.

No Matter the Name, Use What's Available to You!

A Note from Chris

When writing this chapter, we had a key choice to make about terminology. There are many different types of tax-advantaged investment plans offered through employers, depending on exactly what kind of employer is offering it. The most well-known of these is the 401(k), so we could have used the term 401(k) as shorthand for any tax-advantaged investment account offered to you through your employer; that's what many financial writers do. Or, we could have used use the term "401(k), 403(b), 457, or TSP (Thrift Savings Plan) account, depending on the type of employer you work for." Quite a mouthful!

Instead, we chose a middle ground: we refer to tax-advantaged investment plans offered through employers as "401(k)/TSP-type plans." It's just too much of an oversimplification to refer to all of these plans as 401(k) plans. Not everything that's true about 401(k)s is true about the others, so it would be a disservice to those eligible for 403(b), 457, or TSP accounts to lump them in with 401(k)s.

Here's a quick explanation: if you work for a private sector, for-profit employer above a certain size (classic example: a corporation), the kind of retirement account available to you is a 401(k), just as we've been describing. So, who uses 403(b) or 457 accounts? Employers like nonprofit organizations, government (state and local), schools, hospitals, religious organizations, and the like. Most government employees at the federal level, including members of the military, are eligible for TSP accounts. If you work for a very small employer, there are yet other types of accounts that might be offered. Fortunately, you don't have to know the ins and outs of this entire bureaucratic quagmire, you only have to understand which one applies to *you*.

For the most part, all these accounts offer tax treatment similar to 401(k) accounts, and therefore they should play a starring role in your bathtub filling plans. There can be some key differences, though, in things like contribution amounts, eligibility requirements, and other details. And what about one of the key topics of this chapter, employer matching? In 403(b) and 457 accounts, it's often possible for the employer to match, but far fewer of them choose to do so compared with 401(k) plan employers. TSP accounts are a mix; many federal employees are eligible for matching programs, but many are not—it mostly depends what part of the federal government that you're employed by.

The main point is most employers above a certain size offer some sort of tax-advantaged investment account, whether it's called a 401(k) or not. *Find out what it is, research the details, and take full advantage of it!* Yes, you might have to wade through some fine print and ask some questions. The principles you're learning in this chapter will help you zero in on the most important questions to ask. The reward is long-term financial security, and your future self is depending on you!

Here's something that isn't said every day: US Congress to the rescue! What the . . . ? No matter what your political views are, thanks to Congress, you have the opportunity to supercharge your long-term investing. 401(k)/TSP-type plans and IRAs are investment accounts that help you out on the tax side. Don't worry, this is not a tax conversation. Suffice it to say both 401(k)/TSP-type plans and IRAs are designed to make sure you get to maximize your long-term wealth.

The name 401(k) comes from where it is in the tax code books. It's named after a chapter. In that chapter, which was written in the early 1980's, Congress said that you get to take a percentage of your paycheck before they charge taxes on it and then stash it away in your 401(k)/TSP-type plan investment account. Once in that account, you choose from different investment plans provided by your employer. Most of those plans are of the consistent-buying variety we've been talking about all along. You take money from each paycheck and contribute it into your 401(k)/TSP-type plan, where it's then invested into whichever of your employer's plans choices you decide.

An IRA is the same type of account, except that it has nothing to do with your employer; you set it up completely on your own. If you're self-employed, or if you work for one of the few employers who doesn't provide a 401(k)/TSP-type plan, that's when you'd use an IRA. This means you have more freedom to invest those pre-tax dollars how you want. The tax advantages are the same, and the same consistent-buying approach will yield the best results.

A key difference between the 401(k)/TSP-type plan and the IRA is the amount you can contribute every year. For a 401(k)/TSP-type plan, you're allowed to put in up to $18,500 a year, and for an IRA, only $5,500. You can see now why companies are sure to advertise that they have 401(k)/TSP-type plan plans in their recruiting.

By the way, if you're wondering what happens over 40 years if you put in the maximum of $18,500 a year, or $1,542 a month, the answer is a lot. You'd have a little more than $3 million. Nice. Now here's another thing about those contribution limits: The 401(k)/TSP-type plan limit and the IRA limit are completely independent of one another. So, you can contribute $18,500 into a 401(k)/TSP-type plan account, and another $5,500 into an IRA, for a total of $24,000 invested in the same year. If you can swing it, 40 years of maximum contribution gets you into the $4 million-dollar range, after inflation. Even nicer!

These contribution limits change year to year in slight amounts, but no matter how little or much you make, the limits will stay fixed. The fine print and intricate rules may also change year to year, but not enough to make you worry about them, and not nearly enough to make you deviate from the 40-year view.

These two accounts give you some help in your quest for 40 years, but be aware that you can't take any money out without penalty until you're 59 $\frac{1}{2}$. And when you do, depending on the type of account you have, you may have to pay taxes at whatever rate you're being taxed at when you withdraw the money. (Much more on this distinction later.)

To recap, the government is giving you a huge break on taxes for your long-term investing journey! They've decided that it's good for our country to have more people saving and investing for a secure future; that means you get a chance to jumpstart your future wealth. Take advantage of it!

Net Worthy Nugget #7.5

If you work for an employer who offers a 401(k)/TSP-type plan program with an employer match, it's a super-high priority to take advantage of the match as completely, and as early, as possible. That's free money!

We made a point of separating this magical fact from Nugget #7.4. Why? *The employer match is the single best financial deal you will ever get in your lifetime.* There is such a thing as free money, and the employer match is it.

Employers are not required to match your contributions, but about two-thirds of them do, and the proportion is growing. The limits range from 3% - 6%, which means that if you decide to take 6% of your $4,000 a month pre-tax paycheck, your employer will match that $240. If your employer is one of the many which match dollar for dollar, congratulations, you just made an extra $240. Start taking advantage of that *right now* and you'll add more than $450,000 over 40 years even if you never got a raise. Of course, you're free to invest more than 6% of your $4,000 paycheck; it's just that if you do, the additional amount won't be matched.

Let's say this again. Your employer is giving you free money. That money will compound to ever greater amounts down the road. Conclusion: always contribute enough of a percentage of your income to take full advantage of the matching.

One example of not having access to a 401(k)/TSP-type plan is if you are a 1099 freelancer. Freelancing can offer the ultimate in work/life flexibility, and more and more people are either freelancing on the side or diving in full-time. You've probably heard "W-2" around tax time—it's the form you get from being a permanent, official employee. A "W-2" employee will most likely have access to a 401(k)/TSP-type plan. A 1099 employee will not. So, a 1099 employee might have the exact same annual income as a W-2 employee, but the W-2 employee has the potential to fill their financial bathtub up much more quickly because of the higher 401(k)/TSP-type plan contribution limits, and possibly also because of an employer match. This is a key point to take into account when evaluating career choices.

Net Worthy Nugget #7.6

Target-date funds are an excellent choice for you to begin methodically building net worth early in your financial life. These funds offer the safety of extreme diversity and the convenience of automatic adjustments.

Most employers aren't in the business of setting and administering investment plans, so they hire financial services firms, called 401(k) administrators, to come in and run their plans for them. The administrator then provides employees with a list, or "menu," of investment choices. For many people, this menu is as far as they get—one look at the all that complicated jargon, a wall of text a mile long—and they're gone. They may have every intention of coming back sometime and trying again, but the sad fact is that most of them won't. The 401(k) may be the freeway to financial independence, but the infamous investment menu is a very well-travelled off ramp.

We have a suggestion for you to consider: target-date funds. They go by different names in different plans, but they're all based on the same idea, and they're a great choice for young investors, early in their financial lives, looking to get an early start on methodically building financial independence. In other words, perfect for just the kind of person that the Net Worthy book was written for.

Target-date funds are easy to recognize by the 5-year increments on the fund's name. You start by taking an educated guess about what year you'd like to reach financial independence; that's your "target date." The higher the percentage that you're saving and investing, the earlier that year will be. Don't stress much about this; this is easy to change and fine tune as the years go by, so just make a solid estimate and select it. For example, if your target date year is 2045, your employer's investment menu might call the fund the 2045 Freedom Fund, the 2045 Target Retirement Fund, SmartRetirement 2045 Fund—you get the idea.

A target-date fund works on a fundamental assumption: when you're young, you want to grow your savings as much as possible, and you're not very concerned about stock market dips in the early part of your career; but as you get older, you want to start moving towards safer, less volatile—but lower average annual return—sources of income. Hitting a recession in your early 30s is one thing, but having a market bubble pop the week after you've permanently quit your job is quite another. Translating that into investment language, your target-date fund portfolio will be heavy on stocks when you're young, and it will gradually become heavier on bonds as you approach your target retirement date. The target-date funds change this mix automatically as the years go by; it all happens "under the hood," though, so you don't have to do anything but continue to hold that fund.

Target-date funds also offer diversification. This means your investments aren't put at risk by one company doing poorly, because you are invested in hundreds of companies. Likewise, you're not at risk of any one country's stocks doing poorly, or any one industry doing poorly, because you're invested in stocks from most countries, and in most industries. (The telecommunications industry, the restaurant industry, and the pharmaceuticals industry are examples of what "industry" means.) Once you're invested in that many different types of companies, you've now officially invested in the "market."

The S&P 500 is a popular way to invest in 500 of the biggest US companies in the stock market. By investing in a broad index like the S&P 500, which is exactly the type of index featured in many target-date funds, you're choosing the single cheapest way to invest in the stock market. This is called "passive" investing because no one is choosing individual stocks. The fees for passive investing are the lowest you can get.

But, not every target-date fund is based on this low-fee, passive approach. Some target-date funds consist of funds that try to beat the market index but also carry higher fees. Here's our advice: anytime you have a choice, select the target-date funds built from passively managed index funds. If you're investing into an IRA account, you always have a choice, so be sure to open your account somewhere that offers these low-fee passively managed target-date funds. But if you're investing through your employer's program, your selections might be much more limited. If the plan you're in doesn't offer passively managed target-date funds, the next best thing is whatever target-date fund they do offer, even if it's actively managed, with higher fees.

The Incredible Power of . . . Average?

A Note from Chris

Here's a fundamental definition: Funds can be either passively managed or actively managed. Actively managed means that the fund is trying to beat the overall market average (or, maybe the average of some very well-defined subset of the overall stock market). If the stock market goes up this year, the actively managed fund's goal is to go up by more, and if the market goes down, the actively managed fund is shooting to go down by less. In an actively managed fund, there's all kinds of buying and selling going on throughout the year, as the fund's manager constantly fine-tunes the fund's holdings. But a passively managed fund is entirely different—it is perfectly content to simply match whatever the market does. There's no constant fine-tuning of the portfolio. There's not even a full-time manager, just a predefined, automatic algorithm that is running in the background. That's why passively managed funds' expenses are so low. Sometimes passively managed funds are called "index funds," because the goal is to simply match a well-known index like the S&P 500. So why wouldn't the best choice be actively managed? Who wants to be just "average?" You do, that's who. Especially if you're a long-term investor. It may be surprising, but the evidence is very compelling, and it's been that way for a long time. It's really tough to consistently beat the average. When you throw in the higher fees that actively managed funds charge, it's even harder. Every year, a handful of actively managed, high-fee funds find a way to beat the market average, but most of them then fail to do it again the following year. According to MarketWatch, the odds of any one of them beating the average over a fifteen-year period are very slim—about a 1 in 20 chance. The odds over the 30- or 40-year period that you're concerned with are even lower. *Note:* The MarketWatch article referred to here is from May, 2017, and is entitled "This is how many fund managers actually beat index funds." Search for it online for an enlightening look at just how tough it is to beat the average over a long period of time.

This is good news for you, because a long-term investment strategy based on passively managed funds, or index investing, is a snap. It's easy, it's inexpensive, and it's highly effective. It's like going into a restaurant, looking at the menu, and ordering one of everything. Or going to the racetrack and betting on every single horse in the race. You scoop up everything—the winners, the losers, and everything in between. All you're interested in is the overall average, and that's what index funds give you. You're just taking this simple strategy one step further: You're investing in a target-date fund *made up of* passively managed index funds. If you're skeptical, so was I at first. So let's check in with a real expert. The person widely considered to be the world's most successful investor is Warren Buffett. His advice for the average long-term investor hasn't changed in many years: Keep buying shares, year after year, in passively managed funds based on broad indexes like the S&P 500. And if the market tanks? Just keep on buying those same shares.

Hedge funds are the polar opposite of Buffet's advice. They're a very high-end type of investment, which cater to the wealthiest investors and charge the highest fees. The high-profile hedge fund managers aren't afraid of trying to beat the market average; to them it's child's play—or so they say. In 2008, Buffet challenged a group of hedge-fund proponents to a ten year, million-dollar bet, with the proceeds going to charity. His side of the bet? That after all fees and expenses are considered, the return from investing in the plain old S&P 500 would be greater than the high-priced, ultra-sophisticated hedge funds. Nine years into the bet, Buffet and the S&P 500 are so far ahead that it's virtually over already. (Search "Buffet hedge fund bet" or something similar to catch up on the status of the bet. It's a fascinating story, but also sharply highlights the "active vs. passive" debate, one of the most important lessons you can learn about investing.) So, don't think of passively managed target-date funds as a cop-out, or as a placeholder until you have the time to do some serious research; think of them as the very best move that a long-term investor can make!

Net Worthy Nugget #7.7

"Traditional" and "Roth" accounts offer two very different types of tax breaks, for IRA and (some) 401(k)/TSP-type plan accounts. If you have a choice, the earlier you are in your financial life, the more it is likely to be in your interest to lean toward Roth.

Now that you're well on your way to being savvy in all things investing, it's time to get into one of the finer points of tax-advantaged long-term investing: Traditional vs. Roth. If this is new, unfamiliar territory for you, a choice like this might trigger some financial stress. When it comes to anything tax-related, nobody wants to make a wrong choice. Our advice? Relax! This is important enough to put some quality thought into, but here are two reasons why there's no need to stress about it:

1. **You might not even have a choice.** All employers' plans feature the traditional route, but only some offer a Roth option. If you're investing in an IRA, you'll definitely have a choice, but once you've maxed that out, and you go back to your employer's plan to continue investing, you may be forced to go with traditional. No worries, that's still far better than investing outside your employer's plan.

2. **The only wrong choice is neither.** Whether you select traditional or Roth, both your contributions and returns grow tax-free until you withdraw, and that's golden. So, whether you buy a month-long bus pass or pay for each ride, just make sure you get on the bus!

The difference between traditional and Roth comes down to a matter of timing. You're going to pay some taxes; the question is whether it's in your best interest to pay now (as you contribute into your plan), or later (as you withdraw from it). Here's how the two choices break down:

- **Traditional (sometimes called pre-tax):** You can deduct the amount you contribute from your taxable income in whatever year you contribute it. If you're in the 25% tax bracket (*see note below*), for example, and you contribute $1,000 to a traditional 401(k) plan this year, that means that this year's taxes will be $250 lower than they otherwise would be. Think of this as it only costing you $750 to invest $1000 into your plan—such a deal! But after you're 59 ½, and you begin withdrawing from your account, *those* dollars get taxed. If you pull $1,000 out for living expenses, that will add $1,000 to that year's taxable income. This choice makes your current self happy, as opposed to your future self.

    Note: If you're not sure which tax bracket you're in, just use a search term like "2018 Federal Income Tax Brackets." Every fall, the IRS announces the coming year's brackets, and nearly virtually every financial publication, personal finance blog, and finance professionals organization posts an article about it. At the time this is being written, there are seven brackets ranging from 10% to 36.9%, but this is subject to Congressional debate and revision every year.

- **Roth (sometimes called post-tax or after-tax):** In whichever year you contribute to your plan, there's no tax break at all. If you put $1,000 into your plan, it costs $1,000, plain and simple. The benefit comes later, after you're 59½, and you begin withdrawing. When you pull $1,000 out of a Roth account, there are no taxes triggered, at all—the $1,000 is all yours, free and clear. Actually, there's no limit to how much you can pull out in any year, and it's all tax-free. That's why this choice makes your *future* self so happy.

So which is better? Let's make this as simple as possible. This book is written for young adults relatively early in their financial lives. If that's you, then our recommendation is to *begin with the assumption that Roth is the best choice for you*. The fact that you're young and early in your financial life means that (a) your tax bracket is more likely to go up than down over the course of your earning years, (b) your lifestyle after you begin withdrawing from your plan is much too far away to intelligently guess at what your income levels will be, and (c) future tax brackets will depend on the country's economic and political conditions at that time, which are futile to try to predict such a long time from now. All three of these factors point you toward Roth. So here's our Traditional/Roth recommendation for the net worthy reader:

1. If you don't have a choice, you're stuck with traditional—and that's fine.

2. If you do have a choice, choose Roth, UNLESS:

    - You're currently in a high tax bracket (marginal rate of 28% or higher), OR

    - You're within 15 years of beginning withdrawals (age 45 or higher, and anticipate fewer than 15 more years of contributions), OR

- You're planning on doing most of your earning in a high-income tax state, but doing most of your withdrawals in a no (or very low) income tax state (i.e. working in New York or California, and retiring to Florida or Nevada)

- If none of the above three apply, that doesn't automatically mean traditional. It means that it could go either way, and we recommend a consultation with a CPA or CFP, and/or some focused research on your own.

Net Worthy Nugget #7.8

> Small savings in investment fees make a startlingly big long-term difference. Minimizing fees will be your main criterion in selecting an IRA, and may cause you to favor investing in your IRA over your 401(k)/TSP-type plan, at certain times.

Those hedge fund multi-millionaires gorging on large fees may seem like an aberration that likely won't ever affect you, but the fees you face on some plan choices can mean a big difference for your overall savings down the road. Out of all the nuggets we're giving you, this one is perhaps the only one that will take a little work on your end.

We've been saying that target-date funds tend to charge low fees, and they do—but there can be a big difference even within the world of target-date funds. The fee that comes along with whatever fund you're investing in is called the "expense ratio," and it is usually expressed as a percentage. There are hundreds of target-date funds available, and the average expense ratio across all of them is 0.73%. To make that easier to deal with, think of that as a price tag of $73 per year to invest $10,000. Some target-date funds charge over $100. (By the way, the average among actively managed mutual funds is about $129, with some of the super-premium alternatives at $250 and up.) The very lowest price you can pay for a target-date fund is—get this—$16. Is this a case of "you get what you pay for?" Do the higher priced funds give you higher returns? The answer is a resounding "no!" so don't fall for it. Remember, these are passively managed funds, so there's no stock picking involved at all. Bottom line, there are very few aspects of your overall investment return that are completely in your control, but fees are. And when it comes to target-date funds, despite all the fancy advertising claims you'll hear, it makes absolutely no sense to pay any more than you have to.

These fees might seem like very small numbers, but they add up. Every dollar you pay in fees is a dollar that comes right out of that year's investment return—making it a dollar that can't go on compounding year after year for your benefit anymore. Remember the Million Dollar Plan from Chapter 1? If that scenario were changed to add just 1% more in fees, the million-dollar result would be cut down to about three quarters of its former glory. A single percentage point of fees ends up costing that investor $223K over a 40-year period.

Expense ratios are important, but there can be more to the fee story, especially if you go outside your 401(k)/TSP-type plan. Depending where you open an IRA, for example, there may be an annual account fee, and there may be fees for each individual transaction. So, it takes a little homework to compare the fees inside your 401(k)/TSP-type plan to the various IRA options, but most people find that there are very low cost, high quality IRA options available. If that's what you find, then good for you—but remember, the IRA limit is much lower at $5,500, so once you hit that, you'll need to go back into your 401(k)/TSP-type plan to keep investing.

Here's a quick recap of your prioritized strategy. How far along you get on this list depends on your income level, in combination with your magic number (see Net Worthy Nugget 4.4). Don't worry if you don't even get past the first bullet early in your financial life. If you stick with the plan, both your income and your magic number are likely to increase, and you'll progress further and further down this list over time.

- If your employer matches your 401(k)/TSP-type plan contributions, take full advantage until you hit the match limit.

- Then go to the lowest cost IRA alternative (if the total fees are lower than your 401(k)/TSP-type plan), until you hit the $5,500 annual contribution limit.

- Then go back into your 401(k)/TSP-type plan to continue investing, until you hit the $18,500 annual contribution limit.

In Chapter 9, we'll combine this investment sequence together with your other major financial priorities, such as paying off debt and building an emergency fund. This integrated list of priorities will help you decide exactly what to do when as you move through your financial life.

Spotlight on Investment Fees: Part 1

A Mini-Case Study

Keeping fees as low as possible is a huge goal for the long-term investor, but it's easier said than done. Not all fees are called fees, and they can be scattered all over the place. For our purposes, anything you have to pay for in the investment process that doesn't generate a return can be considered a fee—whether it's actually called a fee, an expense ratio, a commission, a load, a transaction charge, or anything else. It can feel a little bit like a scavenger hunt. For any one investment plan, it's up to you to find all the fees—whatever they're called, wherever they're hiding—add them all up, and then shop around to see if you can get a better deal.

In our example above, we said that an expense ratio of 0.73% can seem deceptively tiny, so we expressed it instead as a price tag of $73 per $10,000 invested. Investment pros have their own language for this—they call it 73 basis points. Mathematically, it's all the same, but somehow 73 basis points seems worthier of close inspection than a mere 0.73%. So, we'll stick with the standard investment lingo for the rest of this note.

It's common for newbie investors to get lulled to sleep by fees, because they seem so tiny. But those 73 basis points aren't just applied to the amount that you invest this year, they're applied to the entire cumulative balance in your account, *every* year. Your account balance may be small now, but remember where it's headed. Your investments are going to tap into the mathemagical power of compound interest and eventually grow to an astronomical amount! That's fantastic for you, but it's fantastic for the investment company, too, because they'll continue to draw those same 73 basis points, year after year, out of your prodigiously growing account balance.

Remember, the investment firms you do business with make money only one way: from fees. It's in their interest to keep the spotlight squarely on the wonderful investment returns you can expect and to deemphasize fees. They're required by law to disclose all fees charged. Some of them make it pretty easy, but others force you to look very deep in the fine print to find them all.

Let's look at a couple of examples, starting with the best imaginable fee setup. Vanguard is an investment firm that was founded on the idea of very low fees, and they specialize in passively managed index funds. If you opened a Roth IRA account at Vanguard, and invested in a target-date fund with the estimated retirement year of 2045, you'd pay two kinds of fees.

First, you'd pay an expense ratio on the target-date fund of 16 basis points. Second, you'll pay an annual account fee of a flat $20, but that fee is waived if you agree to electronic document delivery instead of snail mail, which of course, you'd do anyway. So that means your grand total fees are just 16 basis points. Now that's just about as good as it gets!

Now let's say you work for an employer who offers a 401(k) plan. Your employer's plan has a 2045 target-date fund, too, but it's comprised of actively managed funds, and the one available to you carries an expense ratio of 60 points. But that's not all—your employer's 401(k) administrator charges an annual administrative fee of 40 basis points on all investments. So, your 401(k) investment fees will total up to 100 basis points.

Is 100 basis points good or bad? Well, it's much higher than the Roth IRA at Vanguard. But if you want to see how your employer's 401(k) plan compares to other employers, you can use a website like BrightScope.com to compare across similar companies. Usually, the smaller your company, the higher your 401(k) fees will be. A general rule of thumb might be 140 basis points for small employers, 85 for medium-size employers, and 50 for larger employers. Either way, you're investing in a 2045 target-date fund in a tax-advantaged account—but doing so in your employer's 401(k) program will cost you an extra 84 basis points, year after year, compared with the Roth IRA. Everything else equal, your choice is clear. Everything else isn't always equal, though, especially when there's an employer match involved. That's why lots of smart investors follow the three-step strategy described earlier: capture the full match first, then fund an IRA up to the limit, then return to the 401(k). Even more on this coming up in Chapter 9.

Net Worthy Nugget #7.9

> Once you've established your tax-advantaged accounts and selected a target-date fund, you just keep on accumulating shares (always buying and holding, never selling) into those accounts. You do this on a fixed, regular timetable (like every payday), over and over, throughout the yellow phase of your financial life.

OK, let's say you work for an employer who offers a 401(k) plan, you're now sitting at your computer, and you've logged into your HR portal. You've read the first eight nuggets in this chapter, and you have a pretty good idea what you're aiming to do. Now you have the following decisions:

1. **IRA, 401(k) or both?** Remember, are you getting matched? Get as much free money as you can into your 401(k). Have you hit the contribution yet? You have up to $18,500 for the 401(k) and $5,500 for the IRA. If you can, you want to max out both amounts.

2. **Traditional or Roth?** What is your short-term situation, and what are your long-term prospects? If you need money now or expect your tax bracket to lower in the future, then stick with the traditional. If you are just starting out and believe your tax bracket will be higher in the future, take advantage of the lower tax bracket now and go with Roth.

3. **Which target date are you going to use?** Target-dates funds are generally available in 5-year increments: for example, you can pick a 2030 fund, or a 2045 fund, but not a 2033. As a very general rule, choose the 5-year increment that represents the date closest to when you'd realistically like to achieve financial independence. If you were born in 1990, and you're determined to have your bathtub filled by age 45, then choose the 2035 target-date fund. Don't spend a lot of time stressing over this, though! For one thing, it's very easy to change your mind later and move your money to a different target-date. For another, as a practical matter, the real difference in how the target-date funds allocate your money is very minor until

about 10 or 15 years before the target date. Bottom line, you have plenty of time to fine-tune this as you go; the key is simply to get started.

4. **Do you have any existing funds in either your 401(k) or IRA that are just sitting there?** Perhaps you didn't even know you were contributing. Believe it or not, this is common. Or maybe you haven't taken the time to put those funds to work yet. This is the time to set up future contributions and also consolidate existing balances into your funds.

5. **What's your contribution percentage going to be?** The single most important aspect of this whole endeavor is using money now to have exponentially more money later. That means you'll want to live a life where your contribution percentage isn't a burden on your daily activities. Find the highest contribution percentage where you still feel comfortable. And if you get an unexpected bonus or have some supplemental income, make sure to take care of your future self before treating your current self.

You've now gone through the checklist and you've made your choices. Your 401(k) contribution is deducted automatically from your paycheck and you're matched to the maximum amount by your employer. You've logged on to your IRA account and requested monthly contributions from your checking account. Now what do you do? Nothing. You're done. In fact, to do anything would distract from the main goal. By setting up these automatic inputs, you've opted to pay yourself first, or actually, pay your future self. And your future self thanks you.

We apologize for not offering a more exciting plan. We apologize that your heart won't race or your stomach won't knot when a certain stock skyrockets or plummets. Instead, the plan we've given you is as exciting—and as certain—as watching redwood trees grow. Oh, they'll grow, and in fact, they'll soar to majestic, towering heights, eventually. But that will happen whether you stare at them, fret over them, and chart their progress month by month and year by year or not. Let other people brag (or complain) about exactly how much their investment value grew (or shrank) over the past year. That's not something you have to worry about, because you've had the foresight to adopt a fantastic plan that doesn't need your constant attention. For you, every year is a good year in the market, because you have more shares of your target-date fund at the end of the year than at the beginning. Your money is hard at work around the clock, freeing you to focus on your job, your family, your friends, your life.

Net Worthy Nugget #7.10

> Automate the long-term investment process, through preauthorized payroll deductions and similar means, to the greatest extent possible.

You've got everything possible on autopilot. Your 401(k)/TSP-type plan contributions happen every payday, via a preauthorized payroll deduction. Your IRA is funded automatically with each paycheck too, not through a payroll deduction, but through an autopay rule in your checking account, arranged via your bank or credit union. You are all about "set it and forget it." You might miss that money a little bit at first, but in a relatively short time, you get used to a new normal. But automation is not only a setting on a website; it's also a framework of how to protect yourself from your own impulses and urges. Humans are inherently subject to occasional irrational impulses, and there's nothing like the swinging gains and losses in the stock market to trigger colossal spikes of irrationality. "Sure things" and "hot tips" have bankrupted men and women throughout recorded history.

By automating the process, you're taking rational steps to make sure the right things happen *before* your irrational self even has a chance to get into the act. The sure thing may be a winner this time, but it's sure to be a dud the next. None of that will matter to you, because you're on autopilot, and you don't put your future at risk by chasing after hot tips. Essentially, it's out of your hands, which are now free to give yourself a pat on the back for thinking ahead.

Net Worthy Nugget #7.11

> You are a disciplined long-term investor, and you're going to *stick with this plan no matter what*. The stock market is famously cyclical, and market ups and downs—*big ones*—are absolutely inevitable. But you don't care. You just continue to methodically sock away shares of your target-date fund, whether the market is going up, down, or sideways.

You probably looked at Nugget #7.11 and thought, "What, again? C'mon, Colby and Chris, you guys are starting to repeat yourselves." Guilty as charged. We're hitting this point very hard. But that's because *failing* to stick with the plan is such a common reason for long-term investment failure, and we don't want that to be you! You see, now that this plan, and the reasoning behind it, is fresh in your mind, there's little danger. But the problem is likely to come up years from now. Your long-term investment program will be happily and efficiently accumulating shares, because you've wisely set it all up to run automatically. But the reasons behind it won't be so fresh in your mind. And that's when you might be vulnerable to some really bad ideas.

Let's take a look at the last ten years in the market to see how those bad ideas might pop up:

Stock Market Ups and Downs
S&P 500 last twelve years (2006-2017)

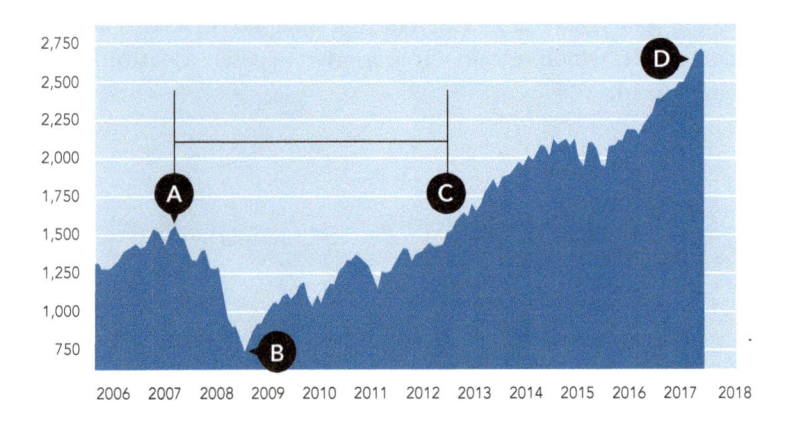

From October, 2007, (A) to March, 2009, (B), a 17-month period, the stock market lost 58% of its dollar value. That means that a dollar invested at point A was only worth 42 cents less than a year and a half later. This was an epic meltdown, and it triggered what we now refer to as The Great Recession. We've emphasized that it's wise to keep an eye on the number of shares you own, as opposed to the dollar value in your account. Those checking their investment balances (at B) saw less than half of what was there 18 months before, and the result was panic. Remember, when it comes to investing, nobody makes any money and nobody loses any money until you *sell*. Well, a lot of these investors panicked and sold. Another way to say this is, those investors *guaranteed* that they lost more than half of their investment.

But for long-term investors focused on *number of shares* instead of dollar amounts, the view was much different. These investors bought shares as they normally did, and they continued to buy shares as usual as the stock market fell 10%, 15%, 30%, and finally well over 50%. The shares they bought in October, 2007, were worth half, but they weren't looking at that. They knew that over time, the long-term trend would prevail, as it always does. By April, 2013, (C), their October, 2007, shares were back to full value. More importantly, the shares they bought in March, 2009, doubled in that same time period. By December, 2017, (D), the October, 2007, shares were up more than 70% (from A to D) and the March, 2009, shares had *more than quadrupled* (from B to D) in value. By consistently buying, you make sure that in the end, it all averages out to at least 10% before inflation, and 6% after, over the long term.

While the market was in freefall (between A and B in the chart), the financial media were *all over* the story. Their job is to maximize clicks, ratings, and circulation, and nothing does that better than a crisis. There's a fine line between covering the fall and fear-mongering. Every investor knows that the objective is to buy low and sell high; if you hold onto your shares for decades, that's exactly what you'll be able to do. But in a hypercharged panic, otherwise rational people can delude themselves into thinking, "sell now, before it goes even lower." *Don't do it!* It may take a few years, but eventually the market will get back to its previous high (C)—this is what's always happened, every time. And then the market will eventually go onto new dizzying heights (D)— that's also what's always happened, every time. Your job is to stick to the plan, regardless of the atmosphere of fear and panic—and that's it.

There's another danger that's just as common, but a little subtler. When the market is enjoying year after year of steady, robust growth (between B and D, and especially between C and D on the chart), investing success stories are common. The financial media, again eager for clicks, ratings and circulation, love to put the splashiest successes squarely in the spotlight. When that's all you see and hear, your little "10% return before inflation, 6% after" plan starts to seem like a complete snoozer. It's easy to start thinking, "everybody else is making so much more than I am, I need to catch up!" Before you know it, you're selling your little redwood grove, and buying into something much more exciting. *Don't do that either!* That "something exciting" is also inherently much riskier. It may take a while, but eventually, the next bubble will pop, and the market will go into freefall once again. This is what's always happened, every time. And if you're fully invested in something exciting when the bubble pops, look out. You'll be left longing for that safe, dependable grove of redwood trees that are undoubtedly headed for great heights—which, sadly, you sold off because you got dollar signs in your eyes. Remember, your job is to *stick to the plan*, regardless of the atmosphere of frenzied opportunity—and that's it.

The best way to avoid both scenarios? Focus on your target-date fund share count, not the dollar balance in your account. All together now: "stick to the plan!"

Net Worthy Nugget #7.12

Most people should be able to get their long-term investment program off the ground without paying for specialized professional help, but there are certain circumstances where such help is highly advised.

All of the advice we've given so far is geared toward helping you set up your long-term investment program yourself. Millions of people get started on their own every year, and as long you're armed with the kind of solid plan that we've described in this chapter, that can be a path to great success for most people. However, there are some special situations where we recommend that you seek the help of a qualified professional.

1. If you make too much to qualify for an IRA or 401(k)/TSP-type plan, you may want help. If you own more than 5% of a company or make more than $120,000 a year, you may face a lower ceiling on how much you can contribute. Speaking with an investment advisor can help you find other ways to maximize your savings long-term.

2. If you own your own company, there are ways to set up "IRA-like" or "401(k)-like" programs on your own, which can offer much higher annual investment limits than

standard accounts. There are choices to make regarding how to go about it, though, and it's best to be guided by an experienced pro.

3. If you have a high net worth or a high value investment portfolio outside of your 401(k)/TSP-type plan, again, there are some restrictions on contributing to your accounts, and thus an advisor would be best suited to give you individualized advice.

4. If your employer doesn't offer a target-date fund in your 401(k)/TSP-type plan or if the expense ratio on that fund is higher than 1% (100 basis points), you probably need to find other options to maximize your savings and investments. For that, we recommend working with a pro.

5. If you know you will stop earning an income in five years or fewer, the contribution math changes significantly, and a retirement or investment advisor is necessary to make sure you have a clear path forward.

6. If some or all of your income comes from outside the United States and is in a different currency, there are nuances that only an investment advisor will be able to help you understand.

Investment professionals can be invaluable allies in your journey to financial independence. But their expertise, and biggest contributions to your financial decision-making are much more likely to come into play once you've already made substantial progress in getting your bathtub filled. Deciding exactly when and how to begin draining from the bathtub can get complicated; relatively speaking, getting started is much simpler. Besides, as a practical matter, if you're just now beginning your long-term investment program, most investment professionals aren't necessarily seeking you out, either. We hope the program outlined in the chapter has given you the knowledge, and the confidence, to get started right away. Happy investing!

Meet Your New Favorite Investment Term: Fiduciary

A Note from Chris

If you're going to hire a financial professional, here's a word that you should become very familiar with: *fiduciary*. A financial advisor acting as a fiduciary is always legally required to act in your best interests, instead of their own. Let's say that you're trying to choose between Investment A and Investment B. You're relying on your advisor to steer you to the right choice. After all, you're the amateur, they're the pro, and professional advice is why you came to them in first place.

So far, so good. But now imagine if you learned that your advisor will get paid a hefty commission if you opt for Investment A, but no commission at all for Investment B. How does that make you feel about the advice you're getting—especially if your advisor is enthusiastically recommending Investment A? This is a classic conflict-of-interest scenario, and it illustrates precisely why it's so important to understand whether your advisor is a fiduciary or not. In this example, a fiduciary would be *bound by law* to recommend whatever fits you and your situation the best. They're required to be fully transparent about any conflicts of interest, and they generally go to great lengths to avoid such conflicts in the first place. But not all financial professionals calling themselves investment advisors are fiduciaries. Those who are not fiduciaries are held to a lower standard (called the "suitability" standard); they might recommend Investment A to you, earn a big commission, never directly tell you about that commission, and still be in full compliance with the suitability standard.

There's much more to the distinction than the simple scenario outlined here. An advisor operating under the suitability standard might be every bit as transparent and trustworthy as a fiduciary; the difference is that they're not *required by law* to be. To make it even more complicated, there is debate going on even now over exactly which types of financial advisors ought to be held to the fiduciary standard. (If you're searching the internet, make sure you're reading the most up-to-date articles—big changes could be in the works.) For all these reasons, we encourage you to do lots of research before engaging any financial professional. But still, after all the research, you'll have a decision to make, and it's fundamental that you know whether any advisor that you're considering hiring is a fiduciary or not. The best way to find out is to ask the question directly: are you a fiduciary? You'll be completely reliant on that person's professional advice, so there can't be any mystery or ambiguity about whether they're acting in your best interests or not.

About the Co-Author:

Colby Howard is currently devoted to a seed-level startup focused on bringing transparency, accountability, and the rigor of buy-side investment analysis to company management teams. His involvement in personal finance stems from his long held interest in making sure he and his friends maximize life while minimizing spending. He enjoys a good rack of barbeque ribs.

"This book reminded me of how much we underestimate taking the long-term view. Millennials have more opportunity than ever to travel, enjoy great food, and have pretty much anything on earth shipped to them in two days. The urge to spend is massive, and I hope this book helps take the focus away from the present and put it on the future."

Chapter 8

Your Financial Dashboard

by Chris Smith with Claire Boyte-White

Net Worthy Nugget #8.1

The Net Worthy Financial Dashboard is your first step to begin taking control of your financial life. This dashboard is your indispensable go-to tool throughout your red phase. It shows your current overall financial condition at a glance, points out where it needs improvement, and allows you to regularly monitor your progress.

Net Worthy Nugget #8.2

The first step in the Net Worthy Dashboard process is to complete a thorough Debt Inventory and Analysis worksheet; update it monthly as you pay down your debts.

Net Worthy Nugget #8.3

Populate your dashboard with these 7 numbers:

- Take-Home Pay [monthly average]

- Total Minimum Required Debt Payments [monthly average]

- Base Living Expenses (household spending excluding debt payments) [monthly average]

- Total Household Spending (item 2 plus item 3) [monthly average]

- Total Debt (excluding mortgage, if any), current balance

- Ideal Eventual Emergency Fund Goal (4, 6, or 9 months' expenses, depending on your risk level)

- Current Emergency Fund Balance

Net Worthy Nugget #8.4

Using the 7 numbers as inputs, you can now calculate your 3 Primary Financial Health Indicators:

1. Your Monthly Gap

2. Emergency Fund
   (months of coverage)

3. Countdown to Yellow Phase
   (months and years)

Net Worthy Nugget #8.5

The value of the dashboard can only be realized by thoroughly completing it to the best of your ability. Don't estimate, guess, or spitball—attack this task head on. If you haven't done so already, complete your first dashboard before moving on to Chapter 9. Continue doing so monthly until you're out of the red phase.

198　I Am Net Worthy

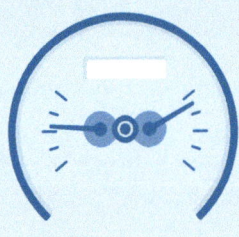

Red Phase Financial Dashboard

Monthly Averages

- **Monthly Average Take-Home Pay**
  $X.X K
- **Minimum Required Debt Payments**
  $X.X K
- **Base Living Expenses**
  $X.X K
- **Total Household Spending**
  $X.X K

Total Balances

- **Total Non-Mortgage Debt**
  + $X.X K
- **Ideal E-fund Goal (in Months)**
  X months
- **E-fund Balance (in Dollars)**
  $X.X K

Primary Financial Health Indicators

Current Monthly Gap:
+$X.X K

Current Emergency Fund (in Months):
X months

Countdown to Yellow Phase (in Months):
X months

Preface to Chapter 8

A Note from Chris

This is where the rubber meets the road! Everything in the previous chapters represents important, necessary pieces of the puzzle. But here in Chapter 8—as well as in Chapter 9 which follows—is where all these pieces come together and you begin to really pick up speed on the road to a bright financial future.

Never underestimate the power of deadlines to spur people into action. It's human nature and always has been. Without deadlines, comfort zones just remain too comfortable—procrastination, distraction, and dithering will prevail, more or less indefinitely. But when specific, unambiguous deadlines are introduced, birthday presents actually get presented, Congress actually votes, and college term papers actually get turned in. Ask any bill collector, late night bartender, or bus driver whether deadlines change people's behavior, and no doubt you'll hear some compelling stories!

Another crucial tool in motivating people is measurement. Measurement matters. Hard numbers get our attention, because they provide the simplest and clearest form of feedback, and feedback is the magic ingredient we humans need to learn, change, adapt, and improve. Whether you're trying to learn a new language, meet your daily Fitbit step-count goal, or make a serious reduction in a troublesome spending category, a well-designed measurement system keeps your eyes on the goal and enables steady progress.

Of course, the real trick with both deadlines and measurements is to choose wisely. Too many deadlines puts people into an "everything's always urgent so nothing really is" gridlock; too few just leads to last-minute flurries of desperate activity. Likewise, deciding exactly what to measure is crucial. With today's explosion in mobile computing power, almost anything can be easily measured, aggregated, and sliced a dozen different ways. What we want to do is to carefully pick the critical few things to pay attention to that make the biggest difference.

What happens when you combine the power of well-chosen deadlines with the power of critical-few measurement? A lot of horsepower under the hood, that's what! With all that roaring force at your command, you'll need an intelligently designed, but simple, Financial Dashboard to ensure your ride is smooth, steady, and under control—and that's exactly what this chapter delivers. The Dashboard directs your attention squarely onto the few most important numbers in your financial world, and you'll look at them carefully on a monthly deadline. Each time you do, you'll make decisions based on what these measurements are telling you. Then next month, you check your Dashboard again, to see whether last month's adjustments created the desired result. With a little practice, the feedback loop is complete, and voilà! You're driving in the right direction, you're picking up speed, and you have the Dashboard numbers to prove it.

The Financial Dashboard as described here is designed to be used with the Net Worthy Navigator App. The recommended sequence is to read about it here, then go to the app and build your personal Dashboard, using your own financial information. Some people might do it the other way around, and that's fine too. Either way, you'll soon reach the point where the visibility that the Financial Dashboard provides you is so indispensable that you wouldn't dream of navigating the financial highway without it. Ready? Let's get this show on the road!

Net Worthy Nugget #8.1

The Net Worthy Financial Dashboard is your first step to begin taking control of your financial life. This dashboard is your indispensable go-to tool throughout your red phase. It shows your current overall financial condition at a glance, points out where it needs improvement, and allows you to regularly monitor your progress.

By now, you've read a lot (seven whole chapters!) about what it means to be in control of your financial life and what you need to do to reach the end-goal of financial independence. Or, maybe you just skipped straight here. In either case, you're probably looking for some guidance on how to take concrete action—those first crucial steps, maybe even an outline for where you need to go from here. Knowledge is a powerful thing, but without the tools to put it to proper use, you're just a very well-informed financial dreamer.

This chapter and its successor, Chapter 9, are aimed at giving you actionable tasks that will help you make meaningful strides toward financial freedom. In Chapter 8, we'll focus on establishing and maintaining a solid, data-based foundation for all your financial decisions. You'll learn how to analyze your current financial situation and how to interpret changes in your financial data as indicators of progress or peril. Most importantly, you'll learn how to use this data to make better decisions by employing straightforward, fail-proof "if-then" rules. There's no mathematics degree required, just some initial information collection and some basic arithmetic.

If you're looking for a how-to guide for taking your very first step toward financial freedom, this chapter is it. We're not saying it will be easy, we're just saying it will be worth it.

Your Financial Dashboard

To begin taking control of your financial life, you need to get comfortable with a few key numbers. They aren't complicated, but they lay the groundwork for everything else you need to do to achieve financial freedom. You can think of these ten figures as your Financial Dashboard.

The first time you see these numbers, you may be a little shocked, even dismayed. And that's OK. If you're reading, it's likely because you know you need a little help getting your financial life on track. Like anything worth having, you'll need to put in the legwork if you're serious about attaining financial freedom.

When you first begin populating the Dashboard with the requested financial information, you may need to pull out some bank statements, credit card bills, or do some simple math to determine your average expenses. Do it. Don't just guess, but really crunch the real numbers.

When you research and input the requested financial data, approach the task ruthlessly; don't leave yourself any buffers for what you think (or hope) will be true next month or the month after. Take a serious and unflinching look at where you stand today, right this minute, and know that it can only get better from here. It may be a pain, but it is the number one most important thing you can do to get yourself heading in the right direction.

The Net Worthy Navigator App or DIY?

Most people learn faster, and start generating real improvements in their financial picture sooner, if they put the maximum time into *using* the Financial Dashboard, as opposed to *building* it piece by piece from scratch. That's one of the main reasons we built the Net Worthy Navigator App; it's specifically designed to prompt you for all the necessary inputs, do all the number crunching, and then display your Dashboard exactly as we're describing it in this chapter. If you haven't begun using the app yet, go to the I Am Net Worthy website (www.IAmNetWorthy.com/app) to get started. It's free. Versions are available for iOS, Android, and for any of the major browsers. By the way, any personal financial data you enter into the

Net Worthy Navigator app is stored on the local device *only*; never online or in the Cloud. The rest of this chapter assumes you have the app in hand and are entering your own financial information section by section as we go through it.

But notice in the paragraph above, we said *most* people, because we know that not everybody learns the same way. Some of you might prefer to take a do-it-yourself approach and build your own spreadsheet-based Financial Dashboard. If that's you, we've got you covered; head for the Guide at the end of this chapter for step-by-step instructions on Dashboard construction. You'll be able to customize, polish, groom, and decorate your Dashboard to your heart's content!

Spotlight: Reaching Financial Adulthood

Now, if you've discovered (or admitted) that you need some help getting your financial house in order, you're likely an adult already, chronologically speaking. Sure, you can drive and go to bars and vote, you pay your own rent, but reaching Financial Adulthood is a whole other ballgame.

Your Financial Life begins as soon as you are primarily responsible for all your own financial affairs, But for purposes of this discussion, think of your Financial Life, right up until this very moment, as your Financial Childhood. You may have spent this time not really thinking or worrying about saving, investing, or planning for your financial future. You might have had some generalized anxiety about what you 'should' have been doing; maybe you've even been seriously stressing about looming debts, or the persistent fear that your financial future will be a series of nasty surprises.

But no matter how you've spent your Financial Childhood, when it began, or how long it's lasted, it's over now. You're ready to move past Financial Childhood. It's time to take control of your financial future, rather than let it take control of you.

The Three-Phase Path to Financial Independence (Chapter 2) begins with the red phase, and it's a tough neighborhood—the kind of place where a kid has to grow up fast! But even though the red phase has more than its share of financial dangers, they are not insurmountable, and you can navigate your way around them. With some sustained and focused effort, you *will* successfully arrive at the yellow phase. *The entire purpose of the Financial Dashboard is to make your journey through the red phase as safe, steady, and direct as possible.*

By committing to the Dashboard process, you're starting on the path to full Financial Adulthood, with four distinct developmental stages:

- **Stage I:** You complete your Dashboard for the first time and establish a habit of checking it regularly. Until you actually add things up and take stock of where you are financially, you're driving blind. The Dashboard allows you to finally see where you are and what direction you're going. You'll begin to develop a much better understanding of how your everyday financial decisions affect your overall financial position. In short—you learn to 'drive.' This is your Financial Adolescence, and just like your actual teenage years, it might be scary at times, exciting at others, and more than a little unpredictable!

- **Stage II:** The good news is now you know where you are financially. The bad news is you're probably sitting precariously on the edge of a financial cliff and didn't know it until now! (Gee thanks, Chris and Claire.) Stage II can mean abruptly shifting from blissful ignorance (or maybe stressful ignorance) into a state of financial red alert. It's not comfortable; real change rarely is. You have to work harder than you ever have before. Through determination, sacrifice, and planning, you force yourself to spend less than you earn, creating a positive gap, which we'll discuss later. You start really getting the hang of things, but you are primarily focused on getting out of immediate danger on the financial basics.

- **Stage III:** By this time, you've become quite familiar with the Dashboard, and you know the ropes. The skills you've built have enabled you to get out of immediate danger, and you're increasingly confident that you can successfully steer clear of those hazards from now on. Now, your attention can turn to longer-term goal setting. For the first time, you're able to thoughtfully assess what kind of fundamental "current self/future self" lifestyle tradeoffs match up best to your real, deepest values and priorities. You're finally able to set specific long-term goals, firmly based on an accurate understanding of your current financial position, and you'll use the Dashboard to chart your progress.

- **Stage IV:** Your Dashboard skills are now so engrained they're second nature. Many key aspects of your financial life are now completely automated, led by your pay-yourself-first savings and investment plan. Your Dashboard provides an effective early warning system if things begin to drift off-course, allowing you to make relatively painless corrections. You're very comfortable with your long-term financial goals and direction, and the progress you're making toward reaching them gives you a strong sense of control and empowerment.

Your financial development will be lifelong, but the progression through these four initial stages is where it all begins. And right here is where it starts.

Net Worthy Nugget #8.2

The first step in the Net Worthy Dashboard process is to complete a thorough Debt Inventory and Analysis worksheet; update it monthly as you pay down your debts.

Before we dive right into the Financial Dashboard, we'll need to lay a little groundwork. One of the most important aspects of your financial life is debt. Do you have any? What kind? How much? The answers to these questions are going to shape your Dashboard and dictate a lot of your financial decisions going forward.

It's possible that you don't have any debt, and if so, great! You can probably skip along to the next nugget and we'll catch up with you there. For others, you may have debts of all kinds—student loans, credit cards, a car loan, and maybe more. In that case, this section is going to be crucial.

Nobody likes to owe money. It's unpleasant to think about, so who wants to be reminded of it on a regular basis? But consider what happens if you *don't* think about it. If your rational self doesn't get a regular, accurate reminder of the key details of your debts, your irrational self will take over. Irrational selves love extremes, so one of two things will happen: either you'll minimize the role that debts play in the financial picture and start believing an artificially rosy version of reality, or you'll magnify the role of your debts, and endlessly stress over a seemingly impossible hole to dig out of.

Neither of these is a winning strategy. Like most things, the best way to conquer debt is to face it head on—know thy enemy, and then defeat it. The Debt Inventory and Analysis worksheet (we'll just call it the DIA worksheet from now on) allows you to do just that.

Mortgages

If you're a renter or are somehow otherwise mortgage-free, you can skip this section. But if you're one of the millions of Americans paying a mortgage—or if you plan to anytime soon—read on. As we've discussed in past chapters, not all debts are created equal. A mortgage on a house that you live in is special, because it:

- Typically carries a much lower interest rate than other forms of debt

- Provides important tax advantages to the homeowner

- Increases your equity stake in an asset that typically appreciates over time

For these reasons, it may not be appropriate to apply the same zealous pay-down strategy to your mortgage that you'll be applying to your other debts. In fact, paying off your mortgage early may actually be a step in the wrong direction—the money you'd use for an early payoff is almost always better deployed in long-term investing, as outlined in Chapter 7.

So, the DIA worksheet that you're going to prepare *excludes* mortgages. Not only that, the Financial Dashboard we'll construct in Nugget #8.3 treats non-mortgage debt differently from mortgage debt, too.

Don't let this confuse you—a mortgage is a debt. But because it's a very special kind of debt, we'll deal with it elsewhere in the Net Worthy Navigator App. If you have a mortgage:

- You'll enter your current mortgage balance as a liability in the Net Worthy Calculator

- You'll include your mortgage payment (principal and interest) as well as all the other costs of being a homeowner described in Chapter 6 as part of your Base Living Expenses in the Financial Dashboard (more on this in the next nugget)

- If you haven't bought yet, but you're considering it, enter the financial characteristics of your *target* house in the "Houses" section of the app; go to Main Menu > Houses > Readiness Tests.

- *Note:* Paying your non-mortgage debts completely off is a requirement to exit the red phase; but paying off your mortgage is not (i.e. you can carry a mortgage into the yellow phase)

Revolving vs. Installment Debt

There are two primary types of debt: installment debt and revolving debt. Neither one is great, but there are important differences between these two liabilities that should inform your financial planning.

Revolving debt is most clearly illustrated by the almighty credit card. You have a set amount you can spend, called your credit limit, but you can use your card and pay off your balance as you like. So, you might spend nothing one month and make no payments. The next month you might spend $2,000 and make one large payment or several small ones over time. While you are required to pay off revolving debts, the amount of your payments will vary depending on how much you spend. There is no end-date for your credit usage—you can keep a credit card open forever—only a limit to the maximum amount you can borrow at one time.

Installment debts are more typically called loans. You borrow a set amount of money up-front and then make payments over time until you've paid back the loan, usually plus interest. There is a pre-determined pay-by date, and your monthly payments are typically identical. Mortgages, car loans, personal loans, or consolidation loans—these are all installment debt.

Having a mixture of debt types can help you build your credit score, but only if you are consistently able to make on-time payments. There can be a fine line between "carrying debt" and "crushing debt." Revolving debt typically carries a higher interest rate than installment debt, so these are the balances you want to pay off first.

Creating Your Debt Inventory and Analysis (DIA) Worksheet

Now that you know a bit more about what kinds of debt do the most damage to your monthly finances, it's time to wrangle all your bills into one place: your DIA worksheet.

Your first step should be to collect all the information you'll need to complete it. Get your credit card statements, or better yet, pull up your online accounts—all of them. Check in on that student loan that you've been blindly throwing money at each month, never really believing you'll ever pay it off. Same goes for car loans, appliance loans, loans from family and friends, everything. However you are best able to check in on the details of your various financial obligations, make it happen. Open eight browser tabs if you need to, pull things out of the recycling. Getting all your information in one place will make everything else much easier.

Once you've arranged your piles of soggy statements and/or logged in to all your various online accounts, you're ready to start. Fortunately for you, the Net Worthy Navigator App is standing ready to help you get everything organized once and for all, and keep it that way.

Once you've opened the app, navigate to the Debt Inventory & Analysis. Here you'll find a separate section for each debt—Debt 1, Debt 2, and so on. We recommend that you put your debt with the highest APR into Debt 1, the next highest into Debt 2, and on. It's not strictly necessary to do that, and it won't change how anything gets calculated—but this will determine the order in which you'll update your progress every month, so seeing the highest APR first every time will reinforce your commitment to start making dents in that one ASAP. (Note: As we discussed in Chapter 2, the other alternative is the snowball method—knock out the debt with the smallest balance first to gain some momentum, then the next smallest, and so on. If that's your approach, list the smallest balance as Debt 1.)

Once you open Debt 1, you'll be prompted for the following:

- **Debt Name:** Nothing formal, just the short and sweet nickname you'll give each debt to keep it straight from the others. Examples: Camry Loan, Capital One Card, Stafford Student Loan.

- **Debt Type (Revolving or Installment):** If installment, you'll be asked if it's a student loan, and if so, whether federal or private.

- **Lender:** Who you make your payment to
  Note: Your lender is the bank or institution that takes your payment. If you have a United Airlines Visa card issued by Chase Bank, for example, then Chase is your lender—not Visa, and definitely not United Airlines.

- **Balance:** The total amount you currently owe
  It's very important not to guess on this; pull this directly from each debt's monthly statement, where it should be plainly labeled, in dollars and cents.

- **APR:** Your annual percentage rate, which should be clearly stated on credit card statements or loan documents

- **"Interest Deferred?":** A common benefit offered to entice new credit card customers is zero interest for an introductory period of 6, 12, or even 18 months. Enter yes or no, and if yes, when the interest deferral period ends.

- **Repayment Interval:** Usually monthly; but here's where you can specify annual, semi-annual or quarterly, if necessary.

- **Minimum Payment:** The minimum amount you must make for your next payment to avoid late fees or delinquency

- **Due Date of Next Payment:** Calendar date for the next required payment

Enter all the prompted information for Debt 1, then repeat for Debt 2, Debt 3, and so on.

The Big Picture – Owning Your Debt

Once all the key information is entered, for each debt that you have, take a deep breath. It might have been a lot of effort to gather all that information up, but it will never be that time-consuming again. That's because the app will store everything you just entered, so from now on, you'll only need to update those few numbers, which will change over time—like your balances, as you consistently pay them *downward*.

The work you've just done to build your DIA worksheet is vital to your quest for financial independence. Here you've got all the key details about the money you owe, all in one place, where it's easy to get at.

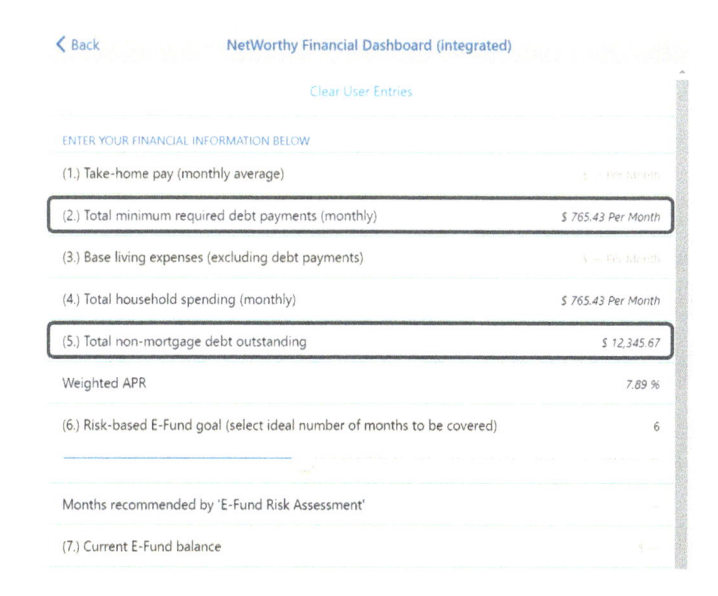

‹ Back	NetWorthy Financial Dashboard (integrated)	
	Clear User Entries	
ENTER YOUR FINANCIAL INFORMATION BELOW		
(1.) Take-home pay (monthly average)		$ — Per Month
(2.) Total minimum required debt payments (monthly)		$ 765.43 Per Month
(3.) Base living expenses (excluding debt payments)		$ — Per Month
(4.) Total household spending (monthly)		$ 765.43 Per Month
(5.) Total non-mortgage debt outstanding		$ 12,345.67
Weighted APR		7.89 %
(6.) Risk-based E-Fund goal (select ideal number of months to be covered)		6
Months recommended by 'E-Fund Risk Assessment'		
(7.) Current E-Fund balance		

And now that the details are all safely stored away, it's time to zoom out and look at the big picture. How does your debt—all of it, *in total*—affect your overall financial position and direction?

For that, we'll go to a different part of the app: Your Net Worthy Financial Dashboard. We'll cover the Dashboard from A to Z in the next nugget, but for now, let's just look at the bottom line when it comes to your debt. Actually, there's not just one debt-related bottom line, but two key, summarized numbers that are calculated from the inputs you made to the DIA worksheet and then carried directly forward into your Financial Dashboard:

Let's start with the lower red circle, labeled as (5.) in the image above: Total Non-Mortgage Debt Outstanding. There it is, in black and white, the actual current amount that you owe all creditors. You can't chart a course until you know where you are. Total Non-Mortgage Debt has to be zero before you can leave the red phase; now you know, exactly, how far you have to go.

The upper red circle, labeled (2.) Total Minimum Required Monthly Non-Mortgage Debt Payments is equally illuminating. It's a mouthful, though—some people just call it "debt service." *This is what your debt is costing you each month.* Usually, when money leaves your financial bathtub, you get something in return for it, that you've just purchased—a month's rent, a new pair of shoes, a concert ticket. But when this amount leaves your bathtub, you get *nothing* in return; this is repayment for money you borrowed in the near or distant past, for purchases you've already made, enjoyed, and possibly already forgotten. But you'll keep on paying anyway, month after month, until you drive your total debt to zero.

Studying these two numbers, and truly owning what they're telling you, is what being financially responsible is all about. Your irrational self can neither minimize nor magnify the role of debt in your financial picture, because you're looking squarely at the truth. No matter how you feel about the numbers you're looking at—good, bad, or ugly—you can realistically resolve from this point forward, your debt picture is going to get nothing but better, month by month. Because now you're in a position, *at last*, to really do something about it.

Now that you've gotten a sneak peek at how immensely valuable these two parts of the Financial Dashboard are, keep reading to dive right in to the whole thing.

Spotlight: Reflecting on Your Debt Inventory

We know that having all your debts staring you in face may be a little overwhelming, but this is also a huge opportunity. Now that you can see exactly how much debt you're in, you're both able and motivated to take a hard look at which debts were necessary and which weren't.

Cars

If you have a car, you might have a car loan you have to pay each month, and you definitely pay for car insurance. Those two things can add up quickly, so maybe now's a good time to consider whether you actually need a car.

Many people—millennials especially—are deciding they can easily do without these expenses. The rise of the sharing economy, including services like Uber and Lyft, means getting around is more than possible without your own vehicle. If you live in a big city, you might even have access to a metro or reliable bus system. Have a good long think about whether you need a car in your life, or whether it's "just one of those things you buy." If you can get to the point of thinking of your car as more of a want than an actual, critically important need, consider it an opportunity to whittle down your total debt and monthly household expenses, all in one fell swoop. And if you don't own one yet, go through the same "want vs. must" thinking—if you can avoid or delay that expense, your financial bathtub will undoubtedly thank you.

Student Loans

There are several options for reducing your monthly student loan payments, and you may hear politicians and others touting monthly payment reduction options as the cure-all for your student loan woes. In reality, those are short-term salves that will probably end up costing you more over time. Like all loans (except mortgages!), your best option is to pay off student debt as soon as possible. Of course, there are times when a deferral or forbearance is going to be your best option, albeit temporarily, and it's OK to use these options when it's really necessary. Even so, you should still be looking for long-term solutions to eliminate your balances as soon as possible.

Depending on what type of loan you have—private or federal, or a combination of the two—there may still be options for reducing your interest rate or even having part of your loan forgiven. If you have private loans, it might be in your best interest (pun intended) to refinance by rolling all your loans into a single package with a lower rate. When it comes to federal loans, get ready to do some research, because there are many repayment programs and options to consider, and these can change frequently. The best place to begin your search is the US Department of Education's Federal Student Aid website (at StudentLoans.gov). The information there is complete and up-to-date but not necessarily the easiest to understand. A great resource for helping you understand these programs better and navigating your choices is the Student Loan section of the NerdWallet site.

Any internet search you do on student loans is likely to bring up ads—or ads disguised as articles—for companies promising to help you sort out your student loan problems. Some are real, but many are the worst kinds of scams. NerdWallet comes to the rescue once again; search for their Student Loan Watchlist for an up-to-date listing of who to avoid.

Credit Cards

Credit card debt is another huge opportunity to completely revamp your thinking. Yes, sometimes expensive emergencies come up unexpectedly. And yes, you may have spent more than you should here and there just because you could. However, credit card balances don't need to be costing you.

If you're in credit card debt, your two new favorite words might well turn out to be "interest deferred." To attract new customers, some credit cards offer an introductory interest deferred period that might run for 6, 12 or even 18 months. During that period, interest is—believe it or not—literally zero. To sweeten it further, minimum payments during that period are often as low as 1% of the balance.

And 0% interest periods aren't always limited to new cards or introductory rates. Many cards offer similar options for balance transfers, which is the term for paying off one credit card with another. If you have access to a 0% balance transfer option, consider rolling your interest-bearing credit card balances over onto a card that offers an interest-free period, especially if that period is 12 months or more. You'll still need to pay off your balance, but you'll have a bit more time before you start paying more than you have to, and you'll have at least one less bill to pay.

Of course, this option isn't free—you will likely pay a balance transfer fee. But, fees can be as low as 1% of the transfer amount, which is a lot cheaper than what you'd pay in interest over the next year.

Above all, you need to be careful and read all the fine print when it comes to taking advantage of these interest free periods. Once the period is over, it's over—and interest is often applied retroactively to the date new purchases were made. Bottom line, the strategy can work great if you succeed in paying off your balance during the interest-free period. But if you lose focus and have a sizeable balance remaining when the music stops, you could be in a worse position than where you started.

A Globetrotting Freelancer . . . Whose Travel is Funded by Savvy Credit Card Hacks? It's True!

Meet Co-Author Claire

You'll already have noticed that each chapter in this book is authored by both Chris and someone else—all of us chiming in like the many voices of some spooky personal finance oracle. This chapter is co-authored by me, Claire (Hi!), and that little section on balance transfers you just read is something I think is pretty important. In fact, given my renegade, freelancing hobo lifestyle, it's been darn near crucial. If you live a non-traditional lifestyle, like me, have seasonal income, or just have (or expect to have) some unavoidable debt that's draining you dry in interest, this little ditty is for you:

A Lesson in Thinking Outside the Checkbook

I write for a living, and I love it—partially because I get to choose my projects and learn about things that interest me, but also because pants are optional. The downside is that my income ebbs and flows quite a bit depending on how many projects I'm working on. I could jam-pack my schedule and maximize my earnings, but I like being semi-retired at 32, so I don't.

Because I travel year-round, however, I regularly incur large up-front expenses followed by periods of blissful bill-less-ness. In particular, my housing costs are often paid in huge multi-month allotments—six month's rent at the lakefront Guatemalan villa, two months Airbnb in Prague, another four in Edinburgh. Awesome as my chosen lifestyle is, I don't always have $6K on hand to pay advance rent, and charging that amount to a regular credit card would be a huge mistake. Enter balance transfers, stage left.

I first discovered this amazing card feature during my inaugural trip to Lake Atitlan, Guatemala. One week in, I found myself needing lodging with actual walls after I discovered that I love the jungle climate but not the night-time wildlife. Walls come at a price, which, frankly, I was willing to pay, just not in cash.

I already had the Barclay Arrival Plus World Mastercard in my wallet, and I remembered that they'd been sending me lots of emails about balance transfers lately. I had never considered this feature before because I don't typically carry large balances on my credit cards. Upon looking into it further, however, I realized that Barclay actually allows you to transfer cash to your bank account, not just to another credit card company. Mind. Blown.

In exchange for a 1-3% transfer fee, I could transfer as much cash as I wanted, up to my credit limit, directly to my checking account and pay 0% interest for 12-18 months. This allowed me to pay for six months of rent in an amazing flat on the lake, and then pay it off over the next six months; essentially I was just paying rent to my credit card company, no strings attached.

Claire Boyte-White: Credit Card Industry Shill

OK, so I'm a big credit card geek and a huge points-and-miles schemer. The upside is I mostly travel for free. The other upside is, knowing what I know now, I have great card recommendations for you. It's all upside!

Best for Transfers

The Barclay Arrival Plus has an annual fee, and I opened it for reasons other than its balance transfer feature. But, if it sounds like a balance transfer card is something your wallet needs, there are a few great fee-free options.

In particular, the Chase Slate card has no annual fee and allows free balance transfers for the first 60 days. That means that if you roll a balance from another card onto the Slate within the first two months after you open it, you get 15 months of 0% interest with no transfer fee. The $150 fee I paid on the Barclay transfer was worth it at the time, but now I know that, with a little planning, I could have avoided paying anything at all. If I had it to do again, I would have opened the Slate right before leaving for Central America.

Best for New Purchases

If you don't yet have a big credit card balance but are anticipating a big up-front expense in the near future, you can get a whopping 21 months of interest-free wiggle room by using the Citi Simplicity card. While the Slate does allow for 15 months interest-free on new purchases, in addition to balance transfers, the Citi card tacks on another six months with no transfer fee and no annual fee.

If you haven't made the purchase yet, go for the Citi card. If you already have a balance, however, stick to Slate since the Simplicity carries a 5% fee for balance transfers.

Not all cards allow cash transfers to your bank account, so if that's going to be a linchpin in your plan, you may want to stick to the Barclay.

Best for You

A balance transfer shouldn't be your go-to when you need cash—and I'm definitely not advocating that you put off paying your debts—but it can be an amazing tool if you just need a bit more time to pay something off. You'll need to weigh your options, but know that you

> *do* have them—you're not stuck paying hundreds of dollars in interest because of past decisions or unavoidable expenses.
>
> It's important to add that any balance transfer strategy shouldn't be pursued tentatively or half-heartedly. Carefully think through what you want to accomplish during the interest-free period, make sure you've got a realistic plan, then make it a top priority to follow through. Opening new credit cards, especially more than one, can reduce your credit score. If a balance transfer can help you punch your way out of the red phase, though, a small and temporary credit score reduction is well worth it. Resolve to get it right the first time, and never look back.
>
> Now, back to the show!

Net Worthy Nugget #8.3

Populate your dashboard with these 7 numbers:

⌂ Take-Home Pay [monthly average]
⊖ Total Minimum Required Debt Payments [monthly average]
⌂ Base Living Expenses (household spending excluding debt payments) [monthly average]
⌂ Total Household Spending (item 2 plus item 3) [monthly average]
△ Total Debt (excluding mortgage, if any), current balance
✳ Ideal Eventual Emergency Fund Goal (4, 6, or 9 months' expenses, depending on your risk level)
⊕ Current Emergency Fund Balance

Now that you've gotten your head around your debt situation, we can really start to build something useful. The information you've gathered to create your debt spreadsheet is going to help flesh out your Dashboard, but there are still some crucial figures we haven't discussed yet, so let's get started.

Using Your Financial Dashboard

‹ Back	NetWorthy Financial Dashboard (integrated)
	Clear User Entries
ENTER YOUR FINANCIAL INFORMATION BELOW	
(1.) Take-home pay (monthly average)	
(2.) Total minimum required debt payments (monthly)	$ 0.00 Per Month
(3.) Base living expenses (excluding debt payments)	
(4.) Total household spending (monthly)	$ 0.00 Per Month
(5.) Total non-mortgage debt outstanding	$ 0.00
Weighted APR	
(6.) Risk-based E-Fund goal (select ideal number of months to be covered)	6
Months recommended by 'E-Fund Risk Assessment'	
(7.) Current E-Fund balance	

As you can see, this part of your Financial Dashboard consists of seven important figures, which, together, help determine the values of the three super-crucial Financial Indicators coming up later. We'll cover why these three metrics are so vital in a moment, but first let's fill in the first seven figures and see where we stand.

Note: There are two different Net Worthy Financial Dashboards available to you in the Net Worthy Navigator Financial App: the manual version and the integrated version. Here's the difference:

- *The Manual Version of the Financial Dashboard is for a quick and easy approximation.* It's probably what you'll start out with, just to get a rough idea of where you stand and how the Dashboard works. The Manual Version is 100% stand-alone; all the required inputs are entered directly, not pulled in from earlier inputs that you might have made in any other part of the app. To find the Manual Version, go to the Main Menu, then look in "Standalone Tools & Calculators."

- *The Integrated Version of the Financial Dashboard, which is the one we'll refer to throughout this chapter, is for when you're ready to regularly use the Net Worthy Navigator App to guide your financial life month after month.* To use this version of the Dashboard, you must first complete the Debt and Inventory Analysis. Once you've completed those inputs, they'll remain there for the Integrated Dashboard to access every time you use it—all you have to do is update the balances as you pay them down. To get to both the Debt Inventory and Analysis, as well as the Integrated Version of the Financial Dashboard, go to the Main Menu, then look in "Integrated Tools & Calculators."

Monthly Take-Home Pay

The most basic case is simple to describe: you've got a single full-time job in which your employer pays you monthly and deducts tax withholding, Social Security, and perhaps a few other items from your gross pay. What's left after those deductions, usually called "Net Pay" on a pay stub, is your monthly take-home pay—and that's what you enter into the Net Worthy Navigator App.

Your situation might really be this simple, but probably not. Any number of factors might come into play in your income picture that will complicate the question of what to enter here. The overriding rule is to enter your very best estimate of the true, sustainable, disposable (after tax and any other withholding) income, from all sources, that will flow into your household every month.

Here are some examples of typical "complications," and how to handle them. It's far from a complete list, but this should be enough to give you the general idea:

- You want this to reflect a level of tax deductions that will roughly equal next year's tax bill(s). If your current withholding level has resulted in big tax bills, adjust your monthly take-home pay downward appropriately; if you've been getting big refunds, adjust it upward. (If you need to make this kind of adjustment, it might be time to adjust your employer's withholding via a W-4 form, instead of just adjusting it in your Dashboard.)

- If you earn any kind of supplemental income (part-time job, freelance work, passive income stream of any kind, renting out your car, home or other assets, or any other side hustles) include your best estimate of a typical month's worth. But pay special attention to whether estimated tax is being withheld from each source of income. If it is, make sure it's the right amount, then include the net (after withholding) amount in your monthly take-home pay. If it isn't, you'll want to *withhold the appropriate amount yourself*, in a separate "hands-off" savings account, so you won't be caught short at tax time next year. Whether you do the withholding yourself, or the payer does, the average *net* amount that you take home every month is what gets added in here.

- If your employer deducts health insurance premiums directly from your paychecks, that's fine—leave that amount out of your take-home pay, and also leave it out of your base living expenses. But if they don't, and you pay your health insurance premiums directly, then *include* that amount in your base living expenses.

- If your income varies a lot month-to-month, track your income for a few months and then take the average. In the case of commissioned salespeople, we'd encourage you to lean to the conservative side here. For example, if last month included an extraordinarily big commission, the type that's unlikely to be repeated often, it's safer to exclude some or all of that from your calculation of the average. You want this figure to reflect the amount you can reliably depend on.

- If your income is very seasonal, the best strategy is to literally adjust your Dashboard up and down during the year to track your income level. This is far from elegant, but since your monthly bills are very unlikely to track your income swings, it's important to have an accurate picture of the high and low points of your annual financial cycle.

- Include investment income, after withholding, if you take cash distributions. Note that we are not encouraging you to take any cash distributions as part of your investment strategy at this point in the red phase—that comes later! But, if you already have investments that pay interest or dividends, then that income is included here.

Total Minimum Required Non-Mortgage Debt Payments

This includes the minimum payments due on your *non-mortgage* debts each month, which was also calculated for your Debt Spreadsheet. If you don't have a mortgage, then you don't need to worry about this distinction. If you *do*, then don't worry, your mortgage payments will be accounted for elsewhere.

Basically, the twin goals of the red phase are to establish a sufficient E-Fund and pay off all your non-mortgage debts. Eventually, your Total Non-Mortgage Debt and Total Minimum Debt Payment figures will both be $0 (huzzah!) but you'll probably still be paying your mortgage if you have one, which is perfectly fine.

Note: If you're using the Integrated Financial Dashboard, you won't need to enter anything here—the proper amount will be automatically pulled forward from your Debt Inventory and Analysis, which you've already completed. But if you're just doing a quick and easy estimate using the Manual Financial Dashboard, this is where you enter your estimate of the sum of your minimum required monthly debt payments.

Base Living Expenses

This reflects how much it would cost you to live your normal life if you had no debt. Look at everything you spend in a month, aside from debt payments, and add it up. The big categories are housing (monthly rent payment, or PITI if you own), transportation-related (except car loan payments), utilities, insurance, all taxes except income taxes, phone/cable/internet, food, entertainment, donations and charitable contributions, "fun money"—basically everything except debt payments.

If you've got every intention of reducing your base living expenses, that's wonderful, and we're in full support of your goal! But don't enter your intended base living expenses here, enter your *actual average* for the past few months.

Total Household Spending

This isn't something you input—the app calculates it for you by adding up Minimum Required Debt Payments and Base Living Expenses.

Even so, it might be wise to calculate this number in two ways the first time you complete your Dashboard. First, add up *everything* you spend in a month—bills, rent or mortgage, daily lattes, monthly Netflix and Spotify charges, whatever—leave nothing out. Second, try simply adding the numbers you got for Nos. 2 and 3, above. You should get the same number both times. If you don't, it's a clear sign you missed something.

Once you've ensured that your methodology is solid, you can let the app calculate this for you for future Dashboard reviews: No. 2 + No. 3 = No. 4!

Total Non-Mortgage Debt

This includes your current balance on all non-mortgage debts, like student loans, credit cards, car loans, and personal loans. As we discussed before, mortgages are a different type of debt and aren't included here.

Note: If you're using the Integrated Financial Dashboard, you won't need to enter anything here—the proper amount will be automatically pulled forward from your Debt Inventory and Analysis, which you've already completed. But if you're just doing a quick and easy estimate using the Manual Financial Dashboard, this is where you enter a quick estimate of the sum of all your current debt balances.

Risk-Based E-Fund Goal (in Months)

Your ideal E-Fund goal is measured in months' worth of average household spending. As we discussed in Chapter 2, the easiest way to approach this is to just assign yourself one of three risk levels—9 months for high risk, 6 months for average, and 4 months for low.

For example, if you have no kids (and aren't planning to anytime soon), earn a good salary in a growing market, have a "layoff proof" union job, have multiple income streams, and have a spouse who is also a good earner in an unrelated field, then you could likely get by with only four months of expenses saved.

If you have kids, work in an unstable or shrinking field, are the sole breadwinner, have health issues or other additional expenses, and don't have any outside income, then you should shoot for nine full months to ensure you have enough cash on hand to weather any storm.

If you haven't done so already, you can easily size up your own risk exposure level and convert this into a personalized E-Fund size recommendation, by using the E-Fund Risk Assessment Questionnaire in the Net Worthy Navigator App. Once you've decided, use the pulldown menu in the app to enter your goal. As the months go by, you might be tempted to lower your goal as a shortcut to exit the red phase. Our advice? Only change the goal if there's been an actual, sustainable change to your underlying risk profile.

Current Emergency Fund Balance

This is how much you currently have saved up as a safety net if things go wrong. At the minimum, you should have enough to cover one month of your Total Household Spending. Eventually, you will have much more.

Note that your E-Fund should not be kept under your mattress. At the very least, this money should be kept in a savings account, separate from your everyday checking and savings. Leaving it in checking is an invitation to spend it, but you also don't want it to be so hard to access that you can't use it when you need to.

Gambling with your E-Fund is never a good idea. However, you may be able to earn a little more interest on your E-Fund than simple savings account rates, without risking your capital, through a CD, or even a series of CDs (known as a CD ladder). Research your options, but remember to keep fees and risk to the absolute minimum.

Let's Take a Breather . . .
OK, the tedious part of completing your first Dashboard is done. Whether you're using the quick and easy Manual Financial Dashboard, or the more elaborately connected Integrated Financial Dashboard, the inputs are now all in! So feel free to take a little break, get a drink, and clear your head—because the next step is the payoff for all the hard work you've just put in.

What's the payoff? Three critically important financial indicators that will tell you, probably for the very first time, exactly where you stand in your financial journey out of the red phase and toward financial independence.

Net Worthy Nugget #8.4

Using the 7 numbers as inputs, you can now calculate your 3 Primary Financial Health Indicators:

(1) Your Monthly Gap
(2) Emergency Fund (months of coverage)
(3) Countdown to Yellow Phase (months/years)

If you're quantitative geeks like us, then these inputs and calculations probably have you all jazzed up to see what's next. If you're like almost everyone else on the planet, however, you're likely covered in a cold sweat, losing hair by the handful, frantically wondering why all this math is happening to you. Worry not! These last three figures are powerful indicators, guiding you directly toward financial independence.

Your Primary Financial Health Indicators
There are 3 Financial Health Indicators that you'll see highlighted on your Financial Dashboard; they're in the RESULTS panel, circled with the solid red outline. These are the most important figures on the entire Dashboard and the ones you should keep top of mind day-to-day. Think of these 3 as your Speedometer, your Fuel Gauge, and your GPS.

‹ Back	NetWorthy Financial Dashboard (integrated)	
	Clear User Entries	
ENTER YOUR FINANCIAL INFORMATION BELOW		
(1.) Take-home pay (monthly average)		$ 0.00 Per Month
(2.) Total minimum required debt payments (monthly)		$ 0.00 Per Month
(3.) Base living expenses (excluding debt payments)		$ -- Per Month
(4.) Total household spending (monthly)		$ 0.00 Per Month
(5.) Total non-mortgage debt outstanding		$ 0.00
Weighted APR		-- %
(6.) Risk-based E-Fund goal (select ideal number of months to be covered)		6
Months recommended by 'E-Fund Risk Assessment'		--
(7.) Current E-Fund balance		$ --
RESULTS		
(A.) Monthly Gap (income - expenses)		$ 0.00
(B.) Number of months covered by current emergency fund value		Months
(C.) Countdown to yellow phase (months)		Months
(C.) Countdown to yellow phase (years)		Years
Networthy Nugget #2.4		
Your goal is to get out of the red phase and into the yellow phase as soon as you can. To accomplish that: permanently eliminate all your (non-mortgage) debt and build up an adequate emergency fund.		
Ideal Emergency Fund Goal		$ 0.00
Amount short of E-fund goal		$ 0.00
Amount remaining until yellow phase is reached		

Your Monthly Gap

Your gap is the difference between money in and money out; it could also be considered your monthly net cash flow, and it's calculated by subtracting (4.) Total Household Spending from (1.) Take-Home Pay, which the app does for you.

At first, it is very likely that your gap will be negative—meaning you're spending more than you're bringing in. While this is not abnormal in the beginning, fixing this is undoubtedly your very first order of business. When your gap is negative, your car may be on the financial highway—but it's moving in reverse! You're getting *further away* from your goals, and you're in a hazardous situation. If your Gap is negative, there's no point in even looking at the rest of the Dashboard—turn that gap from negative to positive ASAP!

What if you do only enough to get your Monthly Gap to zero? You may not be traveling in reverse anymore, but you're stalled. You're watching other cars speeding along toward financial independence, but you're sitting on the shoulder of the financial highway getting nowhere fast. You might notice that there are lots of other cars parked on the shoulder along with you. Vendors of all kinds are walking throughout this roadside parking lot, offering their products as they weave through the maze, because it's well known that these idled drivers are big spenders.

A common term for this getting-nowhere-fast financial condition is "living paycheck-to-paycheck." Millions of people find themselves trapped in this status primarily because they employ a "spend first, save later" mentality. Here are some common symptoms of this mindset:

- When you get paid, do you immediately spend anything you don't need for bills?

- Do you *gasp* sometimes spend money you don't have via credit cards you can't *definitely* pay off within one month?

- Does each month pass by with your checking account hovering near zero, furthering your belief that you "just don't make enough" to save?

Under this mindset, you'll never have anything to devote to paying down your debts, let alone bulking up your savings. To move toward financial independence, you need to shift your mentality to "save first, spend when you need to." When you get your paycheck, your focus needs to be on paying down your debt and building your E-Fund. We'll get into the nitty gritty of how you should prioritize these goals in Chapter 9. For now, however, this mental switch-up has to be your primary objective.

A negative gap is traveling in reverse, a zero gap is getting nowhere, and neither of these is for you. Job One is to get that Monthly Gap positive! Now that you see your gap in black and white, you know exactly how far away you are from positive territory. To get back into the flow of traffic headed toward financial independence, you'll need to either reduce your spending, increase your take-home pay, or a combination of both. And whichever you do, go all in on the pay-yourself-first approach.

> ## Your Monthy Gap:
>
> *The Take-Away*
>
> Your Monthly Gap (A) is your **Speedometer**—it's the very first thing you look at on your Dashboard. If you're traveling in reverse (negative gap) or stuck on the roadside (zero, or near-zero gap), the rest of the indicators on your Dashboard are probably not faring much better, and you need to reduce your base living expenses, increase your take-home pay, or both. The bigger your positive gap, the faster you're heading for financial independence.

It is important to check in on your Monthly Gap any time your income or spending changes for the long-term.

Number of Months Covered by Current Emergency Fund Balance

By now we've drilled into you that the two goals of the red phase are to pay off your non-mortgage debt and to establish a sufficient E-Fund. While that first task has a pretty clear-cut goal (i.e. get your debt down to $0), the second one takes a bit more consideration.

The *wrong* question to ask is: Do I have an E-Fund? That way of approaching it is far too vague, and it's too easy to answer "yes," when all you have is a few hundred dollars squirreled away. Even worse is when people answer "yes" when all they have is a credit card with some breathing space between their current balance and the credit limit. (Raise your right hand and repeat: a credit card is not an E-Fund!)

The *right* questions to ask are: Have I carefully considered how big my E-Fund needs to be, and do I have that amount saved up yet? The Dashboard makes these questions extremely clear. You already answered the first question in Dashboard item (6.), E-Fund risk exposure level (9 months = high, 6 = average, 4 = low). One reason we use months, instead of dollars, is to make your current E-Fund level easy to compare to the goal that you've already established. So now you make the comparison, and it's black and white: If your goal is 6 months, and you've saved 1.2 months—your answer has to be "no." Even if you've saved 5.8 months, it's still no. Ah, but 6.0 months? Now you're talking!

Another reason to use months instead of dollars is that it's self-correcting as your spending level changes. If you're starting a family, you'll probably discover that 6 months of household spending means a very different amount than it used to before your bundles of joy began arriving. But it works the other way, too. As you pay down your debts, your minimum required monthly debt payments go steadily downward too, and this reduces the required size of your E-Fund. It makes sense—any given financial crisis isn't quite as pressing once you're no longer in debt.

E-Fund Months:

The Take-Away

Your Current E-Fund in Months (B) is your **Fuel Gauge**. If it's consistently hovering near zero, you won't be able to deal with any financial detours—like unexpected expenses, medical emergencies, or job loss.

Compare this indicator to (6.) E-Fund Risk Exposure Level to see how full your tank is. As you fill the tank, your financial peace of mind goes up right along with it.

Countdown to Yellow Phase

We've said it before, back in Chapter 2: the red phase is a grind, but the yellow phase is a glide. Especially if you've got a long way to go, the grind can seem endless, and it's human nature to search for the light at the end of the tunnel. So, we know there's likely going to be one question you ask yourself over and over as you progress: "HOW MUCH LONGER?" The Countdown to Yellow Phase indicator is here to answer that question.

The calculation takes into account both of the red phase objectives—completely paying off all of your non-mortgage debts and completely filling up your E-Fund. It also takes into account the effect of interest rates, which work against you on your debts, and for you (at least a little bit) in your E-Fund.

You already know intuitively that the higher your debts (and the higher the interest they carry), and the further you have to go to fill your E-Fund (and the lower the interest you earn on it), the longer you'll stay in the red phase. But now you've got a tool to summarize all those unconnected, intuitive pieces into a single, specific time frame.

Countdown to Yellow Phase:

The Take-Away

The Countdown to Yellow Phase in Months (C) on your dashboard is the **Time to Destination** reading on your **GPS**. This indicator tells you that if you continue paying off debt and building up your E-Fund at your current rate, how long it will be until you reach the yellow phase.

If your Dashboard is telling you that you're going to stay in the red phase longer than you want to, you're going to have to increase your speed. By now you fully understand: that means increasing the size of your monthly Gap, either by spending less, earning more, or some combination of the two.

An Alternate View

At the bottom of the Dashboard on the app, you'll notice 3 additional lines, right below the 3 Primary Financial Health Indicators, circles in a dotted red outline. Always eager to be helpful, your Net Worthy Navigator App is offering up a different way for you to view and interpret a few key aspects of your financial picture.

Earlier, we explained that the reasons for using months instead of dollars were to facilitate comparisons and to self-correct as conditions change. But even so, we know that not everybody thinks that way. When talking about money, you might think that converting everything to months is too abstract—you might be one of those who prefer to see financial information in dollars and cents. That's what these two extra lines are all about.

- **Ideal E-Fund Goal:** In item (6.), you've already entered your risk-based E-Fund goal in terms of months of coverage; this line simple converts your ideal goal from months to dollars, as of today.

- **Amount short of E-Fund goal:** This is the number of dollars you still have to save (or earn in interest) to meet the E-Fund goal appropriate to your risk level, as of today.

- **Amount remaining until yellow phase is reached:** This is the number of dollars you still have to save to meet your E-Fund goal, plus the number of dollars needed to pay off all non-mortgage debt, as of today. (It's calculated as the E-Fund subtotal directly above, plus (5.) Total Non-Mortgage Debt outstanding.)

The "as of today" part of the definitions above is important; these goals are something of a moving target, because of interest. You'll earn a little (probably, very little) interest on the balance in your E-Fund—moving the goal closer. But you'll be charged interest on your outstanding non-mortgage debts, moving the goal further away. Depending on the mix of debt and E-Fund you have to go, and all the various interest rates within those, your goal could be moving in either direction. That's why "as of next month," is a little more complicated of a calculation than "as of today" minus your Monthly Gap.

Spotlight: Financial Dashboard Mini Case Study

So far, all the screenshots we've shown have been empty, unpopulated Dashboards. Let's run through an example so that you can get a feeling for what a filled-out Dashboard would look like, and how helpful that view is. Jen is a fictional reader in her mid-20s, with no financial dependents, and who makes about $40,000 per year working as a dental assistant—which breaks down to $2,250 per month take-home pay. Her only debt is a car loan; the outstanding balance is $15,000, it carries a 6% APR, and her monthly payment is $290. She's done a nice job trimming down her monthly base living expenses, which now average $1,310 per month.

Jen's job keeps her busy, so she hasn't had much time to try to develop any forms of supplemental income. On the other hand, dental assistants are in high demand in Jen's city, so she feels very confident that if her current employer retired or moved, she wouldn't be out of work very long. Taking that into consideration, she's selected a mid-range coverage level of 6 months for her E-Fund. So far, though, she's only put $700 in it.

What does Jen's Dashboard look like? Since she only has one debt, we can use the quick and easy Manual Financial Dashboard in the Net Worthy Navigator App: (See image opposite).

For practice, read down the input panel, from 1 through 7, and make sure you understand where all of those inputs come from. Re-read Nugget #8.3 if you need to reinforce your understanding of any of these important inputs.

Now—let's take a look at Jen's 3 Primary Financial Health Indicators:

1. The first thing to quickly notice about Jen's **Monthly Gap**—it's positive! It didn't start out that way; she's had to carefully examine her spending patterns and make some hard decisions about wants vs. needs. The Dashboard gave her motivation,

< Back NetWorthy Financial Dashboard (manual)	
RESET PANEL	
Clear User Entries	
ENTER YOUR FINANCIAL INFORMATION BELOW	
(1.) Take-home pay (monthly average)	$ 2,250.00 Per Month
(2.) Total minimum required debt payments (monthly)	$ 290.00 Per Month
(3.) Base living expenses (excluding debt payments)	$ 1,310.00 Per Month
(4.) Total household spending (monthly)	$ 1,600.00 Per Month
(5.) Total non-mortgage debt outstanding	$ 15,000.00
Weighted average APR across all non-mortgage debts (best guess)	6 %
(6.) Risk-based e-fund goal (select ideal number of months to be covered)	6 Months
(7.) Current emergency fund balance	$ 700.00
RESULTS	
(A.) Monthly Gap (income - expenses)	$ 650.00
(B.) Number of months covered by current emergency fund value	0.44 Months
(C.) Countdown to yellow phase (months)	38.62 Months
(C.) Countdown to yellow phase (years)	3.22 Years

Networthy Nugget #2.4

Your goal is to get out of the red phase and into the yellow phase as soon as you can. To accomplish that: permanently eliminate all your (non-mortgage) debt and build up an adequate emergency fund.

Ideal Emergency Fund Goal	$ 9,600.00
Amount short of E-fund goal	$ 8,900.00
Amount remaining until yellow phase is reached	$ 25,101.49

because every time she reduced her monthly base living expenses, she immediately saw her Monthly Gap increase. Now, it's at a very healthy $650 per month. She's cruisin'!

2. What about Jen's **E-Fund months**? Uh oh . . . the news isn't so good. The bare minimum level is 1.0 month's expenses, and Jen's only at 0.4 months. That's a problem! Of course, she's miles away from her eventual goal of 6 months, but she can worry about that later. At the moment, top priority is getting her E-Fund "fuel gauge" up to at least the 1.0 month minimum threshold.

3. Jen's made some lifestyle sacrifices to trim her monthly spending. Naturally, she wants to know how long she has to wait for this sacrifice to pay off in the form of yellow-phase status. The answer is right there in the **Countdown to Yellow Phase** of 3.2 years. Jen might feel a little disappointed that it's going to take more than 3 years to get there, but relatively speaking, she's doing great! Millions of people are still in the red phase in their 50s and 60s—some never get to the yellow phase at all. But Jen will! Think of it this way: Long before her 30th birthday, Jen will be 100% debt free, have a fully stocked E-fund, and be completely poised and ready to let the tailwinds of compound interest blow her toward financial independence via her long-term investment program. *Go, Jen!*

There's one more thing we can learn from Jen's situation. The Dashboard allows her to do some very easy *what-if* projections. You might even guess what she's thinking: What if I sold my car?

Anybody who's read Chapter 5 has this question: *You didn't buy that car brand new did you, Jen?* Well, sadly, she did, and so that car is now worth much less than what she paid for it. Fortunately, though, she also made a big down payment when she bought, so she didn't have to borrow the full price of the car. To make a long story short (and simple), Jen spends some time on KBB.com and finds out she can sell her car for $15,000, which is exactly the amount she owes on it. Of course, selling her car will affect her monthly spending too. First, she'll have to spend $150 more per month in public transportation costs, Uber, and taxis. But she'll also save $450 per month! The $290 loan payment, plus $160 more per month savings on gas, repairs, parking, and car insurance. Add all that together, and it means that her Monthly Gap will get $300 larger!

Figuring out the financial effect of selling a car is complicated and has a lot of moving (car) parts to keep track of. But the Dashboard makes it easy! With a few clicks, Jen's in a position to answer the question: What would my Dashboard look like if I sold my car? (See image opposite).

By selling her car, Jen can completely eliminate all of her debt and increase her speed (Monthly Gap) considerably, too—all in one fell swoop! If she does that, her only Red Phase problem to solve is her

< Back NetWorthy Financial Dashboard (manual)	
RESET PANEL	
Clear User Entries	
ENTER YOUR FINANCIAL INFORMATION BELOW	
(1.) Take-home pay (monthly average)	$ 2,250.00 Per Month
(2.) Total minimum required debt payments (monthly)	$ 0.00 Per Month
(3.) Base living expenses (excluding debt payments)	$ 1,300.00 Per Month
(4.) Total household spending (monthly)	$ 1,300.00 Per Month
(5.) Total non-mortgage debt outstanding	$ 0.00
Weighted average APR across all non-mortgage debts (best guess)	0 %
(6.) Risk-based e-fund goal (select ideal number of months to be covered)	6 Months
(7.) Current emergency fund balance	$ 700.00
RESULTS	
(A.) Monthly Gap (income − expenses)	$ 950.00
(B.) Number of months covered by current emergency fund value	0.54 Months
(C.) Countdown to yellow phase (months)	7.47 Months
(C.) Countdown to yellow phase (years)	0.62 Years

Networthy Nugget #2.4

Your goal is to get out of the red phase and into the yellow phase as soon as you can. To accomplish that: permanently eliminate all your (non-mortgage) debt and build up an adequate emergency fund.

Ideal Emergency Fund Goal	$ 7,800.00
Amount short of E-fund goal	$ 7,100.00
Amount remaining until yellow phase is reached	$ 7,093.00

E-fund, and with a Monthly Gap of $900, that won't take long at all. Well under a year, to be exact! With one car sale, Jen has a chance to cut her Yellow Phase countdown from 3.2 years, to 7.5 months.

Before Jen had the Dashboard, if you'd have asked if she'd be willing to sell her car to get to the Yellow Phase faster, she wouldn't have had an easy way to size up the problem, or the opportunity to solve it. Most people don't have the time or the ability to build a detailed financial spreadsheet just to answer one what-if question—so they stick to the status quo. But with the Dashboard, Jen can size this problem up quickly and easily. Goodbye, car!

Net Worthy Nugget #8.5

> The value of the dashboard can only be realized by thoroughly completing it to the best of your ability. Don't estimate, guess, or spitball—attack this task head on. If you haven't done so already, complete your first dashboard before moving on to Chapter 9. Continue doing so monthly until you're out of the red phase.

That was a lot to take in. The upside is that reading through it the first time is definitely harder than actually completing your first Dashboard. And everything about it gets easier every time you do it.

Make a Good Habit

That's right, you'll have to do this again! And again, and again, and again. Just like you learned to occasionally check your speed, fuel level, and rearview mirror as you drive, you have to get in the habit of checking in with your Financial Dashboard regularly. There's no need to recalculate everything daily, but doing a quick rundown once a month will keep your money machine humming along nicely.

In Chapter 4, you learned about your monthly budgeting cycle, and a thorough review of your Dashboard and what has changed should be a part of that habit. Set yourself an appointment each month and keep it. Of course, if you have seasonal income or there are permanent changes to your employment or spending, you may need to revisit your Dashboard more often to ensure you're making decisions based on accurate figures.

If the idea of completing your Dashboard for the first time is giving you the anxiety sweats, remember: It's a learning process, and it gets easier with time. The way to get better is to keep your monthly appointments, even if you're not looking forward to them. The way to stay stuck, or even regress, is to put the monthly appointments off.

No Shortcuts Allowed

Once you get used to the Dashboard process, you may feel a temptation to short-hand the process of collecting the real numbers to input each month. Resist the urge to work off of assumptions or estimates, or to revise your Dashboard in your head during traffic. To make the best use of your financial resources and reach your goal, you need to put in the work. Especially for your first Dashboard, you might need to dig out student loan documents, remember online-banking passwords, go through old pay-stubs, or manually add up all your expenses based on debit and credit card activity.

All of these things are annoying, and all of these things are necessary.

Don't Be Gentle, but Don't Catastrophize Either

Looking at the cold, hard numbers that define your financial situation can be painful. When life isn't exactly as we'd like it to be, we tend to sugarcoat things in our own minds to help us cope with the stress. In this case, however, kindness isn't doing you any favors.

When it comes to your Dashboard and the decisions you need to make based on it, you need to be ruthless. Sit down with your statements and bills and your online checking activity and really let yourself have it. Don't round down on debts or up on savings. Don't give yourself a pass on certain expenses because "it was just a one-time thing." Everything gets counted. If you don't like the numbers you get, implement a plan to make next month's numbers different.

Some people might go to the other extreme and get so discouraged that they start to think of their financial situation as a hopeless mess, not even worth tackling. If that's you, this whole Dashboard process has probably felt like a gut punch. We understand, and we empathize. We're committed to the Dashboard process because in long run, the only real way to improve is to know the truth—the whole truth—about where you stand right now. But seeing that truth for the first time can be devastating.

If you're feeling that way, our advice is to focus on two things. The first is to realize, and appreciate, that at least you know the *truth* now. You can stop living in uncertainty and doubt; now you know exactly where you stand, which puts you, at last, in a position to actually do something about it. This knowledge is *new* to you; sit with it calmly for a while, instead of going with your first emotional, impulsive reaction to it. The second piece of advice to really *shorten* your goal horizon. For now, just forget about becoming debt free, or filling your financial bathtub, or long-term dreams of green phase financial independence. Instead, just think about making a little bit of progress *this* month. It's taken a long time to dig the hole you're in; you won't get out overnight. Your only goal this month is to stop the negative momentum and start moving—no matter how slowly—in the right direction. There will be plenty of time later to start picking up speed.

This is *Not* a Test Drive

Completing your Dashboard isn't actually the hard part. Following through on prudent financial decisions *based on* the Dashboard is much more difficult. You need to commit—to yourself, even to someone else if that helps keep you accountable—to use this data to improve your spending and saving habits, and then stick to that commitment.

We made the Net Worthy Navigator App easy to use on purpose. But the fact that it's so easy can work against you if you're not careful. To get the real, long-term value out of the Dashboard process, you need to do these 3 steps regularly:

1. Update all the inputs.

2. Really understand what happened financially in the last month.

3. Carefully decide what you're going to keep the same, and what you're going to do differently, next month.

Because the app makes step 1 so easy, you might be tempted to do only step 1, stop there, and call it good. "OK, Dashboard's done, all the numbers are up to date!" Not so fast. Steps 2 and 3 require careful, focused thought, and while the app can help you prepare for those steps, no app can do the thinking for you.

Step 3 is where you make important decisions—sometimes really hard decisions—that will make the biggest difference in your financial life. This is where you decide things like: "It's too expensive to live in this apartment alone. I'm getting at least one roommate by the first of next month." "I'm going to commit 20 hours a month to a side hustle starting next Monday." "500 bucks a month, straight into the E-fund, automatically, as soon as my paycheck hits the checking account, no exceptions, starting next paycheck. Boom!" "I want that new iPhone. But I don't need it. That's my decision, and it's final for at least one more year. Next question."

That's why the scheduled monthly appointment is so important. If you just pick up the app from time to time and make sure all the inputs are up to date, you'll feel good because you can convince yourself you've spent time on your financial future. But if you haven't looked at all those "step 3" decisions, long and hard enough to come to definite conclusions or your feeling of making financial progress is just an illusion. This is no test drive—this is your real financial life. Your financial future is at stake, and the financial futures of any dependents you may have, now or in the future, too. So keep your monthly appointment. And the appointment isn't over until all 3 steps are done.

Don't Wait

We know it's tempting to put down this book and mentally check off the "Do Something Good for My Financial Future" box on your to-do list, but don't let yourself stop here. The first step is completing your Dashboard. After that, there's no looking back.

Like any other big goal—weight loss, getting a promotion, earning a degree—the road is long, but you're going to make the most immediate headway . . . immediately. You've envisioned your financial independence, so start taking active steps toward that goal. The hard truth is that the longer you wait to get started, the less likely it is that you'll start at all—so don't let this window of motivation pass you by!

Whether you're a Net Worthy Navigator App user, or a DIY type, gather your documents, roll up your sleeves, and set your first Dashboard appointment for NOW.

Building Your Own Financial Dashboard

A Guide for the Do-It-Yourselfer

Oh, hey there! If you've found yourself here, you're probably the kind of person who likes to see how the sausage is made, so to speak. I'm Claire, your sausage factory tour guide, here to walk you through the whole wonderful, messy process.

The Net Worthy Navigator App aims to streamline the Dashboard process in a way that makes it more accessible for a lot of people. For many, ease of use is the key to actually putting thought into action. But not everyone will choose simplicity over nitty-gritty know-how. If you're the type of person who likes to DIY, or if you just love spreadsheets and math and color-coding, then this guide is for you.

Debt Inventory and Analysis (DIA) Spreadsheet

If you're going the DIY route, the first step is creating a DIA spreadsheet. If you're not using the app, you still need to keep track of your debts. If you're just here to see how the math behind the Dashboard calculations works, you can skip this section.

For the rest of you, start by picking a spreadsheet program to work with. I love Google Sheets because I can access it from anything with an internet connection, so I'll be using that for my examples. The formulas I use to populate the sheet should be the same or very similar to those used in Excel. Assuming you've already gathered all your financial info, as prompted earlier in this chapter, start by creating a column heading for the following data points:

1. **Debt Name**

2. **Debt Type**

3. **Lender**

4. **Balance**

5. **Deferred Interest?**

6. **Deferred Interest End Date**

7. **Current APR:** This is the annual interest rate your card currently charges. If you have consolidated your debt using a 0% interest balance transfer, for example, then your current APR might be 0%.

8. **Standard APR:** The annual interest rate your card normally charges. If you have used a 0% interest balance transfer, this will be the APR your card will charge when the interest-free period is up.

9. **Minimum Payment**

10. **Due Date**

11. **Notes**

I won't go into further detail here about what most of these data points refer to, since you already read about them earlier. If you need a refresher on what information you need to complete this spreadsheet, flip back to Nugget #8.2. Now, create rows for each of your different debts, and fill in all the appropriate information under each column.

Introducing Ben: Jen's Debt-Riddled Twin

This type of project is often easier to visualize with an example. Remember Jen from earlier in this chapter? Well let's assume that her brother, Ben, while having the exact same monthly income, living expenses, E-Fund goal, and current E-Fund balance, has tons more debt to work around. Poor buddy.

Let's say he has two credit cards, a student loan, a mortgage, and an auto loan. His spreadsheet might look like this:

Debt Spreadsheet

fx 5/13/2018

	A	B	C	D	E	F	G	H	I	J	K
1	Name	Debt Type	Lender	Balance	Current APR	Standard APR	Deferred Interest?	Deferral End Date	Minimum Payment	Due Date	Notes
2	Amex Blue	Revolving	American Express	$5,000	0.00%	12.50%	Yes	5/13/2018	$50	12/27/17	Interest deferred
3	Auto Loan	Installment	Wells Fargo	$15,000	8.00%	8.00%	No	N/A	$304	12/31/17	
4	Mortgage	Installment	Citi Bank	$200,000	4.75%	4.75%	No	N/A	$1,043	12/29/17	
5	Student Loan	Installment	MOHELA	$25,000	6.00%	6.00%	No	N/A	$278	12/20/17	
6	United Airlines Visa	Revolving	Chase	$1,200	17.00%	17.00%	No	N/A	$29	12/19/17	

Notice that the Amex Blue card has a note stating that there is a 0% interest rate until May 13, 2018. We've already discussed the benefits of the balance transfer credit card feature, and Ben has clearly taken advantage of it to some degree. (See Claire's little credit card pitch earlier in Chapter 8 for her general recommendations if you need a refresher on just how this works).

In the app, the 0% interest-deferral period is built in. When we DIY, however, we have to make sure we reflect those same little details.

1. For now, simply input your reduced or 0% interest rate under Current APR for any debts to which those conditions apply.

2. Under Standard APR, input the APR that will take effect after your deferral period ends.

3. For all debts that do not have an interest-deferral period, the Current and Standard APR columns will be the same.

Putting This Tool to Use

The most important thing to consider when prioritizing your debt payments is APR, since it is the best reflection of how much all those borrowed dollars are costing you each year. It makes sense, therefore, that you'd always want to pay off the debt with highest APR first.

In the app—while we mentioned it would be wise to input the highest APR debt as Debt 1 to reinforce the urgency of paying that balance down first—it doesn't technically matter which order you input your debts. All of that prioritization is taken care of behind the scenes. For you DIYers, however, it can be useful to be able to see, at a glance, which debts are costing you the most. To arrange your spreadsheet so that the highest APR is first, highlight all the rows and click 'Filter,' which is typically its own button in the toolbar or can be found in the 'Tools' menu.

	A	B	C	D	E	F	G	H	I	J	K
1	Name	Debt Type	Lender	Balance	Current APR	Standard APR	Deferred Interest?	Deferral End Date	Minimum Payment	Due Date	Notes
2	Amex Blue	Revolving	American Express	$5,000	0.00%	12.50%	Yes	5/13/2018	$50	12/27/17	Interest deferred
3	Auto Loan	Installment	Wells Fargo	$15,000	8.00%	8.00%	No	N/A	$304	12/31/17	
4	Mortgage	Installment	Citi Bank	$200,000	4.75%	4.75%	No	N/A	$1,043	12/29/17	
5	Student Loan	Installment	MOHELA	$25,000	6.00%	6.00%	No	N/A	$278	12/20/17	
6	United Airlines Visa	Revolving	Chase	$1,200	17.00%	17.00%	No	N/A	$29	12/19/17	

Small arrows should appear in each column heading. Click the arrow next to 'Current APR' and select 'Filter Z-A'. This will put the highest APR on top and the lowest on bottom, without disrupting all your other data.

	A	B	C	D	E	F	G	H	I	J	K
1	Name	Debt Type	Lender	Balance	Current APR	Standard APR	Deferred Interest?	Deferral End Date	Minimum Payment	Due Date	Notes
2	Amex Blue	Revolving	Ameri Expre	Sort A → Z		12.50%	Yes	5/13/2018	$50	12/27/17	Interest deferred
3	Auto Loan	Installment	Wells F	Sort Z → A		8.00%	No	N/A	$304	12/31/17	
4	Mortgage	Installment	Citi B	▶ Filter by condition		4.75%	No	N/A	$1,043	12/29/17	
5	Student Loan	Installment	MOHELA	$25,000	6.00%	6.00%	No	N/A	$278	12/20/17	
6	United Airlines Visa	Revolving	Chase	$1,200	17.00%	17.00%	No	N/A	$29	12/19/17	

Ben's spreadsheet would now look like this:

	A	B	C	D	E	F	G	H	I	J	K
1	Name	Debt Type	Lender	Balance	Current APR	Standard APR	Deferred Interest?	Deferral End Date	Minimum Payment	Due Date	Notes
2	United Airlines Visa	Revolving	Chase	$1,200	17.00%	17.00%	No	N/A	$29	12/19/17	
3	Auto Loan	Installment	Wells Fargo	$15,000	8.00%	8.00%	No	N/A	$304	12/31/17	
4	Student Loan	Installment	MOHELA	$25,000	6.00%	6.00%	No	N/A	$278	12/20/17	
5	Mortgage	Installment	Citi Bank	$200,000	4.75%	4.75%	No	N/A	$1,043	12/29/17	
6	Amex Blue	Revolving	American Express	$5,000	0.00%	12.50%	Yes	5/13/2018	$50	12/27/17	

Luckily, Ben's United Airlines Visa has the lowest balance of all his debts, because it also has the highest **APR**, by far. Getting that balance down to zero is an obvious priority.

A Note on Notes

Up till now, the Notes column has been sad and lonely, but that's about to change. The primary purpose of this column is to alert you about a potential change in APR, like when your deferral period is up and your balance starts accruing interest.

Now, you could manually enter this data in the Notes column by simply typing "Interest Deferred" and then keeping an eye on the Deferral End Date column as time goes by to ensure you can reorganize your debts by Current APR when the 0% period ends. However, this means you run the risk of not noticing when the Deferral End Date comes and goes. If the Standard APR on your deferred-interest debt is higher than those of your other debts, you may end up mis-prioritizing your Monthly Gap once your deferral period ends.

For example, when Ben's balance transfer period ends, his American Express APR will jump to 12.5%, which is the second highest APR on his DIA. In fact, by the time May 2018 rolls around, he may have paid off his United Airlines Visa entirely, making his Amex the costliest debt he has. If he doesn't reorganize his DIA on May 13, 2018, then he'll end up paying more than he has to in interest by focusing his efforts on his Auto Loan, based on the newly outdated ranking.

All that is to say that, if you elect the manual route, just make sure you keep a close eye on those Deferral End Dates.

Spreadsheet Geek Efficiency Tip!

If you don't want to set little reminders in your phone to make sure you don't miss your Deferral End Date, then maybe we should automate this notes column! With a little geekery, we can easily get the spreadsheet to do the work of alerting you when your interest-free periods are up.

To do so, simply click on the first cell under the Notes heading, which should be cell K2, and enter the following formula:

=IF(ISBLANK(H2),"",IF(H2>TODAY(), "Interest Deferred", IF(H2<=TODAY(),"DEFERRAL PERIOD ENDED, REPRIORITIZE DEBTS","")))

I know this looks complicated, and it kind of is, but all you need to know is that this long string of parentheses and quotation marks tells your sheet to produce the phrase "Interest Deferred" if the date in the corresponding

Deferral End Date cell (in this case, H2) is **earlier** than the current date as read by your computer system clock. If the date in H2 is **equal to or later than** the current date, the sheet will produce the phrase "DEFERRAL PERIOD ENDED, REPRIORITIZE DEBTS".

Once you've entered your formula, test it by inputting a date into a K cell and seeing what pops up under Notes in the same row. Try changing it to a date that's already passed to make sure the Notes column changes accordingly.

fx =IF(ISBLANK(H2),"",IF(H2>TODAY(),"Interest Deferred",IF(H2<=TODAY(),"DEFERRAL PERIOD ENDED, REPRIORITIZE DEBTS","")))

	A	B	C	D	E	F	G	H	I	J	K
1	Name	Debt Type	Lender	Balance	Current APR	Standard APR	Deferred Interest?	Deferral End Date	Minimum Payment	Due Date	Notes
2	United Airlines Visa	Revolving	Chase	$1,200	17.00%	17.00%	No	N/A	$29	12/19/17	Interest deferred
3	Auto Loan	Installment	Wells Fargo	$15,000	8.00%	8.00%	No	N/A	$304	12/31/17	
4	Student Loan	Installment	MOHELA	$25,000	6.00%	6.00%	No	N/A	$278	12/20/17	
5	Mortgage	Installment	Citi Bank	$200,000	4.75%	4.75%	No	N/A	$1,043	12/29/17	
6	Amex Blue	Revolving	American Express	$5,000	0.00%	12.50%	Yes	5/13/2018	$50	12/27/17	

After you've verified that your formula is working, highlight K2 (your first Notes cell) and click and hold the tiny box that appears in the lower right corner of the cell. Drag your cursor down until all the Notes cells are highlighted, then let go. This should copy that formula to all your other cells and automatically change the H cell referenced in the formula to reflect the appropriate row. For example, the formula in K4 won't reference the Deferral End Date for H2 (as in the example above), but it will instead automatically input H4.

Geeking Gets Geekier

For those who really need strong visual cues to help organize information in a meaningful way (like me) or just love playing with the bells and whistles (also like me), you can go one step further and add some color.

First, open Conditional Formatting by highlighting the Notes column, clicking Conditional Formatting under the Format menu. Then add two rules based on the two possible values for Notes.

Now, when a Notes cell reads "Interest Deferred", the font is green (for "Don't worry about it, buddy! You've got time!"). When the Deferral End Date has passed, however, the reprioritization prompt is red (for "ALERT! SOMETHING NEEDS TO HAPPEN!").

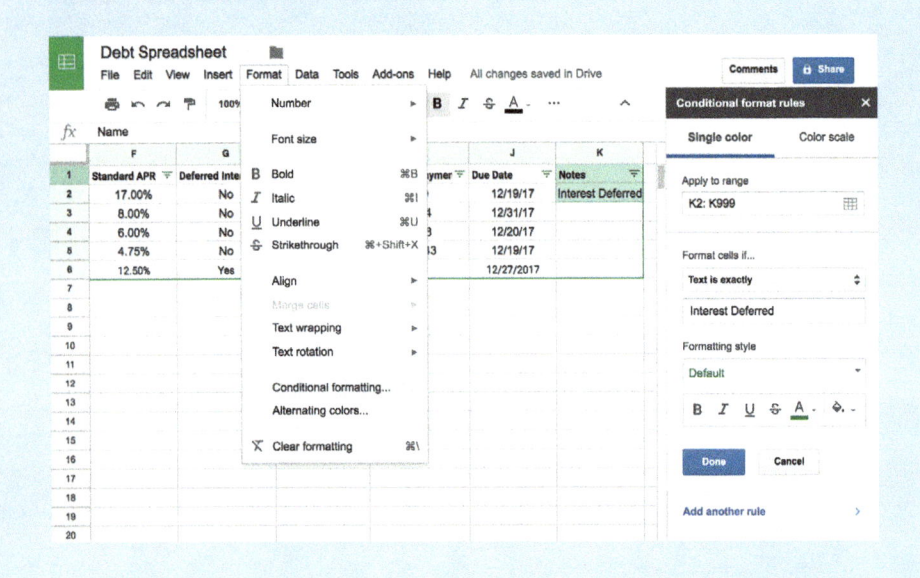

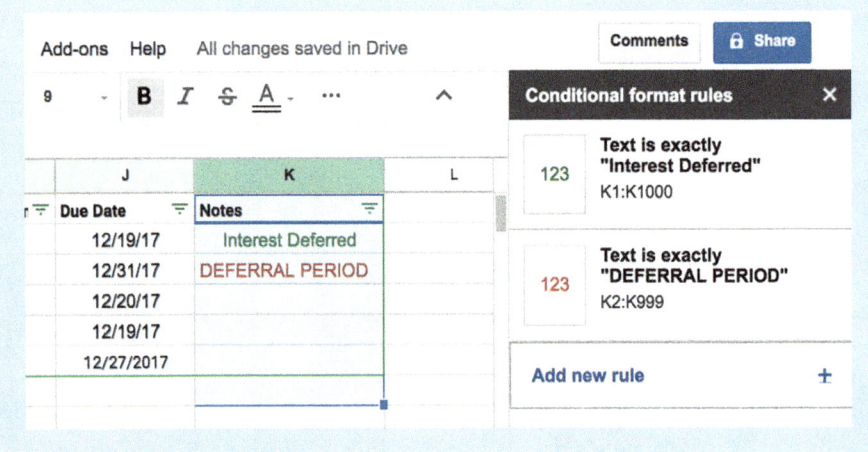

BEHOLD!

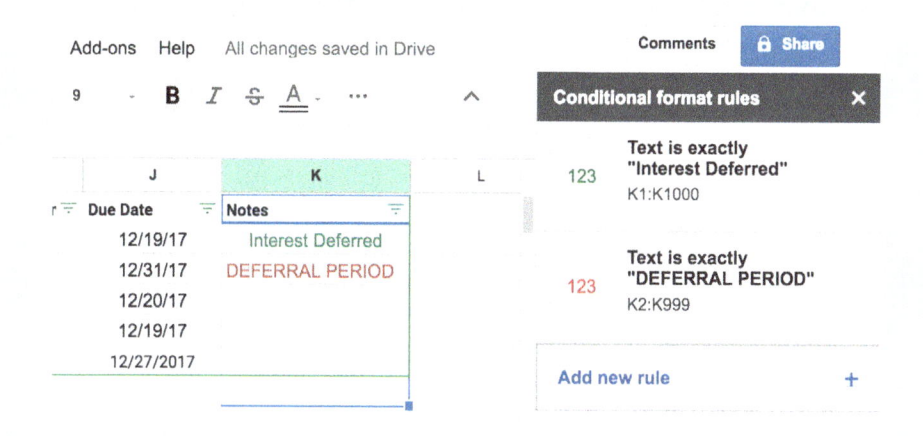

| Add-ons | Help | All changes saved in Drive | | | Comments | 🔒 Share |

| 9 | - | **B** | *I* | S̶ | A̲ ᵥ | ⋯ | | ∧ | **Conditional format rules** | ✕ |

J	K	L			Text is exactly
Due Date	Notes		123	"Interest Deferred"
12/19/17	Interest Deferred			K1:K1000
12/31/17	DEFERRAL PERIOD			Text is exactly
12/20/17			123	"DEFERRAL PERIOD"
12/19/17				K2:K999
12/27/2017				
				Add new rule	+

*Second Deferral End Date added for illustrative purposes. Ben still only has just one deferred-interest balance.

Student Loans

You may have noticed that the interest-deferral period we've been discussing thus far has been focused on credit card balance transfers, with nary a mention of student loan forbearance or deferral. This is by design. Student loans, especially Federal loans, often have pretty complex terms and conditions, which makes a one-size-fits-all approach both inaccurate and potentially ruinous. While your DIY spreadsheet absolutely could be built to accommodate any kind of loan structure, it would take us far, far too long to explain that process here.

Luckily, the Net Worthy Navigator App has all that good stuff built into it already! If you have a student loan with more complicated terms, and you're not already a spreadsheet whiz kid, then we'd recommend just using the app to save yourself the headache.

The Bottom Line(s)

Now that you have all your debt information in one place, we need to use it to look at the bigger picture. What is your total debt situation and how much of your paycheck needs to go to paying down those debts every month? Regardless of whether you fancied-up your Notes column or not, go ahead and add another row labeled 'Total Debt' below your current rows. Then, under the 'Balance' column, add up all your outstanding balances to see what your total debt is.

Next, add another row labeled 'Total Minimum Payment.' Under the 'Minimum Payment' column, add up all your current payments to see what your total debt payments are for the month. These two numbers, Total Debt and Total Minimum Payment, will play a huge role in your Financial Dashboard.

	A	B	C	D	E	F	G	H	I	J	K
1	Name	Debt Type	Lender	Balance	Current APR	Standard APR	Deferred Interest?	Deferral End Date	Minimum Payment	Due Date	Notes
2	Amex Blue	Revolving	American Express	$5,000	0.00%	12.50%	Yes	5/13/2018	$50	12/27/17	Interest deferred
3	Auto Loan	Installment	Wells Fargo	$15,000	8.00%	8.00%	No	N/A	$304	12/31/17	
4	Mortgage	Installment	Citi Bank	$200,000	4.75%	4.75%	No	N/A	$1,043	12/29/17	
5	Student Loan	Installment	MOHELA	$25,000	6.00%	6.00%	No	N/A	$278	12/20/17	
6	United Airlines Visa	Revolving	Chase	$1,200	17.00%	17.00%	No	N/A	$29	12/19/17	
7											
8	Total Debt			$246,200							
9	Total Minimum Payment								$1,704		

Spreadsheet Geek Efficiency Tip!

You can make your spreadsheet do a lot of this work for you by using simple SUM functions. For example, in the image above, you could use a SUM function in cells D8 and G9 to determine your Total Debt and Total Minimum Payments. These functions would look like this:

Cell D8:   =SUM(D2:D6)
Cell I9:   =SUM(I2:I6)

Mortgages

As we've discussed in past chapters, not all debts are created equal. We already mentioned that for those using the app, mortgage debt is entered separately from the rest of the DIA. For those going the spreadsheet route, however, we still need to be able to see the mortgage as a liability and keep track of our progress as we pay it down.

So, while having a complete debt spreadsheet is an important organizational tool, we need to account for the fact that your mortgage payments (if you have them) are not quite the same as your other debt payments. In fact, you've already learned that your mortgage is not even included in the Minimum Required Debt Payments figure on your Dashboard. To make this distinction clear, we need to add a few more rows to our spreadsheet.

Below 'Total Debt' and 'Total Minimum Payments,' add two more rows, labeled 'Total Non-Mortgage Debt' and 'Total Minimum Non-Mortgage Payments.' It's a mouthful, but this will help you a lot later on. Under the 'Balance' and 'Minimum Payment' columns, add up your totals like you did before, but omit the balance and payment for your mortgage, like this:

	A	B	C	D	E	F	G	H	I	J	K
1	Name	Debt Type	Lender	Balance	Current APR	Standard APR	Deferred Interest?	Deferral End Date	Minimum Payment	Due Date	Notes
2	Amex Blue	Revolving	American Express	$5,000	0.00%	12.50%	Yes	5/13/2018	$50	12/27/17	Interest deferred
3	Auto Loan	Installment	Wells Fargo	$15,000	8.00%	8.00%	No	N/A	$304	12/31/17	
4	Mortgage	Installment	Citi Bank	$200,000	4.75%	4.75%	No	N/A	$1,043	12/29/17	
5	Student Loan	Installment	MOHELA	$25,000	6.00%	6.00%	No	N/A	$278	12/20/17	
6	United Airlines Visa	Revolving	Chase	$1,200	17.00%	17.00%	No	N/A	$29	12/19/17	
7											
8	Total Debt			$246,200							
9	Total Minimum Payment								$1,704		
10											
11	Total Non-Mortgage Debt			$46,200							
12	Total Minimum Non-Mortgage Payment								$661		

Spreadsheet Geek Efficiency Tip!

We can automate these cells, too, with one teensy adjustment:

Cell D11:   =SUM(D2:D6)-D4
Cell I12:   =SUM(I2:I6)-I4

*Remember to input the appropriate cells for **your** Mortgage. Depending on how many debts you have and what your mortgage APR is, your mortgage may not be in Row 4, for example.

Of course, many people are renters and have no mortgage at all. If this is you, then you can omit these last two lines altogether. If you do decide to purchase a home at some point, make sure to amend your Dashboard accordingly.

Filling Out Your Dashboard

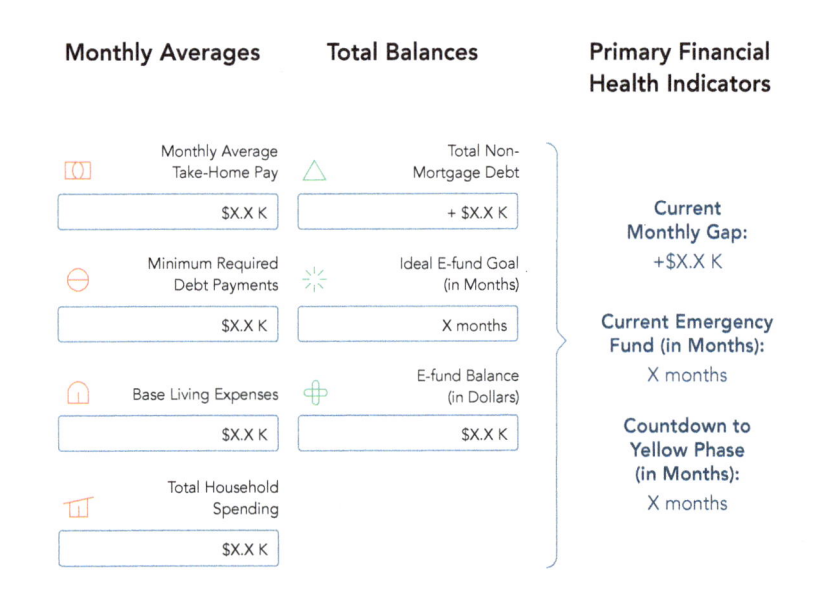

Monthly Averages

Monthly Average Take-Home Pay
$X.X K

Minimum Required Debt Payments
$X.X K

Base Living Expenses
$X.X K

Total Household Spending
$X.X K

Total Balances

Total Non-Mortgage Debt
+ $X.X K

Ideal E-fund Goal (in Months)
X months

E-fund Balance (in Dollars)
$X.X K

Primary Financial Health Indicators

Current Monthly Gap:
+$X.X K

Current Emergency Fund (in Months):
X months

Countdown to Yellow Phase (in Months):
X months

Now that you've gotten your DIA spreadsheet all set up and color-coded and perfectly automated, let's dive back into the Dashboard itself. Since we're DIYing this bad boy, let's use the Dashboard image above as a reference point for how we want your end product to look.

We've already covered Items 1-7 in depth elsewhere, but there a couple data points that you'll need to pull from your DIA spreadsheet in order to populate your Dashboard, so you'll also see a screenshot of Ben's completed spreadsheet, below, to use as a reference.

	A	B	C	D	E	F	G	H	I	J	K
1	Name	Debt Type	Lender	Balance	Current APR	Standard APR	Deferred Interest?	Deferral End Date	Minimum Payment	Due Date	Notes
2	Amex Blue	Revolving	American Express	$5,000	0.00%	12.50%	Yes	5/13/2018	$50	12/27/17	Interest deferred
3	Auto Loan	Installment	Wells Fargo	$15,000	8.00%	8.00%	No	N/A	$304	12/31/17	
4	Mortgage	Installment	Citi Bank	$200,000	4.75%	4.75%	No	N/A	$1,043	12/29/17	
5	Student Loan	Installment	MOHELA	$25,000	6.00%	6.00%	No	N/A	$278	12/20/17	
6	United Airlines Visa	Revolving	Chase	$1,200	17.00%	17.00%	No	N/A	$29	12/19/17	
7											
8	Total Debt			$246,200							
9	Total Minimum Payment								$1,704		
10											
11	Total Non-Mortgage Debt			$46,200							
12	Total Minimum Non-Mortgage Payment								$661		

To complete your DIY Dashboard, you'll enter the following:

- **Monthly Average Take-Home Pay**

- **Minimum Required Debt Payments:**
  Your DIA spreadsheet has already calculated this for you! As you can see in Ben's inventory, Cell I12 shows his total Minimum Non-Mortgage Debt Payments. Input this number from your own inventory into Item 2 on your Dashboard.

- **Base Living Expenses:**
  Remember, this includes your mortgage payment, which can be pulled from your DIA sheet (Ben's is I4), but none of your other debts.

- **Total Household Spending:**
  This includes all your monthly debt payments, so add Nos. 2 and 3 to get No. 4.

- **Total Non-Mortgage Debt:**
  This can also be pulled from your DIA spreadsheet (in Ben's case, Cell D11).

- **Ideal E-Fund Goal (in Months)**

- **E-Fund Balance (in Dollars)**

Using these figures, you'll calculate your three Indicators:

1. **Current Monthly Gap**

2. **Current Emergency Fund (in Months)**

3. **Countdown to Yellow Phase**

All That Sweet, Sweet Math

Now we get to the good stuff. You've completed your DIA spreadsheet, you've input all your basic figures into your DIY Dashboard, and now it's time to break out your calculator and crunch some numbers.

Current Monthly Gap

As you know, your gap is the difference between "money in" and "money out." It could also be considered your "monthly net cash flow" and can be calculated using the following Dashboard items:

- Monthly Average Take-Home Pay
- Total Household Spending

The formula is:

$$\text{Current Monthly Gap} = \text{Monthly Average Take-Home Pay} - \text{Total Household Spending}$$

Current Emergency Fund in Months

One of the twin goals of the red phase is to build up your E-Fund. To help you track your progress toward that goal, you'll need the following Dashboard items:

- Total Household Spending
- E-Fund Balance (in Dollars)

The formula is:

$$\text{Current E-Fund (in Months)} = \frac{\text{E-Fund Balance (in Dollars)}}{\text{Total Household Spending}}$$

Countdown to Yellow Phase

Getting to the yellow phase is work—hard work—and we know there's likely going to be one question you ask yourself over and over as you progress: "HOW MUCH LONGER???" The Countdown to Yellow Phase indicator is here to answer that question.

To calculate your Countdown, you'll need the following Dashboard figures:

△ Total Non-Mortgage Debt

☼ Ideal E-Fund Goal (in Months)

⊔ Total Household Spending

✢ E-Fund Balance (in Dollars)

Current Monthly Gap

The formula is:

$$\text{Countdown (in Months)} = \frac{\left(\text{Total Non-Mortgage Debt} + \text{Ideal E-fund Goal (in Months)}\right) \times \left(\text{Total Household Spending} - \text{E-Fund Balance (in Dollars)}\right)}{\text{Current Monthly Gap}}$$

While we prefer to measure the Countdown in time, we understand that some people work better with a hard dollar amount as a goal. To accommodate different learning styles, the calculation for the Countdown indicator can be done in two stages, which will give you a figure in both dollars and months.

Step 1:

$$\text{Dollars to Go} = \text{Total Non-Mortgage Debt} + \left(\text{Ideal E-Fund Goal (in Months)} \times \text{Total Household Spending}\right) - \text{E-Fund Balance (in Dollars)}$$

Step 2:

$$\text{Countdown (in Months)} = \frac{\text{Dollars to Go}}{\text{Current Monthly Gap}}$$

Example

This metric is by far the most mathematically complex, so let's run through a quick example based on our main man, Ben. Remember we said that Ben had exactly the same finances as his sister Jen, except that he had more debt? Well it turns out that all that debt was giving Ben a depressingly negative gap, which rendered the whole Dashboard process moot. Seeing this, Ben decided it was time to get himself a side-hustle to supplement his income.

Ben already has experience in graphic design and is a quick learner. Using the skills already at his disposal, Ben starts designing and selling witty T-shirts online and doing freelance logo work on the weekends. Together, those side-gigs earn him an additional $800 per month.

Other than his increased income, everything else that Jen entered in her Net Worthy Navigator App earlier in this chapter is still the same for Ben.

- Monthly Average Take-Home Pay = $2,250 (Jen) + $800 (Gigs) = $3,050
- Total Non-Mortgage Debt = $46,200
- Minimum Required Debt Payments: $661
- Base Living Expenses = $1,310 (Jen) + $1,043 (Mortgage) = $2,353
- Total Household Spending = $2,353 + $661 = $3,014
- E-Fund Goal (in Months) = 6
- E-Fund Balance = $700

    Current Monthly Gap = $3,050 - $3,014 = $36

Ben's Countdown can be calculated using the two-step process, rounding to the nearest month:

> Dollars to Go = $46,200 + (6 * $3,014) - $700
> = $46,200 + $14,118 - $700
> = $63,584
>
> Countdown (in Months) = $63,584 / $36
> = 1,766.2 months, or 147.2 years

While Jen has a measly 3.18 years until she's debt-free and ready to take things to the next level, Ben's still got a lot of work to do—he won't even live long enough to see the yellow phase at this rate! Nevertheless, he should be proud of the progress he's made just getting his gap into the black. Before he started his hustle, his Countdown in Months was literally a negative number—he was moving further away from his goal every single month. Ben saw the immediate issue with his finances and fixed it. Now he can focus on widening that gap even further.

Getting a higher paying day job would be an awesome step in the right direction, but that's not entirely within Ben's control. Plus, Ben is rapidly running low on free time. Ben plays around with his Dashboard a bit to see how much of a bump his gap needs in order to reach the yellow phase within a normal human lifespan. He discovers that by getting his gap up to $200, he can drastically reduce his Countdown. To increase his earning potential, Ben decides to take an online course to get a special graphic design certification, which allows him to attract higher paying clients. In the course, he also learns about different types of design products—like brochure layouts, business cards, and creating images for websites—which allow him to offer a wider range of services. By putting in the effort to broaden his side hustle, Ben is able to boost his monthly income by $250.

Now, Ben's Countdown looks like this:

> Monthly Average Take-Home Pay = $2,250 (Ben) + $1,050 (Gigs) = $3,300
>
> Current Monthly Gap = $3,300 - $3,014 = $286
>
> > Countdown (in Months) = $63,584 / $286
> > = 222.3 months, or 18.5 years

By putting in a little extra effort to expand his side gig and increasing income by a relatively small amount, Ben has reduced his Countdown by a whopping **128.7** years! He knocked off more than an entire lifetime of toiling away toward the yellow phase! Seeing that his goal is much more attainable, Ben is inspired to see what else he can do to minimize his Countdown. Clearly, even small changes can have a huge impact.

It may be possible that Ben could eventually devote himself full-time to his side-hustle and earn more than he does at his day job, but he'd need to be sure he could generate consistently high income (at least as much as he earns now), so it would take some time, research, and additional training. For now, Ben should probably focus on cutting down his spending, finding ways to roll his interest-bearing balances onto interest-deferred credit cards, or refinancing his mortgage for a lower rate (if possible). He might begin by playing around with his Dashboard figures again to see how a few other small changes (earning just $100 more per month or cutting his expenses by just 5%, for example) might make an impact on his Countdown figure. Using that info, Ben can (again) strategize the best way to forge ahead.

While Jen may be annoyed at having to wait three years to move forward, that's not an unusual Countdown figure. For Ben, it's time to get creative about cutting costs and amping up earnings. As he now knows, the reality check offered by the Countdown metric might be painful, but it's necessary. To get where you want to go, you have to know where you stand.

About the Co-Author

Claire Boyte-White is a writer, editor, and long-term 'voluntary hobo'. After a backpacking trip to Scotland in 2013, she realized that the standard 9 to 5 grind in her Seattle insurance career wasn't going to lead to the life she wanted. After ditching the fancy job and the high-end apartment, Claire began building a career that would allow her to live life on her own terms. She stumbled into the financial and investment writing niche early on, and found that her natural love of math and analysis made it a perfect fit. Since then, she's traveled the world, married a bonny Scotsman, settled down in Cuenca, Ecuador, and maintained a happily semi-retired lifestyle writing for many well-known financial resources, such as Investopedia, NapkinFinance, CNBC, SmartAsset, and Dividend.com.

"Writing these books was a uniquely rewarding experience. Being on the older end of the Millennial spectrum, I found myself realizing how much books like these would have helped me ten years ago. But it also highlighted how much I'd learned through my own financial journey, and how much joy it brought me to be able to share those tools with others. Because I co-authored the two final volumes, I really got to work with Chris to flesh out the Dashboard tool and fit all these moving pieces together, which made this so much more than just another writing gig. My hope is that I've helped, in some small way, to create something that can help other people free themselves from the status-quo."

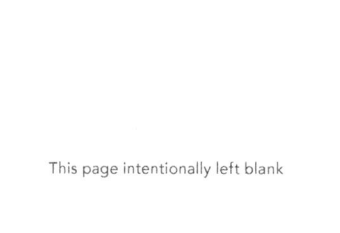

Chapter 09

The Right Things in the Right Order

by Chris Smith with Claire Boyte-White

Net Worthy Nugget #9.0
Priority 0: Total minimum required debt payment

Net Worthy Nugget #9.1
Priority 1: Bare minimum emergency fund of one month's average expenses

Net Worthy Nugget #9.2
Priority 2: Employer matched 401(k)/TSP-type plan contributions, if available

Net Worthy Nugget #9.3
Priority 3: Debts with double-digit APR (10% or higher)

Net Worthy Nugget #9.4
Priority 4: COMBINED priority, paid proportionately: paying debts with single-digit APR and filling your emergency fund to its full eventual required level

Net Worthy Nugget #9.5
Priority 5: Max out IRA

Net Worthy Nugget #9.6

Priority 6: Max out employer 401(k)/TSP-type plan, if available

Net Worthy Nugget #9.7

Priority 7: Advanced savings and investment options

Net Worthy Nugget #9.X

Priority X: Buy a house, if and when it makes sense for you

"Just Tell Me What to Do!"

Preface to Chapter 9 from Chris

You're one of only a few passengers in small private airplane when the plane suddenly veers off course. You're horrified to see that the pilot has slumped over, completely unconscious. In a panic, you jump out of your seat. The only thing you can think of to do is to scramble into the empty co-pilot's seat and try to reach somebody on the radio.

Miraculously, the control tower at a nearby airfield answers your frantic plea for help. You and your fellow passengers might get out of this alive after all! But you can barely believe your ears when you hear the control tower say in an upbeat, cheerful voice, "You know, that dial in front of you is an altimeter, which is probably going to come in really handy before we're finished here. But before we get to any of that 'land the plane' stuff, there's a really interesting story about how altimeters were invented in the first place. It all started way back in . . ."

"Stop!" you scream into the radio. "I don't care! *Just tell me what to do!*" Sometimes, that's the only thing that matters. You need someone who knows what they're talking about to simply *tell you what to do*. Exactly. Step by step. Clearly and succinctly. And nothing else, thank you very much.

Welcome to Chapter 9. This is where we're just going to tell you what to do, exactly, step by step. Compared to the previous chapters, this will read more like a pilot's operating manual. The nuggets are short, in a very specific order, and every word matters. The image that summarizes this chapter's content looks a little bit like a flowchart in disguise—because it is.

Like the other chapters, there's also some color commentary—notes from Claire and me, and a few spotlights—for those who prefer a more complete explanation from the control tower. But they're clearly marked as such, and they're optional. The essential basics are in the nuggets themselves.

It's called "The Right Things in the Right Order" because building your net worth in today's complex financial world really is, at its core, like landing a plane. Trial and error, following your passion, or trying to copy what all the other planes seem to be doing are not great strategies.

When your financial bathtub is full, you can use your financial independence any way you want to, in full accordance with your dreams, your deepest values, and your life priorities. There are countless ways you can express yourself and leave your mark on the world. But how you get the financial bathtub filled in the first place is another matter. There are lots of wrong ways, there are many high-risk/low-probability ways, and there's the Net Worthy way. The Net Worthy way is based on solid, proven principles. It avoids risks, it relies heavily on the immense power of compound interest, it takes full advantage of federal tax incentives, and it emphasizes shielding yourself from the worst kinds of financial danger as early in your financial life as possible. And it will work every time, if you follow the steps in order.

If you want to learn about every single aspect of personal finance that you're likely to encounter throughout your life, with all the context, all the background, and all the reasoning supporting each point, there are some excellent books that we could recommend. Of course, they're huge. But maybe your frame of mind is more along the lines of, "I'm soooo stressed about all this money stuff, and I have no idea where to even start! Would somebody who knows what they're talking about please just tell me what to do?!" If that's you—good. We'll start telling you what to do, exactly, right now. Turn the page.

The Road to Financial Independence

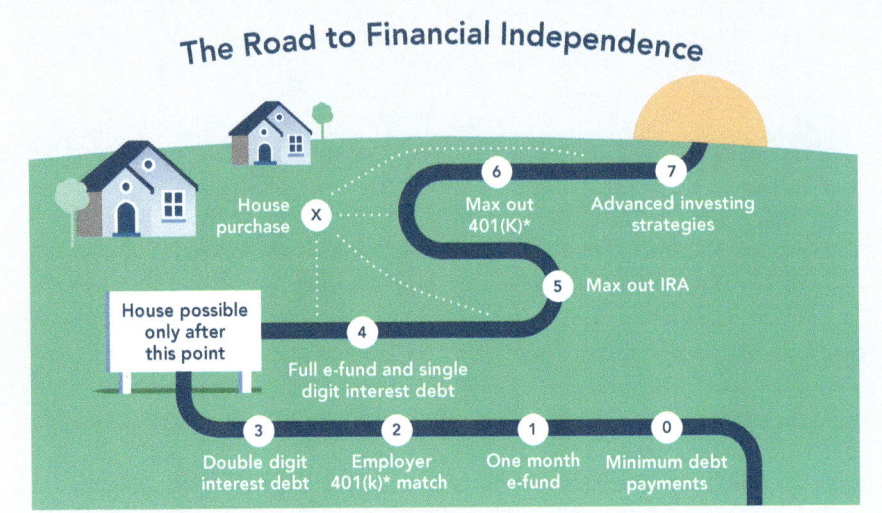

- 7 — Advanced investing strategies
- 6 — Max out 401(K)*
- 5 — Max out IRA
- 4 — Full e-fund and single digit interest debt
- 3 — Double digit interest debt
- 2 — Employer 401(k)* match
- 1 — One month e-fund
- 0 — Minimum debt payments
- X — House purchase

House possible only after this point

401(k)* refers to all 401(k)/TSP type plans, including 403(b) and 457 plans

Spotlight: Chapter 9 Operator's Manual

How this Chapter Works

When your financial life feels like one nasty surprise after another, it can suck the energy and passion out of all the other parts of your life. You probably already understand this. Now imagine the opposite. You're debt free, you know exactly what you're doing financially, and you're making solid, steady progress toward a bright financial future. Even though the journey to your ultimate goal of true financial independence is a long-term proposition, with the payoff far in the future—you get to feel an amazing sense of control, empowerment, and security right now. That peace of mind is profound, and it quickly extends to the other parts of your life. To reap those rewards, though, you need to buckle down and get started, so let's do this.

The starting point for this chapter is for you to have already achieved a positive Monthly Gap, which means that your average monthly income exceeds your average monthly expenses. Congratulations, because that's a huge milestone in itself. It may have been easy, or it may have taken lots of time, struggle, hard lessons, and tough decisions. Maybe you've used every scrap of advice from the previous Net Worthy chapters, including the Financial Dashboard in Chapter 8, or maybe you've arrived here completely on your own.

No matter. Your ins now consistently exceed your outs, so you now have some money each month that you can use to improve your financial future.

The question is: exactly what do you do with that money you've now managed to free up every month? Or maybe another way to put it is, what do you do first? It seems like everybody's got an opinion. Pay off your student loans early. Invest. Knock down those credit card bills. Buy a house. Go on a far-flung YOLO adventure. You're not sure yourself, and at times any of these can sound like a good idea.

So what do you do? Answering that question is the whole purpose of this chapter. It's not enough to just do the right things with your positive gap—you've got to do the right things *in the right order*. Here's the plan: Once you achieve a positive Monthly Gap, use this specific sequence of priorities to decide what to do with the gap dollars:

- **Priority 0:** Total minimum required debt payment (already included in average monthly expenses)

- **Priority 1:** Bare minimum emergency fund of one month's average expenses

- **Priority 2:** Employer matched 401(k)/TSP-type plan contributions, if available

- **Priority 3:** Debts with double-digit APR (10% or higher)

- **Priority 4:** COMBINED priority, paid proportionately: paying debts with single-digit APR and filling your emergency fund to its full eventual required level

- **Priority 5:** Max out IRA

- **Priority 6:** Max out employer 401(k)/TSP-type plan, if available

- **Priority 7:** Advanced savings and investment options

- **Priority X:** Buy a house, if and when it makes sense for you. In this chapter, we'll go through this sequence of priorities, one at a time. If a given priority does not apply to you, just skip it and go on to the next one. In keeping with the structure of the previous chapters, each priority is its own Net Worthy Nugget.

As usual, the Net Worthy Navigator App is designed to be used seamlessly with this chapter; the sequence of priorities is exactly the same. Enter in your own financial picture, and the app will tell you exactly how to deploy your gap, down to the penny. The app does the number crunching, while this chapter explains the exact prioritization sequence, and why.

Net Worthy Nugget #9.0

Priority 0: Total minimum required debt payment

Firstly, you should have already have clocked the fact this first nugget is Priority 0, not Priority 1. This is basement-level, foundational stuff, required before you can even consider building upward. Luckily, it's something you're probably already doing. For one thing, your Minimum Required Debt Payments are included in your Financial Dashboard, derived directly from your Debt Inventory and Analysis (or DIA) worksheet. The Dashboard considers these expenses so non-negotiable that they're counted as *part of* your ongoing monthly expenses. So, if you've been using these Chapter 8 tools to move your Monthly Gap from negative to positive—and we'll just assume you have—making your minimum debt payments each month is already solidly part of your monthly routine. If you haven't been using the Dashboard, the people you owe minimum monthly payments to have an unmistakable habit of making sure you remember each month and setting off alarms if you're late. So either way, it's no surprise to you that these payments are top priority.

But even if you're already doing a pretty good job of this, pretty good isn't good enough now that you've reached this stage of your financial life. To put a checkmark next to Priority 0, you've got to have it completely nailed down, every single month, every single minimum debt payment, without fail. You know you've got this covered when you've reached the point that the process is so automated, you don't even have to think about it. You're miles beyond the point of needing to be reminded by your creditors, let alone ever getting flagged for being late. No matter how tempted you might be to divert some money to other priorities, you never divert it from making your minimum required debt payments—the consequences for doing so are just too extreme. This is no time to start back down the path of increased debt, more interest, and credit score hits. Start here, with just the minimum required payments, and trust the Net Worthy progression to take you where you need to go.

Once you're making your minimum monthly payments consistently, on autopilot, you can move on to the next Priority.

Net Worthy Nugget #9.1

Priority 1: Bare minimum emergency fund of one month's average expenses

Your emergency fund is there to catch you when you fall or when unexpected but unavoidable bills threaten to sink your financial ship. If you lose your job, have a big medical emergency, or just need to get your car fixed so you can get to work, your emergency fund is there to make sure you can keep your head above water.

Eventually, you'll have a big, muscular emergency fund to protect you for several months, just as we discussed in Chapter 2. For now, however, we want to focus on the very urgent business of accumulating just one month's worth of expenses—the barest of bare minimums. While paying off all your debt is generally the highest priority, having some form of financial safety net is arguably even more important when you have creditors to pay. Think of it like your financial seat belt, the most basic safety precaution imaginable. There are a lot of other things you'll eventually need to do to prevent calamity, and we'll get there. For right now, though, just buckle up before starting the car.

Dedicate your entire Monthly Gap to this month after month, until you have one full month of expenses set aside. It's that critical.

Net Worthy Nugget #9.2

Priority 2: Employer matched 401(k)/TSP-type plan contributions, if available

Now that you've laid a foundation—you're paying down your debts and you have a small E-Fund safety net—things start to get interesting.

Saving for retirement is important, but at this stage in your Financial Development there are other uses for your monthly income that are more beneficial in the long run. The sole exception to this is if your employer offers 401(k)/TSP-type plan matching.

Having your employer contribute to your 401(k)/TSP-type plan is basically the only time in your adult life someone who isn't your grandma will give you free money. And it's not just once—they'll keep right on giving you free money, paycheck after paycheck, up to a certain limit. And then they'll do it again next year. The best part is, all you have to do is sign up and make contributions to your own retirement fund—basically paying your future self and getting a bonus for the effort. Not all employers offer this perk, but if yours does, they're essentially saying, "Hey, we found all this extra money laying around. Any chance you want some?"

Find out if your employer offers matching funds for your 401(k)/TSP-type plan contributions. Contact HR, Payroll, Employee Benefits, or whatever part of your employer's organization sends out 401(k)/TSP-type plan-related communications. If you're not sure, ask (gasp!) your boss—or a longer-tenured coworker. If your employer doesn't match, skip this step and move on to Priority 3. But if they do, check to see if your 401(k)/TSP-type plan includes a Roth option.

In Chapter 7, we discussed the difference between traditional and Roth accounts and the relative benefits of paying taxes on your contributions now or after retirement. There are arguments on both sides about which is better, but what was true for your parents' generation no longer really applies. The whole point of the work you're doing now is that you will have more money, and more freedom, down the road. In most cases, therefore, we recommend opting for a Roth account. Go ahead and eat the income taxes now in exchange for tax-free growth and some serious long-term compounding.

If the Roth option is not available, or if you've got your own reasons for opting against it, you should still be taking advantage of employer matching in a traditional (sometimes called pre-tax) 401(k)/TSP-type plan. In either case, now's the time to make sure you're enrolled and start making monthly contributions. Of course, there's a limit to your employer's generosity, and that limit is typically an annual, not lifetime, one. So, keep making contributions until you hit that annual limit, then stop and resume again once a new year begins.

Here's one last twist: Amazingly enough, a few employers will contribute directly into your 401(k)/TSP-type plan account whether you contribute anything or not! This is free money, too, but it isn't a match. Certain federal government employees get automatic contributions into their TSP (Thrift Savings Plan, a program like 401(k)s) accounts each year, in the amount of 1% of their salaries. Some private companies will make direct contributions into your 401(k)/TSP-type plan on a profit-sharing basis—when the company has a good year, they'll share the wealth with their employees. In bad years, they'll share a smaller percentage or maybe nothing at all.

As wonderful as these kinds of direct employer contributions are, don't confuse them with a match. If you're eligible, you're going to benefit whether you put anything in or not—so don't. Instead, go directly to priority 3.

The One Time It Might Make Sense to Say "No" to Free Money

A Note from Chris

Back in Chapter 7, we didn't pull any punches about describing an employer match—we called it "the single best financial deal you will ever get in your lifetime." It's free money, pure and simple. You can't lose. That's why throughout this book, you consistently see the same advice—whatever you do, take full advantage of every employer match dollar available to you. Always. Well . . . almost always. Let's review how employer matches work. All employers above a certain size are required to offer 401(k)/TSP-type plans to their employees. They're not required to offer matches, but about two thirds of them do anyway, to help them attract the best employees. Let's say you work for Grandma's Apple Pie Co, and Grandma offers a 50% match up to 6% of your salary. That means that for every dollar you put into your 401(k)/TSP-type plan account, Grandma puts in another 50 cents, up to a limit of 6% of your salary. For example, if you make $40,000 a year, once you've put in $2,400 (6% of your salary), you've now hit Grandma's limit, and the party stops. Of course, you can keep putting money in, but Grandma won't be throwing in the extra 50 cents past that point. Even so, by that time, Grandma has given—repeat,

given—you $1,200, straight into your account. It gets better. That $1,200 is now all set to grow, tax-free, for decades, so that 40 years from now, even after allowing for inflation, Grandma's gift to you will be worth ten times that amount, *on top of* all the compound interest that your own contributions have earned. And next year, you can repeat this whole happy sequence of events all over again, but your salary will probably be a little higher, so Grandma's gift will be a little bigger. Such a deal!

Hmmm, but wait. There may some fine print in Grandma's plan that deserves some close scrutiny: it's called "vesting." Put yourself in Grandma's shoes. Imagine if you'd hired a brand-new employee, and that person contributed $2,400 into their 401(k)/TSP-type plan account over the next six months, which means you rewarded them with a generous $1,200 match along the way. Now imagine how you'd feel if that employee quit the following day, taking the entire $3,600 and plopping it straight into the 401(k)/TSP-type plan at their new job over at Pete's Pie Palace? That's going to make for a grumpy Grandma, which is why vesting was invented. A vesting schedule determines how much of the match you can take with you if you leave a job, depending on how long you've worked for the matching employer.

A vesting schedule allows Grandma to say, "I can't stop you from leaving. But I can have a say about just how much of my generous match you can take along with you." A typical vesting schedule might specify that you can take 25% of the match with you when you leave, for each year that you worked for that employer. So, work two years there, and you can take half of the match with you. At that rate, the match is all yours to take after 4 years. But sometimes, vesting is set up as an all-or-none proposition. If Grandma had gotten burned a few times too many, she might set up a vesting arrangement of zero vesting before 5 years, 100% vesting after. Remember, matches are purely voluntary on the part of the employer, so they're entitled to set up whatever kind of vesting schedule they want. Grandma's money, Grandma's rules.

If that's the kind of deal you have with Grandma, now you need to carefully consider how likely it is that you'll still be working there past the 5-year point. If you believe it's a long shot you'll still be a member of Grandma's upper-crust team five years from now, then you're better off thinking of Grandma just like any other non-matching employer—in other words, you'd be wiser to attack your credit card debt or E-Fund first. Grandma's free money just has too many strings attached.

Net Worthy Nugget #9.3

Priority 3: Debts with double-digit APR (10% or higher)

OK, by now you have a little bit of a safety net and you've been paying the minimums on all your debt balances for a while, whittling them down bit by bit. You may even be contributing to a 401(k)/TSP-type plan. Things are starting to shape up. Now it's time to tackle the Debt Monster head on.

As if we haven't drilled this home enough already: debt is bad news. The more interest you pay per year, the worse debt is. Most people have multiple types of debt with varying interest rates, and it's important to prioritize paying off those with highest rates—the most expensive debts—first. These are the bills that are doing to most damage to you in the long run—big minimum payments and high interest charges means you have to devote way too much of your income to servicing these debts. Getting rid of the highest-APR balances first will make a huge difference in how quickly you can pay off lower-interest balances and start moving into the yellow phase.

Luckily, in Chapter 8, you learned how to organize your debts by APR in your DIA worksheet. That will come in handy here. Once you've progressed through the first three priorities, you want to focus on eliminating any debt with an APR over 10%. This will include most credit cards and other unsecured debts. Mortgages, student loans, and other types of lower-interest debt will be addressed later.

Once you've established which of your debts meet the Priority 3 definition of more than 10% APR, the next step is to determine whether your stack of high interest debt is small enough to be attacked with traditional measures, or if *advanced* tactics are warranted. Here's how you decide: add up all the outstanding balances that carry double-digit APRs, and then divide that amount by your Monthly Gap. The result tells you how many months it will take to pay this entire debt category down to zero.

If your answer is less than six months, no further words are necessary—go for it. Your gap now goes toward chopping down that debt as fast as possible. But if the answer is more than six months? You'll need to dig a little deeper into the bag of tricks: the *balance transfer* credit card.

Navigating Balance Transfers, the Safe and Smart Way

A Note from Claire

In Chapter 8, I discussed a feature of many credit cards that can be used to give you a bit of extra time to pay off credit card or loan balances that would otherwise accumulate unnecessary interest charges. We don't recommend that you rely on balance transfers as a stalling tactic to put off paying down debts, but they can be a pretty handy tool if you have a high-interest balance that you can't pay off within the next six months. When analyzing your options, you should focus on four important factors:

- 0% Interest

- Lowest possible transfer fee, preferably $0

- Annual Fee

- Interest-free period of 12 months or more

First, take a look at your current credit cards to see if any of them offer an interest-free balance transfer option. The interest-free aspect is crucial, because most credit cards allow for balance transfers, but many of them charge higher interest rates on transferred balances than they do on normal balances.

Secondly, consider the impact of fees. Balance transfer fees are typically anywhere from 1%-5% of the transfer amount. Since we're talking only about debt that you can't pay off in six months or less, we can assume it's a sizable chunk of change. While getting 0% interest is the most important factor, tacking on an additional 5% may end up negating the benefits of the interest-free period altogether, so minimizing transfer fees is almost as crucial.

In the same way, a card with a lofty annual fee isn't really doing you any favors. Depending on how big your balances are, you might prioritize delaying interest charges over a small (relatively speaking) increase in your total balance, but you should generally aim for a card without an annual fee whenever possible.

The importance of the interest-free period term is something you'll need to assess for yourself. We recommend at least 12 months, but the bigger your balance, the longer you'll need to pay it off. In general, the longer the better.

Luckily, there are several options for low-fee (or free) balance transfers that will give you 12 months (or more) of interest-free wiggle room. If none of your current cards offer an advantageous option, consider opening the Chase Slate card, which offers 15 full months of 0% interest on balance transfers. Even better, transfers made within 60 days of account opening incur no transfer fee—which can mean serious savings. Slate also has no annual fee, making it the best of all worlds.

Now, if you didn't raise an eyebrow at these shameless plugs, I'd be a little disappointed. But no, we don't receive any advertising or referral revenue from Chase (or any other credit card issuer). I'm just a big fan of their products, and, after a thorough review of the competition—in both a personal and professional capacity—it's genuinely just the best balance transfer option available right now. That being said, definitely don't apply for a credit card based solely on my recommendations—always do your own research. While the Slate has been the top of the heap for a while now, new credit cards are being offered all the time, so make sure you weigh your options before pulling the trigger.

If you have a high-APR loan balance or other high-interest debt that you'd need to pay with cash, your options may be a bit more limited. Most cards only allow transfers of credit card balances, which wouldn't work for other types of debt. However, some cards—like the Barclay Arrival Plus Mastercard—do allow you to transfer funds to a loan or checking account. Unfortunately, if your high-APR balance isn't on a credit card, you may have to sacrifice something to get flexible transfer options.

The Barclay Arrival Plus, for example, carries an annual fee and a 1%-5% transfer fee, so it's isn't a perfect product. Do the math to determine whether the interest-free period offered by a given product will save you more money than the card will cost in fees. If so, you may have to dig a tiny bit deeper into debt in order to claw your way out of it.

Regardless of whether you can knock out your high-APR debts in less than six months or need a little balance transfer help, focus on paying off these balances completely before you move on to the next step. Other than making contributions to a matched 401(k)/TSP-type plan each month and making minimum payments on your other debts, this should be your sole focus. Eliminating these balances might take a while, and that's OK. Be consistent, and make the biggest payments you can each month. Once those balances are paid off, you can move on to the next step.

Net Worthy Nugget #9.4

Priority 4: COMBINED priority, paid proportionately: paying debts with single-digit APR and filling your emergency fund to its full eventual required level

At this point, you deserve a pretty big pat on the back. For many people, credit card debts are a huge hurdle, so paying off all your high-interest debts is a big achievement. If nothing else, not having big balances accruing interest day after day will reduce your baseline stress level. From here on out, you may even find that this whole process is sort of . . . fun. You still have plenty of work to do, but you'll notice that crushing "I'll never get out from under this" feeling that comes with long-term debt doesn't weigh on you so heavily. And, if you feel like you're picking up steam a lot faster than you did before, that's not just the stress-relief talking, that's real live *math* talking, my friend.

Compound interest is the most powerful force in the financial world, and it can work either for you or against you. Now that your highest interest debt is paid off, compound interest isn't working against you nearly as furiously as it had been. Don't look now, but that positive gap that was so important to establish in the first place? It's growing! This means your other, lower-interest debts can be paid off more quickly. It also means you can take another look at your emergency fund. In fact, those two things are so important—and so crucial to move into the next phase of your financial development—that we've given them equal priority. We'll use a divide-and-conquer approach that will result in you reaching these twin goals simultaneously, launching you into the yellow phase.

By now you should be in the habit of revising your Financial Dashboard monthly, and you might notice yourself smiling a little more each time you do it, because the picture is looking brighter and brighter. Get ready for more of that, because Priority 4 is where your financial improvement momentum really starts to accelerate. For starters, your debt balances are melting away. That will automatically bring down your Minimum Required Debt Payments, which in turn improves your Monthly Gap by still another notch. Your gap is then deployed to reduce your debt still further, as well as to further strengthen your E-Fund—and so this powerful, perfectly balanced, and self-accelerating cycle continues.

All you have to do is maintain your gap (by maintaining your income level and spending discipline), and then use it in the priority sequence we've just described. If you do that, success is inevitable. It's just a matter of time before all of your non-mortgage debt is gone, and you've got an impenetrable, perfectly-sized E-Fund, protecting you and your dependents from any unanticipated financial harm.

Think of how much progress you've made! By powering through Priority 4, you've put yourself in a rock-solid financial position—and you've set the stage for even more explosive progress.

Spotlight on "Combined Priority, Paid Proportionally"

A Mini-Case Study

OK, guilty as charged. We've tried to use geek-free language for all the Net Worthy Nuggets, opting for simple everyday speech wherever possible. But "combined priority, paid proportionally" is a bit of a mouthful. It's simpler than it sounds, though, so let's run through an example.

Kam has worked hard to get his spending down and his income up, and now his Monthly Gap has reached all the way to a positive $1,000. Of course, he always makes his Priority 0 minimum monthly payments on his debt; more about his debt picture in a minute. He's managed to stash away one month's expenses in a savings account, so he can put a check mark by Priority 1. Kam's a freelancer, so he has no 401(k)/TSP-type plan employer match available to him, which means he can skip Priority 2. Priority 3 took a while, but he finally paid off all his credit card balances. He still regularly uses credit cards, but now he pays off the full balances every month and pays no interest at all.

That means Kam has arrived at Priority 4. Therefore, he's focused on just two financial goals: filling up his E-Fund and paying off all his remaining debt.

Let's look at his E-Fund situation first. Kam's expenses now consistently run at $3,000 per month. Since we already know that he has one month's expenses stashed away, that means his E-fund balance is currently exactly $3,000. His risk profile is middle of the road, so he's set a goal of 6 months E-Fund coverage. So his E-Fund goal is $18,000 (6 months x $3,000 monthly expenses). Since he already has $3,000 saved, he has $15,000 more to go before he can consider his E-Fund full.

What about debt? Now that his double-digit APR debt is all paid off, he's down to just one single-digit APR debt—but it's a big one. Kam owes $45,000 in student loans.

Now we're ready to answer the question. Kam's Monthly Gap is $1,000, his E-Fund has $15,000 left to go, and his single-digit APR debt balance is $45,000.

Which is more important, filling up his E-Fund or paying off that student loan? It's a tie! They're equally important; that's what we mean by "combined priority." So what does Kam do with his $1,000 gap each month? That's where "paid proportionally" comes into play.

1. First, add the two goals together: $15,000 + $45,000 = $60,000.

2. The E-Fund proportion is 25% ($15,000 divided into $60,000).

3. The student loan proportion is 75% ($45,000 divided into $60,000)

4. Therefore, every month Kam puts $250 (25% of his $1,000 gap) into his E-Fund, and . . .

5. . . . he pays $750 toward his student loan (75% of the gap).

It may take Kam several years, but he's got his plan: every month, another $250 into the E-Fund, and $750 towards his student loan. If he can increase his Monthly Gap (by earning more money or reducing his monthly expenses), he can pick up speed by paying more—yet he'll continue to *maintain* that 25%/75% split. And, he'll just keep on doing that, month after month, until both goals are met. Then he can move on to Priority 5 and exit the dreaded red phase forever!

Net Worthy Nugget #9.5

Priority 5: Max out IRA

Goodbye, Red Phase!

A Note from Claire

Do you realize what just happened? You may have been working so hard on your financial priorities that you missed an epic milestone If you look fast, you can still see it in your rear-view mirror. That's right—you've made it out of the red phase and into the yellow. Bravo!

I think here you can safely take a small break, have a glass of champagne, and bask in your accomplishment. Paying off all your debt is no small feat. Plus, you've accumulated a healthy emergency fund, which will provide an important sense of financial and emotional security as you move into more aggressive investing techniques. Right now, at this moment, you are better prepared for your future than you've ever been, and you should take the time to feel really, really good about that.

The truth is that many, many people never make it out of the red phase. Stressed out and overwhelmed, the average person just lives with rotating credit card balances and an unending sense of financial doom. Not you! You've finally made it out, so now's the time to set a firm intention to never go back. You've definitely earned a bit of a celebration, but don't let a few glasses of sparkling wine turn into a last-minute trip to the Caribbean courtesy of your E-Fund. It may be tempting to splurge—after all, you've earned it, right?—but delaying gratification now will pay off many times over down the road.

So, no, you're not done yet; there's definitely still work to do. But if you thought you felt good after you knocked out your high-APR balances, then get ready for a burst of dopamine like you've never known. Being debt-free is the No. 1 most important step to reaching

> financial independence, and it's already behind you. From here on out, you'll be picking up momentum like never before, knowing that every month you're making huge strides toward financial freedom. Well done. Now let's get back to work.

Now that's you've one-two-punched your way out of the red phase, you get to start putting your money to work. As usual, we're going to focus on maximizing the power of compound interest to turn your money into . . . more money.

You may or may not already be contributing to a 401(k)/TSP-type plan at work (depending on whether your employer offers matching contributions). Either way, it's time to open a new type of retirement account—an IRA. Just like with your 401(k)/TSP-type plan, we typically recommend that you opt for a Roth account to minimize your tax burden down the road.

The next step is choosing a target-date fund to invest in within your IRA account. In choosing your IRA and your investment fund, your primary goal is to have the lowest possible combination of fees.

Once you've made your selections, devote your Monthly Gap to your IRA, month after month, until you've reached the annual maximum. For 2018, the maximum amount you could contribute to all your IRA accounts (in case you have more than one) was $5,500, or $6,500 if you're over 50. Once you've reached this limit, move on to the next Priority.

If you're married but file separately, earn more than $120,000 as a single filer or $189,000 as a married couple filing jointly, the amount that you can contribute per year may be reduced, so be sure to read up on the limits that apply to you. You can find this information easily by searching for "2018 IRA Contribution Limits IRS." Try to use the IRS website whenever possible, just to be sure you're getting accurate information.

You Want What's Best for Your Kids, But Are You Sure You Know What It Is?

Note from Chris

Life's most stressful, urgent financial priorities are now behind you, once and for all. There are still some serious prioritization decisions to make, but now you're asking yourself intriguing, heady questions like "What's the best thing to accomplish next?" instead of "OMG, which financial demon is closest to catching me?" As we noted earlier, if the red phase is a grind, the yellow phase is a glide.

But if you have kids, or plan to, you might be feeling unsettled about priorities as you enter the yellow phase. Some might think of this as a good problem to have, but it's still a tough question: your own financial independence vs. a college savings plan for your child(ren)? Well, get ready for the fight of the century—it's the battle of the financial priorities, and because both of them have such a strong emotional pull it's going to be a doozy! As this whole chapter is making very clear: You have to be very explicit when it comes to setting financial priorities. High, medium, or low doesn't work. A specific ranked ordering, from highest to lowest, does.

So who's the winner? Which of these two is the highest financial priority? Easy. Your own financial independence comes first. You can also set a goal of paying for your child's/children's college education, but that comes *after* your own financial independence.

"What? Isn't that incredibly selfish? And isn't college for my kids coming up a lot faster than my own retirement? No way am I going to let my past financial mistakes jeopardize my child's chance at a better life!" If that's your initial reaction, I completely understand. No, really, I do. I may be a personal finance fanatic, but I'm also the dad of two adult, college-educated sons, and a veteran of many college expense bills. My own financial advisor dad had to teach me when I was a young parent, that those feelings of "kids first, me last" are well-intentioned, but they're misguided.

Here's the most important reason: Most people overestimate their ability to keep working in their later years. It might sound noble to say, "I'll just keep working until I die if that's what it takes to pay for kids' college," and you probably sincerely mean it. But the truth is that your health, your ability to stay current with ever-escalating job skill requirements, the retirement of your most loyal supporters and proponents, and your willingness to move to where the jobs are will very likely spell the end of your income-earning days whether you're ready or not. And if you're not ready, you're going to need a financial lifeline. Guess who that's likely to be? Yup—your child.

It gets worse, because of the timing. They'll probably need to start providing for you in their 20s and 30s, which is the prime time for them to getting out of their own red phases, which in turn means they'll be late to the best parts of the compound interest party. See what's happening? Your decision to underfund your own retirement could very well end up causing them to underfund their own. This is exactly—*exactly!*—the kind of life for them that you were trying to avoid in the first place. So don't do it.

This logic might seem brutal the first time you hear it. But it's not just me, it's what you'll hear from a consensus of financial planners. Here's a way to think about it that might make it easier to take.

In Chapter 2, where we cover the idea of having "enough" in your financial bathtub, "enough" isn't a fixed, single number—it's a question of degree:

- Point A: Enough for a comfortable, but no-frills lifestyle

- Point B: Enough to maintain current lifestyle

- Point C: Enough for a dream lifestyle

So your first priority is your own financial independence, but only up to point A. Then you can direct money into a 529 (or similar) college savings plan—with similar "point A" thinking about the amount. Once that's locked in, you can go back to putting a little more icing on your own financial independence cake. Take it from me: handling it in this specific order will give you an incredible sense of accomplishment and peace of mind. In this showdown battle of the financial priorities, you've created a way for both to win—but in the prioritized order that makes the most sense for everybody concerned.

Net Worthy Nugget #9.6

Priority 6: Max out employer 401(k)/TSP-type plan,
if available

If you ever thought the path to financial independence was going to be a straight line, think again.

Investing for your future requires doing the right things in the right order, and now's the time to finish what you started a while back—unless your employer doesn't offer a 401(k)/TSP-type plan at all, in which case you can skip ahead to the next Priority.

You've already put in a lot of work establishing some minimum retirement savings, either through an employer-matched 401(k)/TSP-type plan, a Roth IRA, or both. Assuming that you've already maxed out the available free money from your employer and hit the annual maximum for your IRA, it's time to loop back around to that 401(k)/TSP-type plan and start making some unmatched contributions. Or, if your employer only offers an unmatched 401(k)/TSP-type plan and you skipped Priority 2 as a result, now's the time to enroll and start contributing.

Either way, continue devoting your Monthly Gap to your 401(k)/TSP-type plan month after month until you reach the maximum annual contribution limit. For 2018, that's $18,500 a year. Remember, however, that these numbers may change in 2019 and beyond, as the IRS periodically increases contribution limits. Always make sure to verify the maximum contribution limit that applies to you each year to ensure you're making the most of your tax-deferred savings.

Finally, you may be ready to start contributing to your 401(k)/TSP-type plan—but it might not be ready for you. Sometimes, you can only sign up (open your account and begin making contributions into it) during specified periods. In other cases, new hires may need to meet a length-of-employment requirement (six months or a year, for example), before becoming eligible to sign up. If either of these is preventing you from contributing to your 401(k)/TSP-type plan right away, just park that money in your E-Fund until the coast is clear.

Spotlight on Investment Fees: Part 2

A Mini-Case Study, continued (from Chapter 7)

By this time you might well be wondering why we're recommending such a jumpy, back-and-forth investment strategy. 401(k)/TSP-type plan, then IRA, then back to 401(k)/TSP-type plan, all in the same year. There's a one-word reason for that: fees. Back in Chapter 7, we got a close-up view of how investment fees work by considering two different ways of investing in a 2045 target-date fund. To refresh your memory, the two ways were:

- A Roth IRA from Vanguard, where target-date funds carry an industry-low expense ratio of just 16 basis points.

- Your employer's 401(k)/TSP-type plan program, which offers an actively managed 2045 target-date fund with an expense ratio of 60 basis points. On top of that, the plan charges an administrative fee of 40 basis points, so your overall investment fees come to 100 basis points.

If that's the only information you have to work with, then the Roth IRA is the easy choice. But real life is usually a little more complicated, so let's add a few more facts:

- To keep the numbers round and simple, let's say your salary is $50,000, and you're committed to a magic number of 20%. That means you'll invest a total of $10,000 per year (20% of $50,000).

- Good news, and more round numbers: your employer offers a 50% match up to 5% of your salary.

- The 401(k)/TSP-type plan program has a schedule that allows you to be fully vested after 4 years. You like your employer, and you have no intentions of leaving anytime soon. In other words, it's much more likely than not that you'll end up becoming fully vested.

It sounds more complicated than it is. It's actually pretty easy to figure out the sequence that you should step through:

Step 1: Take the match! You'll never get a better deal than an employer match, but it's capped at 5% of your salary. You're going to take every last bit of matching that you're eligible for, so the very first $2,500 (5% of $50,000) you invest goes to the target-date fund in your 401(k)/TSP-type plan. Your employer generously contributes another $1,250 into your account on top of that. By the way, if you're only now realizing that you're eligible for a match but not taking advantage of it, you don't need to wait for the next annual open enrollment period to jump on board. Most employers allow changes to the contribution percentage—either up or down—every pay period. Talk to your employer's HR or Payroll to get the details.

Step 2: Minimize fees! Once that $2,500 has been invested and matched, now you turn to the Roth IRA at Vanguard and its ultra-low fee level of 16 basis points. But the annual limit on IRA contributions is $5,500, so you'll have to stop there.

Step 3: Back to the 401(k)/TSP-type plan! So far, you've invested $2,500 in step 1 and $5,500 in step 2 for a total of $8,000. Since your investment goal for the year is $10,000, you still have $2,000 to go. You don't like those 100 basis points, but it's still your best remaining option—even with the fees, investing inside the tax-advantaged 401(k)/TSP-type plan account is still far better than investing without any tax advantage.

This three-step approach will save you fees, but it complicates your life a little bit compared to a one-step plan of just putting everything into the 401(k)/TSP-type plan program. Is it worth it? The first-year fee savings is only $42. But this fee-saving snowball is just getting started. Thanks to compound interest, you'll end up saving almost $8,000 over 30 years and more than $21,000 over 40! Not only that, your 401(k)/TSP-type plan may not have a Roth option. If it doesn't—and if you prefer Roth—this approach allows you to get more than half of your annual investment into a Roth plan. It may seem like a hassle to keep redirecting your investment dollars from one account to another and then back again every year. But like any habit, it gets much easier with repetition. When you think of it as a habit that will generate thousands of dollars for you in return for a few minutes of work per year, it's a no-brainer. Fees don't just add up, they *multiply* up, and that's why keeping them to a bare minimum is well worth the effort.

Net Worthy Nugget #9.7

Priority 7: Advanced savings and investment options

By now you've exhausted the tax-advantaged retirement savings options available to you, so it may be time to consider diving into other types of investment or saving options. Note that this does not mean that you stop maxing out your annual contributions to your IRA and 401(k)/TSP-type plan. Contributions should be automated to ensure you hit the annual limits through consistent monthly deferrals.

Same goes for your E-Fund and debt. If the balance of the former dips down, or the latter jumps up, prioritize rectifying that situation before you bulk up your investments. It's likely been a while since you started this journey, but you should still be revisiting your Dashboard regularly and making adjustments where necessary. If lifestyle or employment changes have altered your income, expenses, or risk profile, make sure your E-Fund balance accounts for those changes.

All that being said, you've maxed out on your 401(k)/TSP-type plan and/or IRA avenues, and you still have some positive gap dollars to put to work. What now? You move up to the next level, that elite financial category known as *advanced!*

In your new advanced status, you have a choice of three primary directions. There is no one right answer, so it's completely up to you. In other words, it's a nice kind of problem to have.

Here are the three directions:

- **Use tax-advantaged accounts, but not for your own retirement.** You can actually save and invest for other things, using that now-familiar 401(k)/TSP-type plan or IRA magic, without having to wait until age 59 ½ to get at the money! The two most popular examples are Health Savings Accounts (HSAs) and 529 college savings plans.

  You may already know that 529s are a great way to save and invest for your child's (or children's) future college education. What you may not know is that the beneficiary of a 529 doesn't have to be your child, it can be any "qualifying family member" (children, parents, spouses, siblings, first cousins, nieces/nephews and even aunts/uncles). Not only that, it's remarkably easy to change beneficiaries once a plan is underway. This opens up all kinds of possibilities for beginning a college savings plan even before a child is born; it also provides some easy solutions to the potential problem of over-saving for college. (If your child ends up getting scholarships or decides to skip college, you can just re-designate beneficiaries, even multiple times if you need to.) This landscape can be a little tricky tax-wise, so you'll want to check in with a qualified tax professional.

- **Continue to save for your own retirement, but not using tax-advantaged accounts.** Your 401(k)/TSP-type plan and/or IRA provide the best possible protection from taxes, but as you now know, they have annual limits. If your intention is to keep barreling toward financial independence as fast as possible, there are ways to continue investing that won't trigger an avalanche of income taxes. Welcome to the world of tax-efficient investing. It's not the same as a special account, but there are certain types of tax-savvy products and strategies you can utilize to keep the tax bit to a minimum. The range of products and risk-levels means you should speak to a qualified financial professional to ensure you choose the best option. As we discussed in Chapter 7, there aren't many times when we advise you to pay someone for financial help. However, having enough discretionary income to build a substantial non-retirement investment portfolio is definitely one of them. (As discussed in Chapter 7, look for an advisor who is a fiduciary.)

- **Spend more.** Why not? You've been giving your future self plenty of love to reach this point, and maybe your current self could use a little now! Not everyone wants to retire by 40, and some may be willing to delay complete independence in exchange for a little more luxury now. If you're contributing to your retirement accounts at a healthy pace, you may decide that you want to consciously increase your current spending to enjoy a little bit more freedom now. Perhaps you'd like to take a trip, upgrade your living situation, or enjoy a bit more of a social life. Maybe you'd like to give back to some worthy causes that are near and dear to your heart, knowing that you're finally financially able to make a difference in the lives of others.

  If your current Monthly Gap can accommodate those things without the temptation of accruing debt or dipping into your E-Fund, you absolutely can enjoy the fruits of your labor now. The key here is that your retirement contributions are automated and you keep your other Dashboard indicators stable. You'll still be securing your financial future, but you can also enjoy the present in a way you weren't able to before you began this journey.

Decisions, decisions! You may not have reached the green phase of financial independence yet, but you're starting to get a taste of the kinds of freedom and choices that are your reward for the hard work you've done taking control of your financial life.

Net Worthy Nugget #9.X

Priority X: Buy a house, if and when it makes sense for you

Priority X? What the X is *that* supposed to mean?

Here's the deal: buying a house requires some serious saving up—down payment, closing costs, first-time homeowner expenses (see Chapter 6). That's going to keep your Monthly Gap fully occupied for quite a while. But where this falls in the sequence of financial priorities can be very different for different people in different circumstances. So, you're going to evaluate your own circumstances and insert house-buying at the appropriate place for you. The X is a placeholder, up to you to decide on, including whether buying a house makes sense for you *ever*.

All the other financial priorities we're covering in this chapter fall into a natural sequence, because of how closely interrelated they are. But buying a house is a wild card. It can be a fantastic financial move, but not for everybody. In Chapter 6, we stressed that your personal situation, your job situation, and your financial situation should *all* come into alignment to support a decision to buy. If you're single and living alone, but you think that's likely to change in the next few years? Or if you love your job but keep hearing rumors that your employer might be acquired by an out-of-town competitor? These are not good times to buy a house, regardless of where you are in your progression through the other financial priorities.

Here's another bad time to buy a house: when you're still paying off high-interest credit card debt. Yes, renting is throwing money away, but buying a house while you're still wrestling with Visa bills is throwing it away *faster*. Or, when you haven't even built up a bare-minimum one-month E-Fund yet. So if you're an aspiring buyer, it's up to you to add "Buying A House" into your list of priorities, wherever it makes sense for you—but it never makes sense for anyone before Priority 3. Until then, keep chipping away, while continuing to rent as cheaply as you safely can.

So for the geeks in the house, X > 3. Putting it a little differently, the very earliest we advise you to buy would be at Priority 3½. If that's you, be forewarned—it's going to be a squeeze! In an ideal world, you'd have all your debt paid off (not just the high-interest debt), and you'd have your entire E-Fund built (not just the first month's expenses), before you'd start the house-buying process.

But that's just too unrealistic of a standard in today's financial world. Too many people with large but low-interest student loans (as one example) would be left on the house-buying sidelines for too long—and at some point, the missed opportunity to build tax-advantaged equity in a house overtakes the relatively modest interest rates you're dealing with. So if you've decided that your X is 3½:

1. Keep making the required minimum monthly payments on your remaining (low-interest) debt.

2. Go ahead and take your E-Fund down to one month's expenses, but *not below*.

3. Set your house-savings fund goal at 27% of your target price range.

4. Now, pour the entire remainder of your gap into achieving that goal.

5. Once you've bought and moved in, continue to keep expenses as low as possible, so you can . . .

6. Attack Priority 4 (pay off *all* your debt while building your E-Fund all the way up) with high energy!

Following the "Priority 3½" plan can really pay off for you in the long run, but it does take an extended period of serious financial commitment. If there are multiple people in the household, everybody should understand what that means, and be "all in." If that sounds like too much of a grind though, you can slow things down, rent for a longer time, and maybe go for a Priority 4½ strategy. Or 5½. Hey, plenty of people put it all the way off until it's Priority 7½. You can also change your mind along the way as circumstances in your life change. There's no one right answer for everyone, so here's your chance to write this chapter of your path to financial independence in the way that fits you the best.

The Payoff? It's Whatever You Want It to Be

A Final Note from Claire

We said in the beginning that focusing on—really prioritizing—your own financial progress would enable you to participate in and enjoy your own life more fully, and here we are. You're probably not ready to call it quits on the day job just yet, but the work you've put in thus far is going to pay off right away in some unexpected ways. Even though your account balances aren't where you'd eventually like them to be, you have the knowledge that you are consistently doing the right things to get them there, and I can't overemphasize how much of a difference that peace of mind is going to make in your day-to-day stress level.

At 32, I'm still on my own financial journey. Given that I enjoy a more nomadic lifestyle and spend more on jet fuel than I do on gasoline, my financial goals may be different than the average person's. I'm more likely to buy raw land in Guatemala than a house in the Seattle suburbs, and my partner and I prefer corgis to kids. But that doesn't mean carrying around thousands of dollars in student and credit card debt from my unscrupulous (and underpaid) 20s didn't weigh me down.

Being self-employed carries its own challenges—no employer-matched 401(k)/TSP-type plan and HELLO self-employment taxes!—but I've chosen to have unlimited freedom over a higher income. What allowed me to do that, however, was chipping away at all the financial ties that bound me to a regular 9-5 job that was, itself, slowly chipping away at me. With every dollar of debt I paid off, I became more and more free. My student loan balance finally dwindled to zero early in 2016, and that was the final piece to the puzzle.

While I could have stuck it out in the insurance industry (working 60 hours a week and hating every second) and then retired early by using my paycheck to bulk up my savings, I'd rather be semi-retired now and keep doing what I love well into my dotage. Once I was in a financial place to choose without jeopardizing my future, I prioritized current freedom and the ability to pursue my passion over amassing wealth for later.

I probably won't ever "retire" in the traditional sense, but the independence I have now is, for me, well worth the trade-off. I mean, if I can work from a lakeside villa in Guatemala, or a sunny pied-a-terre on the coast of Croatia, or a gorgeous Georgian flat in Edinburgh's city center, is it really even work? Yes, it definitely is, but it sure beats the cubicle I inhabited in my 20s. My point is that putting in the blood, sweat, and tears to get to this point is far from easy, but once you get here, you get to choose the kind of life you want to have. If you want to have a big family and a beautiful suburban home, you know what you need to do to get there, and you're already doing it. If you want to be a wandering nomad, like me, you can do that, too. If you've been wanting to change careers, or move to part-time, or pursue a passion, you have all the tools you need to plan those changes without putting your future security at risk. Not all of these options may be possible for you right now, but they are options, and the emotional and psychological benefits of having that kind of control over your own future are invaluable.

Now, we all know life throws us curve balls when we least expect it, and we certainly don't expect that you'll blast through this process in less than a year and then be a perfect financial specimen for the rest of time. Life happens, and most people will take several years to get to a place of financial freedom. But now, with the help of the guidance we've provided through these chapters, you know what you need to do to get where you want to go—and you've already established the habits that will help you get there.

You're well on your way, and I wish you the very best in whatever you choose to do with the awesome financial future you have ahead of you.

CBW

Phone Message from A VIP

A Final Note from Chris

"Hello, Self? Past Self? It's me, Future Self!

Listen, I've got to keep this short. I'll get in big trouble if I get caught leaving this message. Even though we've had the technology for quite a while, nobody's supposed to communicate directly with the past—something about screwing up the space time continuum or something. Whatever. But I just couldn't resist contacting you, so I could say thank you!

You'll never guess where I'm calling from. What am I saying, *of course* you know where I'm calling from, you're the one who sent me here in the first place. That's right, I'm smack in the middle of the green phase! I knew it was going to be awesome, but man, it's even better than I—I mean we—ever thought it was going to be. I just had to sneak in a call to tell you about it!

You thought the green phase was leaning back in a recliner, sipping Martian tea and playing virtual shuffleboard? Not even close! At least not for me . . . us, I mean. I'm busier than ever! But now that I'm financially independent, I'm not busy earning an income. Instead, I'm busy doing all the things we've always wanted to, but didn't have the time or money. Well now, I've got *both*—and it's fantastic. I've seen the world. I've gotten involved in causes that are really making a difference where it's needed the most. I've found out that I have some talents that neither of us ever knew we had. Best of all, I'm helping the people we love—some of whom you've never even heard of yet. Oops, I better not say any more about that!

But none of this would have been possible if it weren't for you. You took the initiative, you made the decisions, you kept everything on track—all for the benefit of me. That's why I just had to leave you this thank-you message. I can't tell you any of the details, and I really don't want to give anything away, but I just wanted you to know, without a doubt that everything you're doing now to assure our financial future, is going to be so, so worth it—beyond your wildest dreams. So keep at it, Young Self. The payoff is going to be fantastic!

OK, I gotta go before I get caught. Don't worry about the future, just stick with that nice healthy magic number, keep paying ourselves first, and compound interest will take care of the rest. Have a blast in the past, and take care of ourselves, OK? Later, Self!"

CCS

About the Co-Author

Claire Boyte-White is a writer, editor, and long-term 'voluntary hobo'. After a backpacking trip to Scotland in 2013, she realized that the standard 9 to 5 grind in her Seattle insurance career wasn't going to lead to the life she wanted. After ditching the fancy job and the high-end apartment, Claire began building a career that would allow her to live life on her own terms. She stumbled into the financial and investment writing niche early on, and found that her natural love of math and analysis made it a perfect fit. Since then, she's traveled the world, married a bonny Scotsman, settled down in Cuenca, Ecuador, and maintained a happily semi-retired lifestyle writing for many well-known financial resources, such as Investopedia, NapkinFinance, CNBC, SmartAsset, and Dividend.com.

"Writing these books was a uniquely rewarding experience. Being on the older end of the Millennial spectrum, I found myself realizing how much books like these would have helped me ten years ago. But it also highlighted how much I'd learned through my own financial journey, and how much joy it brought me to be able to share those tools with others. Because I co-authored the two final volumes, I really got to work with Chris to flesh out the Dashboard tool and fit all these moving pieces together, which made this so much more than just another writing gig. My hope is that I've helped, in some small way, to create something that can help other people free themselves from the status-quo."

About the App Developer

Andy Crosby is a recent graduate of the University of Puget Sound in Tacoma, Washington, where he developed a passion for personal finance. As a Certified HERO financial counselor, Andy enjoys volunteering in his community to encourage and promote financial literacy. Andy also served as President of Four Horsemen Investments, a student-run, non-profit that manages a portfolio of investments to raise money for peer scholarships. To learn more about Andy's HERO certification and his involvement with Four Horsemen Investments, visit soundoutreach.org and 4hinvestments.org.

"Helping with the Net Worthy project has been an incredible experience. When school ends and 'real life' begins, we are all expected to have a complete understanding of our personal finances, yet only a small percentage of students have access to financial education. Financial independence should be available and accessible for everyone, and that's what I hope this project will do!"

About the Editor

Ashley Strosnider is a writer and editor living in Nebraska, where she is Managing Editor at *Prairie Schooner* and the African Poetry Book Fund at the University of Nebraska. She holds an MFA in creative writing, and her work has appeared in multiple literary journals. She freelance edits for the love of the game (and for the love of discretionary income).

"When I first signed on to edit, all I was hoping for was to earn a little extra money. I had no idea that I was about to change my entire perspective about earning, saving, and investing to one that not only serves me well today but sets me up for a much more capable, informed, and confident financial life for years to come. I'm thrilled to be a part of this project and hope others will learn as much as I did."

About the Author

Chris Smith is a man on a mission to increase the financial IQs of young adults everywhere. He's a lifelong financial professional, a former senior financial executive with Hewlett Packard, the creator of the I Am Net Worthy series, and the author of *Securing Your Financial Future: Complete Personal Finance for Beginners* (Rowman & Littlefield, 2012).

"I believe that before we send young adults out into the financial world, we owe each and every one of them a solid, practical education about exactly how that financial world works. But we, as a society, have done a really poor job of providing it. Most young adults just don't get taught the fundamentals through the educational system. Parents would love to teach their children, but most of them were never taught either. The kicker is, in today's do-it-yourself financial world, this kind of financial know-how is now a must-have.

All this really hit home for me when my own two sons reached college age—and I saw the financial world from the perspective of their generation. I saw that not enough was being done about the financial knowledge gap for young people, and that it was just too important to wait any longer.

I can't say enough about what an incredible experience it's been for me to collaborate with this amazing group of I Am Net Worthy co-authors. I selected them hoping they'd inspire you, but along the way they've ended up inspiring me. They're all young adults themselves, and they come from all over the country and represent a wide diversity of backgrounds and perspectives. They all believe the same thing that I do—that financial knowledge should be widely available to all, and that financial independence is for everyone."